1989

University of St. Francis
GEN 111.850924 E195

P9-CBH-063
3 0301 00054190 0

The Aesthetics of Thomas Aquinas

Woodcut from Leandro Alberti, *De Viris Illustribus Ordinis Praedicatorum Libri Sex* (Bologna, 1517). Department of Printing and Graphic Arts, The Houghton Library, Harvard University.

LIBRARY
College of St. Francis
JOLIET, ILL.

THE AESTHETICS OF

Thomas Aquinas

Umberto Eco

Translated by Hugh Bredin

Harvard University Press

Cambridge, Massachusetts · 1988

LIBRARY
College of St. Francis
JOLIET, ILL.

Copyright © 1988 by the President and Fellows of Harvard College
All rights reserved
Printed in the United States of America
10 9 8 7 6 5 4 3 2 1

Previously published as *Il problema estetico in Tommaso d'Aquino;* © Gruppo Editoriale
Fabbri, Bompiani, Sonzogno, Etas S.p.A., Milan, 1970.

This book is printed on acid-free paper, and its binding materials have
been chosen for strength and durability.

Library of Congress Cataloging-in-Publication Data

Eco, Umberto.
   [Il Problema estetico in Tommaso d'Aquino. English]
   The aesthetics of Thomas Aquinas / Umberto Eco ; translated by
Hugh Bredin.
   p. cm.
   Translation of: Il problema estetico in Tommaso d'Aquino.
   Bibliography: p.
   Includes index.
   ISBN 0-674-00675-5 (alk. paper)
   1. Thomas, Aquinas, Saint, 1225?–1274—Contributions in
aesthetics. 2. Aesthetics, Medieval. I. Title.
B765.T54E3313 1988
   111'.85'0924—dc19   88-658
                 CIP

111.850924
E195

Contents

134,035

Preface

This book was published first in 1956 and a second time in 1970.[1] It is therefore an "old" book, not just by virtue of its date, but also because it is a typically youthful work, with all the faults that this implies: a convoluted style, a tendency to equate the readable with the unscientific, the headstrong insistence of a young scholar upon technical-sounding phrases instead of plain language, and an overblown apparatus whose purpose, often enough, was merely to show that the writer had read everything he could find on the subject.

Still, none of this makes me feel that the book is out of date. The important things, its historical method and its conclusions, are still valid. And this is no small satisfaction. For I began the work in 1952 in a spirit of adherence to the religious world of Thomas Aquinas, whereas now I have long since settled my accounts with Thomistic metaphysics and the religious outlook. Interestingly, this settling of accounts was made possible precisely by my investigations of the Thomist aesthetic. The book began as an exploration of an area which I considered to be living and contemporary. But as I proceeded, it gradually assumed the character of a remote past, though a past which I reconstructed with passion and affection, rather as one might sort through the papers of someone deeply loved and respected, but nonetheless deceased.

This came about because of my methodology, which I still hold to be the correct one. I decided to explain and clarify every term and every concept in the original texts in the light of the historical circumstances to which they belonged. I wanted to be genuinely faithful to Aquinas, to avoid the falsifications and distortions of his words by his multitudes of biased interpreters. I returned him to his own time. In so doing, I rediscovered his authentic visage, his "truth"; except that his truth was no longer mine. I had set out to explore a realm of metaphysics, and I emerged with a twofold methodology. There was my own method, which I would still use for research in the history of philosophy; and there was Aquinas's method, his exemplary rigor and clarity, whose value was quite independent of his philosophical system, his faith, or his conclusions. This rigor, this clarity, were for me the great lessons of medieval philosophy. I still accept its clean style of argument, and I suspect that I am still under its influence, so that, far from disowning this book, I can repeat the words of the original introduction:

> I believe that a philosopher's significance appears most fully when he is placed in his own time, considered as a representative of his period, and when his ideas are seen as part of a problematic peculiar to that period. His greatness consists in his ability to encompass the spiritual temper of his age, and to carry it forward, through his personal cultural consciousness, both to maturity and to the threshold of further and deeper developments. And what we can learn from him is above all the lesson of his humanity, which is also a lesson in method in a somewhat wider and deeper sense of that term than is usual.

But aside from these autobiographical details, I still have to explain why I have decided on a new edition of this work. The first reason is purely practical: the first edition is out of print and there is still some demand for it. When it first appeared, distinguished medievalists such as Etienne Gilson and Edgar de Bruyne described it as a useful work. Since then, the only study devoted specifically to Aquinas's aesthetics has been Francis J. Kovach, *Die Aesthetik des Thomas von Aquin* (Berlin, 1961);[2] so my own work can still be of some value.

A second reason is that the Structuralist methodologies which are increasingly used in the social sciences have some affinities with certain aspects of Scholasticism. Thus, reflection upon the Scholastic *forma mentis* can serve as a kind of litmus test, both for analyzing and refining certain contemporary theories, and also for disclosing in some cases their medievalist subtleties. It would certainly be interesting to rewrite this book in the light of these new methodologies; but we would then have a different book. I am sure that interested readers can, with the help of my exposition of Scholastic thinking, draw their own conclusions on this matter. In any case I have added an extra section in this edition, in which I briefly address these issues.

There is a third reason, which I have gone into in subsequent works such as my *Le poetiche di Joyce*.[3] It is that the Thomist aesthetic has had considerable influence on contemporary thought, both in its "pure," accurately reconstructed form and through a multitude of ecclesiastical popularizations, theological manuals, and neo-Scholastic modifications. Joyce is the main example of an avant-garde writer whose aesthetics, in his youth, was based upon Scholasticism. Gerard Manley Hopkins is another. Elements of the Scholastic theory of rhetoric, taken over by, for instance, the Chicago school, have influenced the poetics of American New Criticism. More recently still, Thomas Aquinas has returned, through the medium of Marshall McLuhan, to haunt discussions of the mass media. But neither the philosopher nor his aesthetics is a ghost in the library. We have here a fact of our culture, and since it deserves study it should be studied by correct historical methods.

All these considerations might seem to require that the book be rewritten. But this is merely a new edition of a book which was quite obviously written in 1954. I have updated the bibliography only where, in making some additions, I happened to be working with more recent material. It will be apparent from the notes that even in the first edition most of the bibliographical references involved interpretations that I found unacceptable. Aquinas has had the misfortune to be read by "fans" rather than by historians. Three-quarters of what has been written about him has served to obscure rather than to establish a sense of historical perspective. So in this edition I have reduced my comments upon his interpreters in order to focus more intently upon Aquinas's own writings (although I have retained them in the Bibliography). This edition, then, presents a certain reading of Thomas Aquinas which occurred in 1954. If someone should have read him since then with greater insight, so much the better. This book has the faults and the virtues of having been written first.

Nonetheless, this second edition corrects the first in several ways, and above all in its style. I did not want to rewrite the book, but I was able to polish it, to eliminate redundancies and pedantic turns of phrase (and if some still remain, the reader may imagine what the original, unexpurgated version must have been like). I removed anything that was too emotive. Thus, where the original text might have read "We may, perhaps, at this point, feel enabled to advance the hypothesis that this is how things might be," I now prefer "Perhaps this is how things are," or even, "This is how things are." For if I put my name to a book I assume responsibility for it; I did not know that then.

I have also enlarged the chapters comparing Aquinas's views with the medieval aesthetic tradition as a whole. Research for my contribution to the 1959 anthology *Momenti e problemi di storia dell'estetica* considerably enlarged my knowledge of the period,[4] and I have exploited that knowledge to strengthen the central purpose of this book—namely, to place Thomistic thought in its proper historical setting, and thus construct a "code," as it is now called, of medieval aesthetic terminology.

Another change is my addition in 1970 of the Conclusion in order to deal with an issue whose importance was not as clear to me then as it is now. It concerns a central contradiction which undermines the Thomist aesthetic system from within. I had identified it at the time, but in the form of a doubt which could be left in the background, about which one might legitimately keep silent. I could not conceive that a system constructed with such acumen might not be fully coherent. I did not accept that my own reconstruction of the system, which aimed at a similar perspicuity, could end by uncovering an *aporia*. I was as yet too much of a Scholastic, believing that the discovery of a contradiction within a system meant repudiating its validity.

By now I have learned that philosophers should not eliminate contradictions; indeed they should seek them out, if they are not immediately apparent. Above all I now know that every system has a contradiction within itself, so that finding contradictions is not a defeat, but rather a victory for those who believe that philosophy must constantly remake itself. For philosophy always contains within itself something that is not philosophy, which can never be fully eliminated try as one may. A system *must* have a contradiction to undermine it, for a system is a structural model which arrests reality for an instant and tries to make it intelligible. But this arrest, necessary for communication, impoverishes the real instead of enriching it. The model is of value only if it stimulates an advance to a new level of understanding of reality, a level on which it then seems inadequate.

This is an insight which contemporary Structuralism, some of it at any rate, tends to reject. In this respect it resembles Scholasticism. The aim of Scholasticism, its ideological goal, if you like, was to demonstrate that reality could be construed as a motionless system of relations, fully intelligible and not subject to further change. The period was deficient in a sense of historical development and dialectical contradiction; and its picture of reality was rather like its social structures, hierarchical and fixed in immutable relations. Thomas Aquinas pursued his goals with vigor and integrity, aiming to prove that everything possessed the immutable and perfect form that God had assigned to it. Today we should likewise pursue our own goal, which is to show that the only satisfactory proof that we have a satisfactory conception of things is that, when the conception is explored further, it generates a contradiction. This is why, in this second edition, I build upon a suggestion contained in the first, and show how a contradiction in the Thomistic system leads to the history of aesthetics after him.

But these additions do not alter the substance of the book. It undertook to show that Aquinas's philosophical system included a coherent aesthetic theory. And his aesthetics *is* coherent, to the same degree as his general philosophical system. It is the notion of coherence that has changed. When I was writing the book, however, the question of Aquinas's coherence did not seem to be the most important one. At that time the issue was the very possibility of a medieval aesthetics. Things are different in Italy today, but in 1954 there was still a feeling that aesthetics had been born with Baumgarten, that before him aesthetics had been a morass of infantile chatter. What I wanted to show, and what historians now know, was that there was no morass, but instead a coherent body of thinking about beauty and the arts—coherent to the maximum degree attainable by the human intellect when bound to the ideal of coherence that regulated medieval thought.

So I am still content to put my name to the book, with just a touch, perhaps, of the *ennui* that attends the victor when he returns to the field of an ancient conquest. The passionate convictions of yesterday have become academic, respectable.

U. E.

Translator's Note

In translating from Latin, I have used existing English translations whenever possible. However, I have not hesitated to modify these translations, either in order to compensate for the effect of quoting a passage out of context, or in order to make the passage more intelligibly related to the author's commentary upon it. Relatively little of Aquinas has in fact been translated; when not otherwise specified, all translations of his texts are my own.

For the most part, I have copied Aquinas's Latin from Roberto Busa's edition of his *Opera Omnia* (Stuttgart, 1980), which in most cases diverges only slightly from the editions used by Umberto Eco. Where there are more substantial divergences, I have employed other editions as indicated in the notes and bibliography.

Because a translation is necessarily aimed at a somewhat different readership from that of the original, I have taken the liberty of adding a very occasional footnote, and also a Glossary, for the benefit of those who may be unfamiliar with the medieval period. I have also updated the bibliographic references and given English translations when available and appropriate.

My thanks are due to Sinead Smyth, who typed the manuscript; and to my wife, Isabel, for translations from the Greek; also to my colleague, Tim Lynch, and to Umberto Eco, for assistance with the Glossary.

I am greatly indebted to Judith Landry for assistance in the preparation of this translation.

H. B.

The Aesthetics of Thomas Aquinas

I

Aesthetics in Medieval Culture

In 1931 Benedetto Croce wrote and published in his journal *La Critica* a review of Nelson Sella's *Estetica musicale in San Tommaso*.[1] Much of the review was favorable; Croce praised it as a serious work. But his overall judgment was a repetition of what he had written previously about Aquinas and the history of aesthetics.

> The fact is that his [Aquinas's] ideas on art and beauty are, not false, but extremely general. This is why they can in a sense be always accepted as correct . . . The essential thing is that the problems of aesthetics were not the object of any genuine interest, either to the Middle Ages in general, or to St. Thomas in particular. Aquinas's labours took him in quite a different direction, so that he was satisfied with the generalities in question. For this reason, studies of the aesthetics of St. Thomas and other medieval philosophers make dull and unhelpful reading when (as is usually the case) they lack the restraint and good taste that characterize Sella's work.

During the years when Croce's views still carried weight in Italy, such a judgment was enough to discourage any research on medieval aesthetics. Even if someone should happen to agree that the medievals did write about aesthetic issues, issues moreover very similar to those addressed in the classical world, it was common to dismiss them in a perfunctory manner. The medievals, it was said, simply repeated the debates of the classical authors parrot fashion, debates which in any case meant little to them.[2] This kind of judgment amounted almost to a denial of the claim that medieval thinkers continued with the questions of classical aesthetics, on the ground that medieval philosophy was smothered in theology.[3]

The hollowness of all of this has been revealed in recent histories of the medieval period. In fact, even the medieval history of a century ago would have revealed the same error, if it had been read with any care. But careful reading is a difficult matter, as this book will show.

However, in order to eliminate any possibility of misunderstanding I wish to make the nature of my inquiry perfectly clear. The title of the book refers to an "aesthetics" of a medieval author. I therefore want to define my use of this term; and this definition will establish in turn whether the medievals, when they wrote about art and beauty, were engaged in "aesthetics" or not.

Baumgarten described aesthetics by means of such expressions as *scientia cognitionis sensitivae, theoria liberalium artium, gnoseologia inferior, ars pulcre cogitandi, ars analogi rationis* (the science of sense knowledge, the theory of the liberal arts, the epistemology of the lower level of knowledge, the rules of thinking aesthetically, the rules of reasoning by analogy).[4] If aesthetics is conceived of in these ways, then indeed the medievals, with perhaps a few notable exceptions, did not have an aesthetic theory. Again, if aesthetics is thought to signify philosophical discussion of the lyrical intuition of feeling,* it follows that the medievals had no interest in it.

But if, instead, aesthetics refers to a whole range of issues connected with beauty—its definition, its function, the ways of creating and of enjoying it—then the medievals did have aesthetic theories. It is true that these theories were entangled in their theology as well as in their philosophy; but to disentangle them, all one has to do is to read their theology in a philosophical light. This way of reading them is quite in keeping with their own intentions.

Aesthetics also deals with questions about art; and here again we find that medieval treatises, philosophy, and theology were filled with discussion of such questions. However, the medieval theory of art was not very different from the classical theory, so in this book I shall concentrate for the most part upon issues that are aesthetic rather than artistic.

The distinction between the artistic and the aesthetic, a distinc-

---

*"Lyrical intuition" (*intuizione lirica*) was a term used by Benedetto Croce to signify that the unity of the object of an intuition was determined by feeling. For Croce, intuition constituted the realm of the aesthetic.

tion which was obscured in Idealism, is today perfectly clear. It was clear also to the medievals, even though they did not possess the word *aesthetic*. The concept of the aesthetic refers to the problem of the possible objective character, and the subjective conditions, of what we call the experience of beauty. It thus refers also to problems connected with the aesthetic object and aesthetic pleasure. The experience of beauty does not necessarily have art as its object; for we ascribe beauty not just to poems and paintings but also to horses, sunsets, and women—or even, at its limits, to a crime or a gourmet meal.[5] And conversely, we employ the word *art* to refer to such things as educational projects (for example, in Socialist Realism) or to functional solutions (industrial design), life experiences (happenings), linguistic experiments (Joyce), and the manipulation and combination of mathematically generated entities (computer art).

The medievals, then, concerned themselves with the psychological and ontological conditions of aesthetic pleasure, but they distinguished this from the problem of artistic creation. Medieval thought, like classical thought, did not consider that art necessarily had to do with the production of beautiful things or the stimulation of aesthetic pleasure. *Ars* signified the technique for constructing objects. If some of these objects appeared to be beautiful, this was a side issue. Of course this "side issue" is central in modern philosophy, to which it appears that artistic experience is always somehow connected with aesthetic experience. And this is why we shall have to look at the relation between the Scholastic theory of art and the Scholastic philosophy of beauty. But initially I will keep them sharply distinct, just as the medievals did, and just we do now, albeit in a rather different way.

Of course, the fact that the medievals had theories of art and beauty might still be of little significance. Perhaps they were no more than a frigid reworking of ideas inherited from the classical world, now converted into theological abstractions, with no application to concrete experience. In view of this possibility, we must establish whether medieval terms such as *pulchritudo* (or *pulcritudo*), *suavitas*, *proportio*, and *harmonia* actually referred to the concrete experiences which today we describe as aesthetic pleasure or the perception of beauty.

Even a short and cursory examination of the everyday aesthetic sensibility of medieval people will show that their aesthetic terminology did in fact relate to their experience. Whether they felt pleasure in looking at things or in engaging in activities, whether they spoke of philosophical entities such as "form" or theological realities such as "beauty," medieval thinkers employed the same concepts that we do today, with all their connotations and implications.

Historiography

A survey of the history of medieval aesthetics provides ample evidence of two of the elements in medieval culture: philosophical reflection on beauty, and also a concrete and conscious awareness of the beauty of things and the aesthetic reality of art. Both of these elements are of interest to us, although often enough they are treated separately. Some historians even assert that they were in fact independent, that metaphysical reflection on beauty was something quite separate from the everyday, concrete aesthetic sensibility of the time.[6] Others consider that the two elements were intimately connected; a notable example is H. H. Glunz, although he tends to concentrate upon the poet's consciousness of his art.[7] Glunz also examines the evolution of literary taste in the Middle Ages, from its didactic use of pagan stories, and the advent of a genuine Christian ethos, to the rise of the allegorical sensibility that ruled unchallenged in the twelfth century. It was after this that poets became ever more aware of their own creative and expressive activity.

Other historians have concentrated on the self-awareness of the medieval artist, or, more precisely, the degree of awareness of poetic creation that found expression on the level of theory. Eugenio Garin, for instance, discerns in medieval poetry both a special tone and an effort to confer upon poetry a revelatory value, as if it were the highest point of human experience, a supreme vision, "becoming one with the living rhythm of things, as if sharing that rhythm, and also being able to translate everything into the images and forms of human communication." This poetry of "penetrating insight" coexisted with a poetry of rhetorical skill, whose value lay in pleasure and ornament. Medievals, he concludes, had a twofold poetic consciousness.[8]

Considerations of this kind belong to a large field of inquiry which remains controversial because the textual evidence is neither consistent nor clear. Moreover, they concern the twelfth rather than the thirteenth century. And they are somewhat extraneous to the problem of Thomas Aquinas, whose interests lay, not with poetry, but with the ontological character of beauty.

The historian who has examined most fully and deeply all the constituents of the medieval aesthetic sensibility, together with its various metaphysical theories of beauty, its treatises on the rules of art, and all the texts which dealt with problems of art and beauty, is undoubtedly Edgar de Bruyne in his *Etudes d'esthétique médiévale*.[9] Unlike Glunz, de Bruyne takes the view that the aesthetic movements of the medieval period did not follow one another in chronological succession, but coexisted with one another throughout. Only the interactions among them changed with the passage of the centuries. De Bruyne's work is larger both in size and in scope than any of the others cited. It deals not just with literature but with all kinds of artistic phenomena, and in particular with philosophical reflection upon art. He is especially revealing about the quite crucial influence upon the whole period of the Pythagorean aesthetics of proportion, the neo-Platonic aesthetics of light, and the Augustinian aesthetics of quality.

But it is inevitable that even a work as dedicated as de Bruyne's should arrive at some restrictive conclusions. One is that the medieval philosophy of beauty was often a purely verbal matter—that, whereas the Greeks had examined our immediate experiences of concrete beauty, the medievals often deployed Greek theory within the framework of medieval metaphysics. This would mean that they failed to take account of particular concrete instances of the very value of beauty, which was, after all, the object of discussion.[10]

Bernard Bosanquet was influenced by similar considerations. In his view, the concept of beauty in medieval philosophy was always an abstraction, and thus failed to provide any effective account of the beauty of creatures and art.[11] And Maurice de Wulf, despite his much greater sympathy with the medievals' thought, considered them incapable of genuine reflection upon the human creation of beauty, surrounded though they were by art of the highest stature.[12]

So we must now ask whether this "abstraction," this predominant and undeniable interest in the metaphysics of beauty, really had nothing to do with the beauty of concrete objects.

The Medieval Aesthetic Sensibility

The medievals took over various themes, problems, and solutions from the classical world and used them in the context of a quite new and different sensibility. It is also true to say that they took them over bodily, and that in many ways medieval philosophy seems less a phenomenology of experienced reality than a phenomenology of a cultural tradition.

One consequence is that the medievals were disposed to conceive of beauty as a purely intelligible reality, as moral harmony or metaphysical *splendor*. When we come to look at Aquinas we shall find that this conception is indispensable for an understanding of medieval aesthetics. E. R. Curtius writes: "When Scholasticism speaks of beauty, the word is used to indicate an attribute of God. The metaphysics of beauty (e.g., in Plotinus) and theories of art have nothing whatever to do with each other. 'Modern' man immeasurably overvalues art because he has lost the sense of intelligible beauty that Neo-Platonism and the Middle Ages possessed . . . Here a beauty is meant of which aesthetics knows nothing."[13]

On the other hand, an abundance of medieval literature demonstrates an awareness of sensible beauty, the beauty of natural objects and of art. The problem is not one of contrasting one type of sensibility with the other as if they were mutually exclusive, but rather of integrating them. They were two features of a single realm of the aesthetic, a realm incomparably wider than ours. Paradoxically, it is not that the medievals did not have an aesthetics, but that modern aesthetics is excessively narrow. This is one way of replying to an Idealist historian such as Croce.

Medieval thinkers were quick to point out that sensible beauty could not be discarded simply because a higher value was ascribed (on the theoretical level at least) to spiritual beauty. In fact the tension between the theoretical and the practical, which was a feature of the medieval outlook, generated an attempt to reconcile these two irrepressible aspects of their aesthetic experience.[14] An illuminating example of this is found in the attitude of medieval mystics and rigorists,* people who by definition should have been closed, whether by vocation or by choice, to the attractions of earthly beauty, sensuous pleasure, and emotional gratification. In fact, mystics and rigorists in all periods have not been at all insensitive to worldly "temptations." In a sense they feel them more strongly than other people do. The drama of asceticism is grounded in just this interaction between a responsiveness to worldly values and a straining after the supernatural.

A relevant example is the twelfth-century campaign against excessive ornamentation in churches, conducted by the Cistercians and the Carthusians. A well-known Cistercian statute prohibited the use in churches of silk, gold, silver, paintings, stained glass, and carpets.[15] St. Bernard of Clairvaux and Alexander Neckham attacked the *superfluitates,* the excesses, which interfered with the concentration of the faithful. But it would be wrong to look upon these strictures as showing a dislike of beauty; on the contrary, beauty is here recognized and admired, and is rejected precisely because its attractions are judged to be dangerous. Hugh of Fouilloi described it as a wondrous but perverse delight ("mira sed perversa delectatio").[16] St. Bernard throws light upon the peculiar features of this psychological stance, in a passage dealing with the moral character of the monastic life.

> Nos vero qui jam de populo eximus, qui mundi quaeque pretiosa ac speciosa pro Christo reliquimus, qui omnia pulchre lucentia, canore mulcentia, suave olentia, dulce sapientia, tactu placentia, cuncta denique oblectamenta corporea arbitrati sumus ut stercora . . .

> But we [monks] who have now come forth from the people; we who have left all the precious and beautiful things of the world for Christ's sake; who have counted but dung, that we may win Christ, all things fair to see or soothing to hear, sweet to smell, delightful to taste, or pleasant to touch—in a word, all bodily delights . . .[17]

This passage needs no comment. The scatological rejection is forceful, yet the things rejected are brilliantly seductive. The mystic

*Rigorism (*rigorismo*) refers to any kind of moral, intellectual, or religious absolutism.

knew what it was that he was giving up. This ambivalence in St. Bernard is splendidly illustrated in another well-known passage from his *Apologia ad Guillelmum*. Here, he is attacking the "Cluny style" of church, a church excessively rich in sculpture and painting—and so, incidentally, opposed also by the aesthetic ideals of Suger, which I discuss below.

> Omitto oratorium immensas altitudines, immoderatas longitudines, supervacuas latitudines, sumptuosas depolitiones, curiosas depictiones: quae dum orantium in se retorquent aspectum, impediunt et affectum, et mihi quodammodo repraesentant antiquum ritum judaeorum.

> I say naught of the vast height of your churches, their immoderate length, their superfluous breadth, the costly polishings, the curious carvings and paintings which attract the worshipper's gaze and hinder his attention, and seem to me in some sort a revival of the ancient Jewish rites.

This passage displays considerable skill in its use of the rules of rhetoric, its handling of *color rethoricus* [sic] (rhetorical color), and the techniques of *determinationes* (definition). We shall see more of these qualities in a moment. St. Bernard considers excessive ornament to be a kind of trap designed to attract generous donations. The eyes are dazzled by gold, and purses open: "Ostenditur pulcherrima forma sancti vel sanctae alicujus, et eo creditur sanctior, quia coloratior" ("They are shown a most comely image of some saint, whom they think all the more saintly that he is the more gaudily painted"). It is not a bad analysis of the Cluny publicity technique, the style of hidden persuasion which made use of beauty and of aesthetic pleasure in order to manipulate the emotions. And when St. Bernard describes the aesthetic stratagems exploited by this technique, he shows himself to be a gifted prose writer extremely alert to the form of language, and a critic extremely sensitive to the rich iconography of the figurative arts.

> Caeterum in claustris coram legentibus fratribus quid facit ridicula monstruositas, mira quaedam deformis formositas, ac formosa deformitas? Quid ibi immundae simiae? quid feri leones? quid monstruosi centauri? quid semihomines? quid ma-

culosae tigrides? quid milites pugnantes? quid venatores tubici-
nantes? Videas sub uno capite multa corpora, et rursus in uno
corpore capita multa. Cernitur hinc in quadrupede cauda ser-
pentis, illinc in pisce caput quadrupedis. Ibi bestia praefert
equum, capra trahens retrum dimidiam: hic cornutum animal
equum gestat posterius. Tam multa denique, tamque mira diversarum formarum ubique varietas apparet, ut magis legere li-
beat in marmoribus quam in codicibus, totumque diem occu-
pare singula ista mirando quam in lege Dei meditando. Proh
Deo! Si non pudet ineptiarum, cur vel non piget expensarum?

But in the cloister, under the eyes of the Brethren who read
there, what profit is there in those ridiculous monsters, in that
marvellous and deformed comeliness, that comely deformity?
To what purpose are those unclean apes, those fierce lions,
those monstrous centaurs, those half-men, those striped tigers,
those fighting knights, those hunters winding their horns?
Many bodies are there seen under one head, or again, many
heads to a single body. Here is a four-footed beast with a ser-
pent's tail; there, a fish with a beast's head. Here again the fore-
part of a horse trails half a goat behind it, or a horned beast
bears the hinder quarters of a horse. In short, so many and so
marvellous are the varieties of divers shapes on every hand, that
we are more tempted to read in the marble than in our books,
and to spend the whole day in wondering at these things rather
than in meditating the law of God. For God's sake, if men are
not ashamed of these follies, why at least do they not shrink
from the expense?

We are reminded by this that St. Bernard was like many other
mystics and theologians of the time—Peter Damian, Aquinas, the
Victorines, St. Bonaventure—in knowing how to utter condem-
nations of poetry with all the style of a poet. In fact some of these
poet-theologians produced works which are among the most remarkable in medieval Latin literature.[18] There is something more
in St. Bernard, however, a certain gusto in his descriptions of the
sculptural flora and fauna of abbeys and cathedrals; he has the in-
quisitive eye of a mystic *voyeur*, denouncing objects which provoke
his ardor and his aesthetic gratification. What he attacked also fascinated him. St. Augustine also had warned against the seduction

of music while at prayer;[19] And, as we shall see, Aquinas returned to the same theme, though with more moderation. Aquinas advised against the use of instruments for sacred music only because, instead of awakening in the soul a feeling of piety, "they move it rather to a sense of delight" ("magis animum movent ad delectationem").[20] The thing that is repudiated is recognized to be an object of pleasure and desire. It is one thing to maintain that aesthetic pleasure is in some circumstances out of place; it is quite another to have no aesthetic sensibility in the first place.

Furthermore, even when the mystics were rejecting the pleasures of sensible beauty, they were elevating their aesthetic sensibilities to another level. They rejected the beauty of outward things only when those were contrasted with inner beauty. "Inward beauty," wrote St. Bernard, "is more comely than exterior ornament, more even than the pomp of kings" ("Pulchrum interius speciosius est omni ornatu extrinseco, omni etiam regio cultu").[21]

The bodies of martyrs might be terrible to look at, but they had a splendid spiritual beauty; what was lost in one aspect was regained in another. Also, the loss by rejection or by nature of sensible beauty evoked a profound regret. The transience of earthly beauty did not make it inferior, but produced instead a sharp feeling of sadness. Boethius, for instance, when he was facing imminent death, reaffirmed the primacy of spiritual values; but he was also compelled to elegiac lamentation: "Formae vero nitor ut rapidus est, ut velox et vernalium florum mutabilitate fugacior" ("The beauty of things is fleet and swift, more fugitive than the passing of flowers in spring").[22] Boethius was here voicing a sentiment prevalent throughout the medieval period, the moralistic theme of *ubi sunt:* where are the great of yesteryear, the magnificent cities, the works of the mighty . . . ? Moralistic, but pervaded also by a note of aesthetic yearning. Underlying the *danse macabre* and death's triumph we find an autumnal sense of the beauty that passes away, the feeling that pervades François Villon's *Ballade des dames du temps jadis:* "Mais où son les neiges d'antan?"[23]

Thus the emphasis on an interior beauty which does not die was more than a simple opposition to an aesthetic of the sensible. It was, rather, a kind of reinstatement of such an aesthetic. If a permanent, inner essence of beauty could be established (and, as we shall see, Thomist hylomorphism was to provide its philosophical ground), then, once rid of the transience of the everyday world, this essence became the source of the beauty of sensible appearances. As Gilbert of Hoyt put it, the light of a virtuous soul diffuses itself through the external appearance of the ideal Christian.[24] St. Bernard put it even more effectively:

> Cum autem decoris hujus claritas abundantius intima cordis repleverit, prodeat foras necesse est, tamquam lucerna latens sub modio: immo lux in tenebris lucens latere nescia. Porro effulgentem et veluti quibusdam suis radiis erumpentem [lucem] mentis simulacrum corpus excipit, et diffundit per membra et sensus, quatenus omnis inde reluceat actio, sermo, aspectus, incessus, risus—si tamen risus mixtus gravitate et plenus honesti.

> When the brightness of beauty has replenished to overflowing the recesses of the heart, it is necessary that it should emerge into the open, just like the light hidden under a bushel: a light shining in the dark is not trying to conceal itself. The body is an image of the mind, which, like an effulgent light scattering forth its rays, is diffused through its limbs and senses, shining through in action, discourse, appearance, movement—even in laughter, if it is completely sincere and tinged with gravity.[25]

The beauty of humankind and of nature thus reappeared even in the teaching of rigorists. So it is understandable that it should be found more widely and positively still in a mysticism of the intellect which attained the serenity of the spirit to turn back to the world of the senses. This was the case with Hugh of St. Victor, for whom intuitive contemplation was a feature of the human intellect whose operations were not confined to moments of mystical experience, but could take the form of "an easy and clear-sighted penetration of the soul into the objects of perception" ("perspicax et liber animi cointuitus in res perspiciendas").[26] The soul recognized in material objects a harmony identical with that of its own structure, and this recognition was the genesis of aesthetic pleasure. The intellect was in this way brought face to face with the marvelous spectacle of the world and its forms.

> Aspice mundum, et omnia quae in eo sunt: multas ibi species pulchras et illecebrosas invenies . . . Habet aurum . . . fulgo-

rem suum, habet decor carnis speciem, [habent] picta tapeta et
vestes fucatae colorem . . .

Look upon the world and all that is in it: you will find much
that is beautiful and desirable . . . Gold . . . has its brilliance,
the flesh its comeliness, tapestries and dyed garments their
color . . .[27]

We can see, therefore, that the philosophical and theological literature of the Middle Ages contains more than just academic discussions of beauty. It is filled also with admiring and exclamatory
passages which mediate between purely philosophical thinking and
concrete expressions of taste and sensibility. We have only to think
of the numerous medieval commentaries on the Canticle of Canti-
cles, in which the commentator dwells upon the beauty of the
Bride. Of course, the passage about the Bride has precise allegorical
meanings, and it was always the intention to bring these to light.
But the mystical-rigorist sensibility was bound in the exercise of
chastity, and the Marian cult constituted an ambiguous element in
a sublimated eroticism. We often find that discussion of the dark
but comely maiden (Cant. 1:4) is filled with a discreet appreciation
of feminine beauty. Baldwin of Canterbury, for instance, even
though he is mainly interested in allegorical significance, gives a
description of plaits in which his knowledge of fashion combines
with a keen aesthetic awareness.[28] And Gilbert of Hoyt digresses in
order to describe what makes the female breasts most pleasing. His
ideal is remarkably close to that of certain medieval miniaturists, in
whose illuminations we see a tight corset binding and raising the
bosom: "breasts are most pleasing when they are of moderate size
and eminence . . . They should be bound but not flattened, restricted gently and not allowed to wobble too freely" ("Pulchra
enim sunt ubera quae paululum supereminent et tument modice
. . . quasi repressa sed non depressa, leniter restricta, non fluitantia
licenter").[29]

There was, therefore, an everyday sensibility whose recognition
of beauty was grounded upon ordinary taste, and not just upon
theory. And often, quite irrespective of theory, this ordinary sensibility made a connection between the concepts *formosum* or *pul-*
chrum and the concept *ars*. We need only look at the records of cathedral construction, letters about artistic problems, and the com-

missions given to artists by their patrons.[30] In due course I shall consider whether medieval theory really ignored this assimilation of the artistic and the aesthetic, which was taken for granted in day-to-day practice. Initially, however, I shall adopt the method of doubt, embarking upon my textual analyses with the assumption that the two were kept distinct.

When we talk about the medievals' taste and spontaneity, their immediate sensuous pleasure in the beauty of the world, we at once raise another problem. Did they always think of art as didactic, or were they capable of disinterested aesthetic experience?

Huizinga writes, "The consciousness of aesthetic pleasure and its expression are of tardy growth. A fifteenth-century scholar like Fazio, trying to vent his artistic admiration does not get beyond the language of commonplace wonder."[31] But this means only that the medievals were not equipped with a body of technical terminology suitable for the articulation of aesthetic pleasure. It does not mean that they felt no such pleasure. To put it more precisely, the medievals did not succeed in devising a terminology for distinguishing between the admiration produced by a sunset, or God's grandeur, and the admiration they felt for a statue (that is, in our language, a work of art) or for the beauty of a porphyry vase (a work of craft). This is undeniable. The semantic range of the term *ars,* which had been inherited from the Greek word technē, is sufficient evidence. But the fact that the extension of the concept of the aesthetic was greater then than it is now is not a proof that they had no idea of the aesthetic, nor a lived experience of it. At the most, one is justified in talking about a cultural model whose values, though distinct for us, were integrated for them. Thus, beauty and goodness were integrated in the Greek notion of *kalokagathia.*

Suger, the abbot of St.-Denis, may be taken as typical.[32] Suger's views were in complete contrast to the unbending rigorism of St. Bernard. He was enamored of the beauty of his house of God, built on the model of Solomon's Temple. He wrote his description of the treasures gathered in St.-Denis "lest Oblivion, the jealous rival of Truth, sneak in and take away the example for further action."[33] He listed the chalices adorned with hyacinth and topaz, and the vessels "made admirable by the hand of the sculptor and polisher."[34] He loved the brightness of the precious stones, the carbuncles, topaz, diamond, jasper, chrysolite, onyx, sapphire, beryl, emerald. However, he saw all of these splendors as the sensible vestment of the divinity whose altar they adorned. Suger combined his taste for the *kolossal*—Huizinga's "commonplace wonder"—with an integrated feeling for a splendor which was at once material and theological. It is not clear whether he loved God as beauty, or loved beauty as a secondary revelation of God. As we shall see, when I come to discuss the allegorical and symbolical element in the medieval sensibility, this lack of clarity was valid within the medieval framework. Suger's attitude is not clear because it was not supposed to be. We shall see, in connection with the neo-Platonic elements in Aquinas, that for the medievals the aesthetic moment was characteristically theophanic. They had a sense of universal harmony, in which all beings sing of the presence within them of an emanating Principle in whose power they share; this is the significance of St. Francis's *Cantico delle creature.* It was also the reason for the commercial equivalent, their love of collecting. Collections were made with a lack of discrimination which today would earn a museum curator dismissal or contempt. But then it earned fame for notable treasuries such as that of the duc de Berry, which contained the horns of unicorns, St. Joseph's engagement ring, whales' teeth, coconuts, and shells from the seven seas. Other collections might list as many as 3,000 items, including 700 paintings, a stuffed elephant, a hydra, a basilisk, an egg found by an abbot inside another egg, and manna fallen in the desert.[35]

Another element in medieval aesthetic pleasure appears in a passage in which Suger relates what it is like to contemplate the beauty of his church. It is an experience which unites the sensuousness of beautiful materials with an awareness of the supernatural, in a manner which he describes as "anagogical." In the medieval *Weltanschauung* there was a direct connection linking the earth with heaven, and this must be taken into account when one considers their aesthetic perceptions.

> Unde, cum ex dilectione decoris domus Dei aliquando multicolor speciositas gemmarum, ab extrinsecis curis me devocaret, sanctarum etiam diversitatem virtutum de materialibus ad immaterialia transferendo, honesta meditatio insistere persuaderet . . . videor videre me quasi sub aliqua extranea orbis terrarum plaga, quae nec tota sit in terrae faece, nec tota in coeli

puritate demorari, ab hac etiam inferiori ad illam superiorem anagogico more, Deo donante, posse transferri.

Thus, when—out of my delight in the beauty of the house of God—the loveliness of the many-colored gems has called me away from external cares, and worthy meditation has induced me to reflect, transferring that which is material to that which is immaterial, on the diversity of the sacred virtues: then it seems to me that I see myself dwelling, as it were, in some strange region of the universe which neither exists entirely in the slime of the earth nor entirely in the purity of Heaven; and that, by the grace of God, I can be transported from this inferior to that higher world in an anagogical manner.[36]

It is in this light that we must interpret the medievals' failure to distinguish between the beautiful and the useful or fitting (*pulchrum* or *aptum,* and *decorum* or *honestum*). Their constant intermingling of these two aspects of things permitted Suger to see the beauty of his church as simultaneously aesthetic and didactic. In this perception he was following the dictates of the Synod of Arras in 1025, which stated that whatever simple people could not grasp through the scriptures should be learned by means of images. As Honorius of Autun put it, "Pictures are the literature of the laity" ("pictura est laicorum litteratura").[37] If art could simultaneously instruct and delight (*prodesse et delectare*), this was because the medieval sensibility, like medieval culture as a whole, was an "integrated" sensibility.

It is only to be expected, then, that one of the main problems for the philosophy and the theology of beauty was the problem of integrating it with other values. Philosophy struggled to establish that beauty was not distinct from the good and the true—an enterprise just the opposite of what is accomplished nowadays. Medieval distinctions among these values emerged only in the context of attempts to unify them. It is this conception of value which explains, in the pages that follow, how the problems of aesthetics were posed within the Thomistic system.[38]

Thomas Aquinas

Thomas Aquinas displays a competence in and a love of art which, if by no means unusual, are noteworthy nonetheless. He lived in the thirteenth century, when, as Gilson has shown, the taste for classical literature was considerably less than in the century preceding. Despite this, Aquinas was exposed to an education in letters. In his early youth he attended a school in Naples where he studied the *trivium* and *quadrivium*—that is, rhetoric, grammar, with exercises on the major texts, and music. In fact he had received a musical education from his infancy, at Monte Cassino, where there was a flourishing *schola cantorum* using the method of Guido d'Arezzo. There were numerous stories of Aquinas's cultivation in music, including a spurious attribution to him of the anonymous treatise *De Arte Musica*.[39] And John of Meurs, in his treatise *De Tonis* (c. 1323), referred to Aquinas as an expert on music.[40] More direct evidence, however, is found in Aquinas's own works—quotations from the musical treatises of Boethius and Augustine, and various passages which reveal an undeniable mastery of the subject.[41]

So far as poetry and literature are concerned, the documentary evidence is more than sufficient. We know that at school in Naples Aquinas studied the rules and methods of rhythmic composition. And we have the direct evidence of his prayers, and of his *Office of the Blessed Sacrament,* which is one of the finest instances of medieval Latin literature. These reveal a masterly knowledge of technique, combined with an ability to breathe life into the traditional rules. They possess both an expressive strength and an innate sense of music. And again, they display a creative breadth which is able to exploit traditional precepts in the interests of expressiveness. For example, in the hymn *Verbum supernum prodiens* Aquinas adopts the metrical scheme *abab*. In the fourth stanza, however, which refers elliptically to the mystery of the Redemption, he realizes that a repetition of the same assonance at the end of all four lines will create a verbal music more in keeping with the dense, compacted rhythm of the utterance. In this way, he implements the metrical scheme precisely by breaking it.[42]

One could continue in this vein. We might observe, for instance, that Aquinas was compelled to make his poetic creations follow existing melodies, with each syllable corresponding to a change in pitch, in the classical manner of the plainchant sequence. In fact this put him in vital contact with a creative process in which music leads to the birth of poetry and imposes on it the imperatives of consonance and proportion. However, all of these considerations are by way of introduction. They show that when Aquinas wrote about beauty and artistic form he was not dealing with mere abstractions, cut off from experience. He was referring, implicitly, to a world which he knew well.

The Possibility of Aesthetic Pleasure

For Aquinas, then, beauty was not just an abstract reality, known on the conceptual level but not experienced empirically. In fact he was familiar with beauty under several aspects, such as music, poetry, and perhaps natural phenomena. But there are other areas of Aquinas's thought which are even clearer and more helpful—for instance, his reflections on human psychology, the appetitive mechanisms and the hierarchy of human pleasures, together with the moral judgment and rational control which should govern our appetites and pleasures. Aquinas was always conscious of the possibility of a pleasure which was pure and disinterested. He identified it with the pleasure produced by the apprehension of beauty in objects. Disinterested pleasure means pleasure which is its own end, which is not connected with the satisfaction of animal needs or with utility. An embryonic form of such pleasure already exists in play. What is play? It is an activity whose end is its own fulfillment, and which causes a psychic relief necessary for our biological rhythms. "The activities of play," Aquinas writes, "are not aimed at some extrinsic end, but aim rather at the well-being of the player" ("Actiones ludicrae non ordinantur ad aliquem finem extrinsecum, sed tantum ordinantur ad bonum ipsius ludentis").[43]

Pure, disinterested contemplation is similar to play, because it is an end in itself. It also resembles play in that it is not a response to some compulsion rooted in the exigencies of life, but is rather a higher activity appropriate to a spiritual creature.

It is in Aquinas's discussion of temperance that he addresses this particular issue. Pleasure, he says, accompanies all activities which proceed from our inner nature; and the more an activity corresponds to a natural need, the stronger the pleasure. The most spontaneous activities are those pertaining to vital needs such as nutrition and reproduction. Temperance has to do with just these activities and these pleasures; and its rule extends to all other pleasures insofar as they relate to these primary pleasures. What unifies them all is that they are connected either directly or indirectly with the sense of touch. However, in animals the pleasure of each of the senses has a necessary connection with touch, and thus with natural needs; in humans alone there exists the possibility of a pleasure quite extraneous to tactile pleasure. And this is aesthetic pleasure.

A lion experiences pleasure when he sees a stag, but it is not a pleasure in its shape nor in the sounds it makes. Rather, he immediately refers these sensations to his tactile wants. "Man, however, enjoys these sensations not just because they promise a prey, but also because they are pleasing to sense" ("Homo autem delectatur secundum alios sensus non solum propter hoc, sed etiam propter convenientiam sensibilium").[44] Also, although we have a duty to control our sense pleasures by temperance, there is no such duty in the case of the latter type of pleasure.

> Inquantum autem sensibilia aliorum sensuum sunt delectabilia propter sui convenientiam, sicut cum delectatur homo in sono bene harmonizato, ista delectatio non pertinet ad conservationem naturae. Unde non habent huiusmodi passiones illam principalitatem ut circa eas antonomastice temperantia dicatur.

> These sensations are pleasurable in themselves. This is the case, for example, when we listen to music. It is not a pleasure, therefore, connected to the preservation of our nature. So it follows that feelings of this kind do not possess the fundamental character which would enable us to connect them with temperance, not even by an antonomasia.[45]

Thus, only human beings are capable of pleasure in the beauty of objects: "solus homo delectatur in ipsa pulchritudine sensibilium secundum seipsam" ("Man alone takes delight in the beauty of sense objects for its own sake").[46]

All of this is part of a discussion on an ethical question. The underlying aesthetic consciousness in Aquinas's discussions of ethics is what constitutes the object of our inquiry.

Plan of the Research

Now that I have established the existence of a medieval aesthetic sense, widely diffused throughout the culture, accredited by the works of Aquinas both in his psychology and in his artistic personality, and now also that his works have testified to the possibility of a disinterested aesthetic pleasure—now at last we can turn to what he has written about beauty.

Aquinas did not formulate a clear, specific aesthetic theory in a homogeneous, explicit body of writings. It is necessary, therefore, to choose an appropriate pathway through his works. Such a pathway is suggested by traditional interpretations, but also by the structure of Aquinas's own system. This system begins with God, considered in himself as exemplary cause and the fullness of being, and proceeds to deal with God in relation to his creatures, God as efficient cause and redeemer. It then passes on to the human actions which pertain to eternal life, considering them both generically and in particular, as passions and habits, virtues and vices.

Following this plan, I begin with an analysis of beauty as a transcendental attribute of being and then consider it in relation to man and the natural world. I look at it from the point of view of the psychology of perception and also examine its ontology, its formal properties.

I then examine beauty in relation to the operative virtue *ars,* in relation to the moral life, and in relation also to judgments of the intellect. This perspective will enable us to see the fundamental role of beauty for Aquinas, as the restoring of order and of an equilibrium brought about through a synthesis of random events and empirical contradictions. If we are to unearth the philosophical theories and their historical significance, which interest us here, then we must give full weight to Aquinas's metaphysical vision, his image of a universe hierarchically ordered in a perfect harmony of causes and ends. It is only in paying close attention to what he knew and wrote that we can bring to light, not just what he actually said, but also what he did not know how to say, and indeed what he was unable to say. Thus shall we frustrate the many commentators who indulge in the presumption of Aquinas's omniscience by pointing out things that he never said at all.

II

Beauty as a Transcendental

The Problem

At the very beginning of his *De Veritate,* Aquinas confronts the problem of being and its transcendental properties in the following words.

> Illud autem quod primo intellectus concipit quasi notissimum, et in quod conceptiones omnes resolvit, est ens . . . Unde oportet quod omnes aliae conceptiones intellectus accipiantur ex additione ad ens. Sed enti non possunt addi aliqua quasi extranea per modum quo differentia additur generi, vel accidens subiecto, quia quaelibet natura est essentialiter ens.

> That which the intellect first conceives as, in a way, the most evident, and to which it reduces all its concepts, is being . . . Consequently, all the other conceptions of the intellect are had by additions to being. But nothing can be added to being as though it were something not included in being—in the way that a difference is added to a genus or an accident to a subject—for every reality is essentially a being[1]

Being, therefore, is not a genus, and nothing can be predicated of it in an adjectival sense. Nonetheless, Aquinas goes on, there do exist certain properties which, it might be said, can be added to being ("dicuntur addere supra ens") in the sense that they express a mode of being or of presence which the term *being* (*ens*) itself does not make explicit.

Aquinas further distinguishes between properties which express a particular and partial mode of the being of being—namely the categories, which define being in determinate areas and apply to a particular set of beings—and a different kind of predicate, which applies to every being ("ita quod modus expressus sit modus generalis consequens omne ens"). In the Scholastic tradition, this second type of attribute is given the name "transcendental," or "transcendental property of being." In his *De Veritate* Aquinas distinguishes among and discusses the transcendentals *unum, res, ens, aliquid, bonum,* and *verum* (the one, a thing, a being, something, the good, the true).

The transcendentals add nothing to being. Nor do they in any way diminish its totality and extension. They inhere in being coextensively and can be discerned in every being, and they determine the character of beings both in themselves and in relation to other beings. They are a bit like differing visual angles from which being can be looked at. This is why they differ from one another conceptually or logically (*ratione*), according as it were to the particular point of view that one adopts to being. But each transcendental is nonetheless the whole of being and is found in everything that exists. This is why they are convertible into one another.[2]

It is well known that the problem of the transcendentals originated in Aristotle's *Metaphysics,* where he discussed being and the one (*ens* and *unum*) in several places.[3] Later on the Arab philosophers, who transmitted the problem to Latin Scholasticism, enriched the list of transcendentals by adding *res* and *aliquid* (thing and something). All Scholastic thinking manifests in various ways the fundamental belief that being (and also God, the most perfect being) possesses certain properties.[4] However, the problem was of interest to the medievals in the first place primarily in connection with apologetics. The Catharist heresy, with its revival of Manichaeism, divided the universe into opposing forces of good and evil. To combat this heresy, it was necessary to reaffirm the inner value and above all the goodness of all being.

The result was that all medieval discussion of the transcendentals led back to a metaphysical issue of enormous significance. This is true also of Aquinas, by whose time the problem was fairly clearly defined in its general outlines. The issue of the transcendentals was in fact the issue of the fullness of being, of the indissoluble union of being and value. To remove any terms from the traditional list of transcendentals was to diminish being.

It was therefore necessary that the transcendental properties of being should be enumerated with great care; the manner in which the question of truth is posed in Aquinas's *De Veritate* is proof of that. But of course this treatise is neither exhaustive nor definitive, and we may with some justice inquire why it is that *pulchrum* is not to be found in classical accounts of the transcendentals. Is beauty also a property coextensive with being, a mode universally attendant upon being in all its manifestations?

If beauty is considered to be a transcendental, it acquires a metaphysical worth, an unchanging objectivity, and an extension which is universal. As a result, the aesthetic pertains to the universe as a whole. The problem of beauty then takes on an importance that cannot be ignored, and any solution to the problem has decisive implications for metaphysics. This means in turn that our investigations here can be conducted only in the light of Aquinas's entire system.

If beauty is a transcendental, there are two fundamental consequences, one having to do with being, the other with beauty itself. First, the various determinations of being are affected: the universe acquires a further perfection, and God acquires a new attribute. Beauty, for its part, acquires concreteness and a quality of necessity, an objectivity and dignity. This is why the question has been of interest not just to historical commentators but also in neo-Thomist apologetics, in which it is thought necessary to combat aesthetic subjectivism by reaffirming the objectivity of beauty. In fact contemporary neo-Thomists are inclined to insist that beauty is a transcendental, whereas those of a generation ago tended to exclude it.

Contemporary Thomists, therefore, tend to look upon the transcendentals in a doctrinal rather than a historical and interpretative manner. They are somewhat more polemical, and more influenced by a particular aesthetic problem (that of the subjectivity or objectivity of the aesthetic), than the medievals were. For the medievals, the fact that goodness was a transcendental meant that there could be nothing evil in being—not, that is, in the metaphysical sense. In the same way, defining beauty as a transcendental implied the elimination of the seeming deformities and dissonances in the universe. Such an enterprise involved a kind of ardor and an aesthetic optimism which, on its own theoretical level, reflected the sentiments of St. Francis's *Cantico delle creature*.

The Aesthetic Vision of Things

These beliefs and sentiments entered the Middle Ages from many sources. First and foremost was the Bible, in which the beauties of God's creation were constantly extolled. Similar views were common also in the classical world. The medievals had no direct acquaintance with the works of Plato, save for his *Timaeus,* but this was enough to generate a certain kind of aesthetic sensibility. The cosmology of the *Timaeus,* articulated as it was in terms of mathematics, produced an image of the world as something endowed with artistic order and resplendent with beauty.[5]

The *Timaeus* and the Bible were not the only sources. For example, we should not overlook a number of influences derived from Pythagoras. These were most fully articulated in Boethius, whose idea of the universe was aesthetic in character, combining the musical with the mathematical.

Yet another source gave rise to what de Bruyne calls "l'esthétique sapientale"—an aesthetics based upon a verse in the Book of Wisdom, "But thou hast ordered all things in measure, and number, and weight" (11: 21). This verse inspired the Augustinian concepts of *modus, forma,* and *ordo* (dimension or quantity, form, and order), which appear everywhere in Scholasticism, employed sometimes in the definition of beauty, sometimes to define the good.[6]

However, the strongest impulse underlying the medieval aesthetic conception of the world came from neo-Platonism—to some extent from Proclus and Porphyry, but principally from Dionysius the Areopagite, in whom the aesthetic vision of things found its fullest meaning and its fullest, and most influential, expression. The very obscurity of his language, which lent itself to multiple interpretations, for long prevented any critical awareness of the metaphysical principles upon which his thought was based; but it also helped in the formation of an aesthetic outlook on things by way of the emotions. Dionysius may not have been fully understood, but his authority was unquestioned.

The whole of Chapter IV of Dionysius' *The Divine Names* (especially IV, 7 and 10) presents the universe as a cascade of beauties springing forth from the First Principle, a dazzling radiance of sensuous splendors which diversify in all created being.

Supersubstantiale vero pulchrum pulchritudo quidem dicitur propter traditam ab ipso omnibus existentibus iuxta proprietatem uniuscuiusque pulchritudinem; et sicut universorum consonantiae et claritatis causa, ad similitudinem luminis cum fulgore immittens universis pulchrificas fontani radii ipsius traditiones, et sicut omnia ad seipsum vocans, unde et càllos dicitur, et sicut tota in totis congregans.

That, beautiful beyond being, is said to be Beauty—for
   it gives beauty from itself in a manner appropriate to each,
   it causes the consonance and splendor of all,
   it flashes forth upon all, after the manner of light, the
     beauty producing gifts of its flowing ray,
   it calls all to itself,
     when it is called beauty.[7]

This abundance of images fascinated and won over medieval readers. Not only did they take from it many of their ideas on aesthetics; it also seemed to them to reflect the sensibility which was being formed in them in any case by other influences.

One of these influences, and one that cannot be ignored, was John Scottus Eriugena. Eriugena's thought was in essence that of Dionysius the Areopagite, but rendered more congenial to the medievals, assimilated and translated into a system of enormous breadth. Eriugena taught the Middle Ages to look upon things with a penetrating eye, to read the universe, to read nature, as if it were a vast store of symbols. For him, the relations between God and things were not solely causal, but were also like the relations between sign and signified.[8] The created world is a revelation. Nature is a theophany. In this theophanic harmony, objects are symbols, disclosures, indicators. It is their nature to point toward God, and to God conceived of as Beauty revealing itself through harmonious design. It is a theophanic vision which is openly and profoundly aesthetic.[9] Eriugena's aesthetic perspective was the most far-reaching and the most lively in the whole of the Middle Ages. When the influence of his thought is added to elements from Plato, Pythagoras, neo-Platonism, Augustine, and Boethius, all of these together explain the widely-felt need for beauty which accompanied the medievals' observations of the world, a need which manifested itself in the search for proofs of this beauty. This outlook was

University of St. Francis Library

always part of the medieval mentality, although it has not always been sufficiently noticed. It was also part of the Christian mentality. For if the First Cause is conceived of as creative and provident, the created comes to be seen, in the words of scripture, as "exceedingly good"; and this conception quickly leads to the notion of the exceedingly beautiful.

The vision of the universe that is at issue here may be described by the term *pankalia,* the beauty of all things. It is a very interesting notion, and one which in a religious context is both edifying and stimulating. If it is looked at on a critical level, however, it is seen to have certain dangers. There are dangers involved in defining it, for all too often the attempts to establish the validity of pancalism are emotive and uncritical, and depend upon a conception of the created world which is mythical and anthropomorphic rather than philosophical. It is dangerous to handle in general, for the diffuse image of constantly emerging beauties can lead to the loss of a hard, concrete sense of the aesthetic.

The medieval need for beauty, to which I referred above, created the need also for a metaphysical verification. The perception of the world in terms of its beauty came to birth as a sentiment which was at once religious and aesthetic. But this initial passion came to infuse itself into various theoretical systems, and then later on became the object of rigorous metaphysical and ontological inquiry. Medieval aesthetic feeling had to be tested, and this occurred with the revival of Aristotle. With this there arose metaphysical structures and a rigor of method which would permit only those concepts of totality which were subject to law, classification, and measure.

Aquinas's Texts

The medieval need for beauty in all things was, in the beginning, vague and uncomplicated. But no philosophical system could ignore it. Even philosophers who were personally insensible to the beauty of things found that the problem of beauty was forced upon them by works such as those of Dionysius the Areopagite (Pseudo-Dionysius).

During the period that Aquinas spent in Cologne, he attended

134035

College of St. Francis Library
Joliet, Illinois

Albertus Magnus's lectures on Pseudo-Dionysius. This was in the years 1248–1252, before he embarked upon his career as a bachelor of arts, and therefore before his earliest writings. Thus, it was Dionysian thought which first presented the philosophical issue of beauty to the student Aquinas. It would seem to follow that, although his *Commentary on the Divine Names* dates from 1265–66, the influence of the Areopagite's thought was present in earlier works—for instance, in the infrequent references to beauty in Aquinas's *Commentary on the Sentences* (1252). It will be best, however, to begin with the *Commentary on the Divine Names*. Here we can discover how Aquinas assimilated, and attempted to justify systematically, the medieval pancalistic sensibility, the sensibility which had been so vividly expressed in Pseudo-Dionysius' work. We can see that Aquinas's approach to the Dionysian text consisted in the attempt "to reduce to homogeneous mental categories the mystico-metaphysical attire of the Oriental doctor." [10]

The Divine Names is filled with references to beauty. Wisdom and beauty appear early in the list of divine names: "Sapientem autem et pulchram, quoniam existentia omnia propriam naturam incorruptam servantia, omni harmonia divina et sancto decore sunt plena" ("Wise and beautiful. For all beings are preserved in what is incorruptible of their own nature and indeed are filled with every divine harmony and sacred good form"). [11] Aquinas, influenced as he was by the Augustinian aesthetics of wisdom, refers the concept of harmony to the operations of Wisdom, "whose function is to order and measure things" ("cuius est ordinare et commensurare res"). [12] But he also accepts the close identification of the two terms, the view that God's ordering of things is both an operation of his wisdom and also the source of beauty.

The question of beauty is raised specifically, however, in chapter IV of *The Divine Names*, "Concerning the Good, Light, Beauty, Love, Ecstasis, and Zeal." Initially it deals with the good, which is conceived of in the first instance as a name which is properly and preeminently predicable of God. Next it is attributed to angelic powers, who possess it in a manner that is more evident and accessible than in the divine nature. Finally, it belongs to all corruptible creatures. This hierarchy of living beings, a hierarchy which depends upon the degree of participation in the most perfect Being, is subsequently presented, not just as a hierarchy of goodness, but also as a hierarchy of beauty. In IV, 7, Dionysius examines beauty as a divine attribute, and also its causal role and its diffusion throughout creation. In IV, 10 (after an interlude concerned with the divine and the human intellects), he returns to an analysis of the causal efficacy of beauty. Beauty is attributed, at once and without equivocation, to God. The Dionysian text (IV, 7) reads:

> Hoc bonum laudatur a Sanctis Theologis et sicut pulchritudo et sicut pulchrum, et sicut dilectio et sicut diligibile, et quae-cumque aliae convenientes sunt pulchrificae et gratiosae habitae pulchritudinis nominationes.

> This good is celebrated by the sacred theologians as beautiful and as beauty, as *agapē* and beloved, and by many other divine names which are suitable to its beauty producing and rich character.

Aquinas stresses in his *Commentary* that "this good" is *ipsum bonum,* God himself. He sets out furthermore to show that the beautiful and beauty (*pulchrum* and *pulchritudo*) belong in a different way to God and to his creatures. In God, these two attributes are not divisible: "deus tamen utrumque comprehendit in se, secundum unum et idem" ("God enfolds both in himself as one and the same").[13] But in the case of creatures, Aquinas writes,

> pulchrum et pulchritudo distinguuntur secundum participans et participatum, ita quod pulchrum dicitur hoc quod participat pulchritudinem; pulchritudo autem participatio primae causae quae omnia pulchra facit: pulchritudo enim creaturae nihil est aliud quam similitudo divinae pulchritudinis in rebus parteci-pata.

> the beautiful and beauty are distinguished with respect to participation and participants. Thus, we call something "beautiful" because it is a participant in beauty. Beauty, however, is a participation in the first cause, which makes all things beautiful. So that the beauty of creatures is simply a likeness of the divine beauty in which things participate.

The distinction is clear: the beauty which we find in all things is a participation in (rather than a mere reflection of) a beauty which is identified with the First Good and therefore with Being. God is *supersubstantiale pulchrum* (*hyperousion kalon,* supersubstantially beautiful, beautiful beyond being). He is called Beauty because, as Aquinas comments, "he gives beauty to all created beings, according to the properties of each" ("omnibus entibus creatis dat pulchritudinem, secundum proprietatem uniuscuiusque"). In God there is no defect. In him, beauty is not present in one part rather than in another, nor is it present under some particular aspect. Rather, God is beautiful simply and in all respects ("Deus quoad omnes et simpliciter pulcher est"). He is, Aquinas goes on, *pulcherrimus* and *superpulcher.* He is beautiful in himself and not in respect of anything else: "Deus est pulcher in seipso." And in God, this preeminence of beauty is the same thing as a preeminence in the generating of beauty, "for he has within him, wonderfully and before all else, the source of all beauty" ("inquantum in seipso excellenter et ante omnia alia, fontem totius pulchritudinis").

God, then, is the creator of beauty in the world. And he creates it by means of consonance and light. I shall consider this latter aspect of the theory in due course, for, as Aquinas said, it concerns the nature of beauty ("in quo consistat pulchritudinis ratio"). But for the present, we should note that God, the Supreme Beauty, creates all things in accordance with the order and the effulgence which are constitutive elements in the value which he shares with others. The divine beauty is creative because it produces order and harmony, and "it is always the case that whatever creatures may have in the way of communion and coming together, they have it due to the power of beauty" ("universaliter omnes creaturae, quantamcumque unionem habent, habent ex virtute pulchri"). Furthermore, beauty is the effective cause of being, and the final and the exemplary cause of the created world. As Aquinas writes,

> Omne quod est, est ex pulchro et bono quod est Deus, sicut ex principio effectivo; et in pulchro et bono est, sicut in principio contentivo vel conservativo; et ad pulchrum et bonum convertitur, ipsum desiderans, sicut ad finem . . . et omnia quaecumque sunt et fiunt, propter pulchrum et bonum sunt et fiunt et ad ipsum omnia inspiciunt, sicut ad causam exemplarem, quam habent ut regulam suae operationis.

> Everything that exists comes from beauty and goodness, that is from God, as from an effective principle. And things have their

being in beauty and goodness as if in a principle that preserves and maintains. And they turn toward beauty and goodness and desire them as their end . . . And all things are and all things become because of beauty and goodness, and all things look to them, as to an exemplary cause, which they possess as a rule governing their activities.[14]

Here we might pause to note how laboriously (and incompletely) Aquinas's commentary strives to impose an order upon the riotous and hermetic imagery which throngs the Dionysian text. The whole matter could be summarized in a few sentences, with the term *pankalia* as a central point of reference: everything is beautiful and comes together in beauty; everything is constructed in accordance with beauty; everything shines with beauty and declares and manifests beauty; the order which the creator Good has assigned to things—the combining of parts, their unifying communion, their harmony—constitutes the rationale of being, goodness, and beauty.

This, at any rate, is how Aquinas understands it. In his *Commentary* he identifies the creator Good with being and regards it as the foundation of single, finite goods in their existential concreteness—in short, he identifies the Divine Goodness, or the divine essence, with the fullness of being.

> Unumquodque enim bonum est, secundum quod est res actu; Deo autem proprium est quod sit suum esse, unde ipse solus est sua bonitas.

> Everything is good according to its function. It is the nature of God, however, to be what he is; and so, he alone is his own goodness.[15]

We cannot look more closely here at the extent to which this is a misinterpretation of the Dionysian text. For Pseudo-Dionysius, *esse* was an effect of the act of creation and was not identified, in its fullness, with God. God was *super esse* in the sense that he was beyond being; he was the cause of the existence of things in their goodness and their beauty. However, the fact remains that Aquinas very clearly held that God was being, goodness, and beauty, and that things participated in these attributes.

The identification of God with the fullness of being went against the spirit of Pseudo-Dionysius. But this could happen easily enough; all that was needed were slight alterations in certain terms. In the case of beauty, however, it is rather different, for here the Areopagite's text is, so to speak, expansive; the idea of the beautiful (*pulchrum*) is ubiquitous in chapter IV of *The Divine Names*. I am not concerned to decide here whether *pulchrum* is one of the divine names by way of hyperbole or by way of analogy—two interpretations which might be attributed, with all their implications, respectively to Pseudo-Dionysius and Aquinas. Rather, I wish to establish whether *pulchrum* was, to put it crudely, a divine name or not. And in fact Pseudo-Dionysius presents his readers with this name, and Aquinas accepts it as a name: "beauty," Aquinas writes, "which is God" ("quod est Deus"). There is no hesitation. The God of St. Thomas—*ens realissimum,* Oneness, Goodness, Truth—is also, therefore, Beauty. The identification is implicit in his overall acceptance of the Dionysian work.

However, in the economy of the Thomist system there was no allowance for vague or poetic expressions; so that his *Commentary,* reflecting as it did something of the Dionysian text, could not help being a trifle overblown and allusive. As a consequence, the view that beauty was an attribute of God found expression in the only manner that Thomist coherence and rigor could permit—and that was, by adding beauty unequivocally to the attributes of being. The rubric involved here is one which we have already seen in the passage from *De Veritate* examined at the beginning of the chapter. We should recall that *De Veritate* belongs to the period 1256–1259, just before the *Commentary on the Divine Names*. The discussion of the transcendentals in the earlier work ignores beauty; so the *Commentary* would seem to be the right place to make amends for the oversight.

Let us see how Aquinas does this. The Dionysian text reads:

> Propter quod et idem est bono pulchrum; quoniam bonum et pulchrum secundum omnem causam cuncta desiderant, et non est aliquid existentium quod non participet pulchro et bono . . .

> The beautiful and the good are the same:
> all beings desire the beautiful and the good with respect

to every cause,
no being fails to partake
of the beautiful and good.[16]

Aquinas's commentary emphasises this passage. Here, evidently, the beautiful and the good are one and the same. Both, as we have already seen, are efficient and final causes. And it seems natural to identify them because both attributes are predicable of the divinity.

However, when Aquinas finishes his actual commentary he adds another sentence, concerned not with the Dionysian text but rather with the clarification of his own earlier remarks.

> Quamvis autem pulchrum et bonum sint idem subiecto, quia tam claritas quam consonantia sub ratione boni continentur, tamen ratione differunt: nam pulchrum addit supra bonum, ordinem ad vim cognoscitivam illud esse huiusmodi.

> Although the beautiful and the good are the same in the subject—because both clarity and consonance are included in the nature of the good—they are conceptually different. For beauty adds something to the good, namely an order which enables cognition to know that a thing is of such a kind.[17]

The beautiful and the good are identical in the subject. *Claritas* and *consonantia,* which are sources of beauty, are also an aspect of the good, insofar as they are effects of the Good which creates and orders. Nonetheless, the beautiful and the good differ conceptually (*ratione*)—that is, according to the way in which they are conceived, according to the chosen point of view.

This should not surprise us. For these two features—being identical in the subject, but differing *ratione*—are features appropriate to transcendental attributes; this, for example, is the case with the good and the true.[18] Still, this explanation seems rather to assimilate the beautiful into the good than to identify both of them with being. The claim that they are distinguishable *ratione* is compatible with either view, but the former interpretation is suggested by the statement that *claritas* and *consonantia,* the criteria of beauty, "are included in the nature of the good." And this interpretation seems to get extra support from a passage earlier in the *Commentary.*

The earlier passage occurs at the beginning of Aquinas's discussion of chapter IV of *The Divine Names.*

> Item, cum bonum sit quod omnia appetunt, quaecumque de se important appetibilis rationem, ad rationem boni pertinere videntur: huiusmodi autem sunt lumen et pulchrum, de quibus etiam in hoc capitulo agit.

> Since the good is what all things desire, anything which has the explanation of its appetite within itself can be seen to pertain to the notion of the good. Of this sort are light and beauty, which the author also discusses in this chapter.[19]

The beautiful, therefore—like light, love, ecstasy, and zeal—is considered as the object of an appetite and as assimilable to the good. It seems reasonable to say, therefore, that in his commentary upon chapter IV Aquinas thinks of the beautiful as a way in which the good makes itself manifest.

This is a view which is not to be found in Pseudo-Dionysius, at least not expressed in these terms. Here we encounter the thinking of Aquinas himself, or rather the language which he uses to clarify, in terms of his own system, the ideas of the Areopagite.

Language of this kind was nothing new in Aquinas. In his *Commentary on the Sentences* (which takes us back to 1252), he had written:

> Pulchritudo non habet rationem appetibilis nisi inquantum induit rationem boni: Sic enim et verum appetibile est: sed secundum rationem propriam habet claritatem.

> Beauty is not an object of desire except insofar as it assumes the nature of the good. Truth is the same. But beauty does possess clarity of its own nature.[20]

This passage is quite clear. The beautiful is desirable, and so is the true, insofar as both take on the aspect of the good. These three values are thus established as equivalent and convertible. Beauty, furthermore, has its own distinctive logic (*ratio*). These remarks, let us note, were written in 1252, when Aquinas had scarcely left Cologne and was still under the influence of Albertus Magnus's comments on *The Divine Names*. In the later *De Veritate* (1256–1259), beauty makes no appearance in the section dealing with the properties of being.[21] It reappears later in the work, however, when Aquinas, referring explicitly to Pseudo-Dionysius, asks whether beings desire anything other than the good. The answer according to Augustine was that they also desired peace, and according to Pseudo-Dionysius that they also desired beauty. Aquinas writes:

> appetitum terminari ad bonum et pacem et pulchrum, non est eum terminari in diversa. Ex hoc enim ipso quod aliquid appetit bonum, appetit simul et pulchrum et pacem: pulchrum quidem, in quantum est in seipso modificatum et specificatum, quod in ratione boni includitur; sed bonum addit ordinem perfectivi ad alia. Unde quicumque appetit bonum, appetit hoc ipso pulchrum.

> If appetite terminates in good and peace and the beautiful, this does not mean that it terminates in different goals. By the very fact of tending to good, a thing at the same time tends to the beautiful and to peace. It tends to the beautiful as it is proportioned and specified in itself. These notes are included in the essential character of good, but good adds a relationship of what is perfective in regard to other things. So anyone who desires the good, by that very fact desires the beautiful.[22]

This passage does not of itself add much to what was quoted above from the *Commentary on the Sentences*. But it does have two peculiarities. First, in a work which contains a discussion of the transcendentals, this passage confers upon the beautiful a status of subordinate identity with the good. Second, the distinctive property of the beautiful (that a thing "is proportioned and specified in itself") is included in the notion of the good. This is similar to the *Commentary on the Divine Names,* in which *claritas* and *consonantia* are included in the notion of the good.

In the *Commentary on the Divine Names,* in the very middle of an explicit identification of the beautiful with the fullness of being, the only thing that is exclusively and genuinely Thomistic is not this identification at all, but rather the cautiously worded sentence referred to above. The beautiful is presented as something identifiable with the good in its constitutive features; and yet it is likened to the true because of its relation to cognition. One can only wonder whether this anodyne and ambiguous feature is all that is distinctive of the beautiful.

*   *   *

But Aquinas's mature thinking is found in the two *Summae,* so we must now look at the *Summa Theologiae* to see whether there is anything more. In I, 5, "De Bono in Communi," Aquinas examines the relations between being and the good (*ens* and *bonum*). In what sense, he asks, can these two be identified? If the good is that which everyone desires, it is clearly desirable because of its perfection. But something has perfection when it has plenitude; and the actuality of a thing is its *esse.* It therefore follows that the good is an *esse* whose specific character it is to be desirable. Every being is good as such.[23]

As Aquinas continues, it emerges that the notion of the good can be defined also in terms of *modus, species,* and *ordo* (measure, species, and order). His reasoning is as follows. A thing is called good insofar as it is perfect; and a thing is perfect when it lacks none of the perfections which pertain to it. Further, this complete adherence to its own nature comes to be realized by its form. Form, however, is something which is determined according to *modus* (measure or proportion), which also assigns the thing to its *species,* and which directs the thing to its end according to an *ordo.* These three characteristics, then, which a thing acquires from the concreteness of its *esse,* are good insofar as they are desirable, and the reason why the thing is good. These considerations show why, in the passage quoted above from *De Veritate,* beauty was included in the notion of the good because it was "proportioned and specified in itself."

In the light of all of this, we can now look in greater detail at *Summa Theologiae,* I, 5, 4. Here Aquinas asks whether the good, which is a final cause, is also any other kind of cause. In *objectio* 1 of the article he refers to chapter IV of *The Divine Names,* in which the beautiful and the good are identified; since the beautiful has the aspect of a formal cause, it seems to follow that so also does the good. This reference to beauty as a formal cause is something new in Aquinas. It is true that in his *Commentary on the Divine Names* he had written, "Particular things are beautiful according to their own nature, that is, according to their own form" ("Singula sunt pulchra secundum propriam rationem, idest secundum propriam formam").[24] But he meant by this that form, insofar as it is constitutive of the being of a thing, participates in divine beauty according to its nature. Here in the *Summa Theologiae,* by contrast, we find it stated as received opinion that beauty has the character of a formal cause: "Pulchrum importat rationem causae formalis." In due course I shall examine the reasons for and the implications of this. But for the moment, and since Aquinas accepts the view without difficulty, we will look rather at how his thought develops on the question put in article 4.

In the corpus of the article, Aquinas begins by saying that the good is indeed an end. For it to be an end, however, it must presuppose both the existence of the thing whose end it is—and therefore an efficient cause—and also the thing's formal cause. In the causal process there is in fact a hierarchy, in which the end toward which the thing is ordered comes first. Second, there is a formal factor, owing to which the thing comes to be adequate to itself. Last there is an existential factor, in virtue of which the thing has being. But on the other hand, when I confront a thing which has been caused I consider first of all that it exists; next I consider what it is in accordance with a particular perfection; and finally, and in consequence, I consider the fact that it is desirable. What, then, is Aquinas's reply to *objectio* 1? It goes as follows:

> Ad primum ergo dicendum quod pulchrum et bonum in subjecto quidem sunt idem, quia super eandem rem fundantur, scilicet super formam, et propter hoc, bonum laudatur ut pulchrum. Sed ratione differunt. Nam bonum proprie respicit appetitum; est enim bonum quod omnia appetunt. Et ideo habet rationem finis; nam appetitus est quasi quidam motus ad rem. Pulchrum autem respicit vim cognoscitivam: pulchra enim dicuntur quae visa placent.

> To the first *objectio* I reply that the beautiful and the good are the same in any subject. For they are grounded in the same thing, namely form, and this is why the good is esteemed as beautiful. They are different notions nonetheless. For the good, which is what all things desire, properly has to do with appetite. So, too, it has to do with the idea of an end; for appetite is a kind of movement toward an end. Beauty, however, has to do with knowledge, for we call those things beautiful which please us when they are seen.

The remainder of the article deals with the properties of the beautiful and the modalities in which it is known. Here, however, I wish to compare the passage just quoted with a passage further on in the *Summa Theologiae*.

The context of the second passage is another problem about the relation of *bonum* and *pulchrum*, whether the good is the only cause of love. Aquinas writes:

> Pulchrum est idem bono, sola ratione differens. Cum enim bonum sit quod omnia appetunt, de ratione boni est quod in eo quietetur appetitus: sed ad rationem pulchri pertinet quod in eius aspectu seu cognitione quietetur appetitus . . . Et sic patet quod pulchrum addit supra bonum, quendam ordinem ad vim cognoscitivam; ita quod bonum dicatur id quod simpliciter complacet appetitui; pulchrum autem dicatur id cuius ipsa apprehensio placet.

> "Good" and "beautiful" have the same reference but differ in meaning. For the good, being what all things want, is that in which the appetite comes to rest; whereas the beautiful is that in which the appetite comes to rest through contemplation or knowledge . . . "Beautiful" therefore adds to "good" a reference to the cognitive powers; "good" refers simply to that in which the appetite takes pleasure, but "beautiful" refers to something the mere apprehension of which gives pleasure.[25]

It would seem from these two passages that any confusion about the good and the beautiful has been dispelled. Each of the two values has its own *ratio,* or sense. Furthermore, and this is of great importance, both of them are grounded in form, which means that they are grounded in actuality, in the concreteness of being. They can be identified, therefore, with *ens* or being. And the beautiful is distinguished by the fact that it refers to knowledge, to the *vis cognoscitiva*. In the *Commentary on the Divine Names* this reference to knowledge was the only thing which was used to distinguish beauty, so that the reader might be inclined to wonder how beauty differs from truth. In the two passages just quoted, however, the reference to knowledge is given a special sense, in that beauty gives pleasure in the act of being apprehended.

Returning now to the question of whether beauty is a transcendental, these two passages seem definitive, though only implicitly so. They are definitive because, if we interpret them in the light of the *Commentary on the Divine Names,* they establish that beauty is a constant property of all being. It is a property of being, not because it appears this way in aesthetic intuitions of the world, nor in some emotive sense of beauty without rational justification; rather, it is a property of being in a precise and categorical sense of these terms— or, better, in a kind of metacategorical simplification. That is, beauty is identified with being simply as being. This theory is implicit rather than explicit, however; Aquinas never expressly states that *ens* and *bonum* and *pulchrum* are interchangeable. Instead, beauty adheres to being only through the mediation of the good.

My insistence on precision in this matter might seem overdone, were it not for a phrase which occurs in one of the passages quoted from the *Summa Theologiae*. The phrase is *visa placent* (beautiful things *please us when they are seen*), and it is a disturbing intrusion into the whole question and its context. As we shall see, it introduces a subjective condition for beauty, and thus points to a denial of its transcendental status. At the very least it brings uncertainty to a theory which otherwise might seem satisfactory enough.

Modern Interpretations

There is another factor which encourages us to probe the question of transcendentals somewhat further: the long-standing debate on the subject among students of Aquinas. There is a divergency of views, and often enough a sharp contentiousness, which warn us to be very cautious in how we interpret the relevant texts. The various accounts of Aquinas's ideas are not lacking in penetration and insight; but their presuppositions are not those of a historical inquiry, but rather those of an autonomous and renovated body of theory. In other words, these students of Aquinas, almost all of whom are neo-Thomists, are guided by systematic rather than historical concerns. This is why they frame the question about beauty absolutely rather than exegetically: they ask, not whether Aquinas considered beauty to be a transcendental, but whether beauty is in fact a transcendental. Many replies have been given to this question, and it would be tedious to list them all.[26] But there are two in particular whose divergence is particularly sharp, and which also are helpful to the present inquiry. These are the views of Marc de Munnynck and Jacques Maritain.[27]

De Munnynck holds that Aquinas did not add beauty to the list of transcendentals, and that it would be foolhardy to ascribe any such view to him. Aquinas's notional distinctions (distinctions *ratione*) among the transcendentals are inadequate, so that any arguments about them based upon empirical facts are fallacious. Not all being gives us aesthetic pleasure, and some objects are incapable of being enjoyed by us. Also, the notion of divine beauty, which is something that we cannot know, casts no light upon the notion of a participated beauty. The state of affairs is just the reverse—we start with the beauty of created beings and then attribute this quality to God. Furthermore, the term *placet*, "pleases," which refers to aesthetic experience, is different in different subjects, so that beauty does not possess the universality of the true and the good. And again, whereas the true and the good pertain to the whole of being, including the possible, the beautiful refers to human nature and so is not predicable of the possible. All of these arguments are very shrewd. Yet I do not find them conclusive, not least because de Munnynck concedes that in the end everything is beautiful, at least for God.

The reason he is so negative lies in the importance he gives to the phrase *visa placent*. He considers this to refer to the constitutive element of beauty. This is why his views have been variously called psychologistic, sensationalist, subjectivist, and empiricist. He begins on a subjectivist level, with a desire to evaluate the function and outlook of the observer and the personal quality of his enjoyment; as a result, the dispute about transcendentals moves into the background. De Munnynck's conclusion is that all things are beautiful, but only for God and not for us. Aquinas's views are made dependent upon the notion *visa placent;* it is this, for de Munnynck, which constitutes their novelty.

Maritain is quite different. In *Art and Scholasticism* he argues exhaustively for the view that beauty is a transcendental. His arguments are based upon passages in Aquinas with which we are by now familiar. He insists on this view even though he gives weight also to the phrase *visa placent*. He conceives of beauty in the mode of analogy. "Like being and the other transcendentals, it is essentially *analogous,* that is to say it is predicated by divers reasons, *sub diversa ratione,* of the divers subjects of which it is predicated: each kind of being *is* in its own way, is *good* in its own way, is beautiful in its own way."[28] Maritain bases his interpretation upon, in particular, the *Commentary on the Divine Names* and arrives at the following important definition: "[Beauty] is in fact the splendour of all the transcendentals together."[29]

I call it important for various reasons, although "interesting" might be more accurate. The definition has certain peculiarities. I am not aware that it has any ancestry either in Aquinas himself or in neo-Thomism. Nowhere else do we find a theory which, instead of putting beauty side by side with the other transcendentals, says that it is the splendor of all of them together. And indeed we might think it possible also to say that truth is the truth of them all together or that the good is their goodness and desirability; perhaps Aquinas in a certain sense did say something like this. Still, the definition does seem especially appropriate to beauty, for various reasons, and in due course we shall discover that if it is not in the nature of a conclusive discovery it is at least well expressed.[30]

As I have already said, however, this kind of theory arises when the issue of the transcendentals is posed as a question of apologetics rather than as one of historical interpretation. If our desire is instead to arrive at a cautious estimate of Aquinas's actual thinking, conducted as it was in a certain period and in response to certain problems, then of course the question is whether he himself considered beauty to be a transcendental. And we must also ask whether by any chance an affirmative answer would be at variance with his philosophical system as a whole. If so, then we ought to note the inconsistency rather than deny its historical accuracy—something that has always seemed to neo-Thomists to be not just objectionable, but unthinkable.

Beauty as a Transcendental in Thirteenth-Century Philosophy

Aquinas's own words have so far left us with some degree of perplexity. It will advance our inquiry, therefore, if we next examine the sense of his language in the light of the philosophical tradition preceding him. It is not fully clear to the modern reader, so we will try to capture the resonance which it possessed in its own time.[31]

According to de Bruyne, the view that beauty is a transcendental had already appeared in the eleventh century, in Otloh of St. Emmeran's *Liber de Tentationibus Suis et Scriptis*.[32] But the passage which he cites adds nothing new to what was already being said in numerous commentaries on Pseudo-Dionysius. In fact, the problem of the transcendentals did not genuinely make its appearance until the thirteenth century, with Philip the Chancellor's *Summa de Bono*. There was no mention of beauty in it, however, not because the treatise was incomplete, but because its principal theme was the relations of the good and the true.

Philip was influenced by the anonymous *Summa Douacensis*[33] and by William of Auxerre's treatise *De Bono*, but the latter work did not make the good fully coextensive with being. Philip was the first to describe them as identical, using the verb *convertuntur* and suggesting that they differed *ratione*—logically or notionally. This terminology was to have much success. The thirteenth-century dispute with Manichaeism led him to give particular emphasis to the concept of the good, and he was inspired by Arab philosophy to suggest that the transcendentals were identical and interconvertible, and that they differed *secundum rationem*—that is, according to the way in which a thing is considered. "Good is convertible with being . . . It is the nature of being to overflow with goodness" ("Bonum et ens convertuntur . . . bonum tamen abundat ratione supra ens").[34] The good is being seen in its perfection, in its effective correspondence with the end to which it tends. The one (*unum*) is something apprehended in its indivisibility.

Philip himself did not discuss the question of beauty. His contemporaries, however, who were writing commentaries on Pseudo-Dionysius, were compelled by his constant references to beauty to inquire whether it also might be a transcendental.

In the early Middle Ages, writers were willing enough to talk about beautiful objects and the beauty of all things but reluctant to formulate the relevant aesthetic concepts. An interesting example of this is the manner in which translators of Pseudo-Dionysius dealt with his terms for beauty, *kalon* and *kallos*. In the year 827 Hilduin, the first translator of *The Divine Names*, rendered one passage as follows: "Bonum autem et bonitas non divisibiliter ad unum omnia consummante causa . . . Bonum quidem esse dicimus quod bonitati participat" ("Goodness and that which is good are not sepa-

rately referable to their single all-encompassing cause . . . for a
thing is called good because it participates in goodness"). Here,
kalon was taken to refer to an ontological goodness. Three centuries
later, however, Johannes Saracenus translated the same passage as
"Pulchrum autem et pulchritudo non sunt dividenda in causa quae
in uno tota comprehendit . . . Pulchrum quidem esse dicimus quod
participat pulchritudinis" ("Beauty and that which is beautiful are
not separately referable to their single all-encompassing cause . . .
for a thing is called beautiful because it participates in beauty").[35]
Saracenus wrote in a letter to John of Salisbury that he had translated according to the sense rather than according to the letter.[36]
Translation in accordance with sense, however, means subjecting
the text to one's own way of understanding. As de Bruyne remarks,
Johannes Saracenus was a whole world away from Hilduin.[37] And
he is not referring just to a difference in theoretical outlook. The
centuries between Hilduin and Saracenus encompassed the end of
the Dark Ages, the Carolingian Renaissance, the humanism of Alcuin and Rhabanus Maurus, the passing of the terrors of the year
1000, an economic revival in agriculture and manufacture, a new
sense of the positive in life, the evolution from feudalism to civic
life, the first Crusades, the opening of trade routes, the Roman-
esque period with its great pilgrimages to Santiago de Compostela,
the first flowering of Gothic art.[38] The medievals' sensitivity to aesthetic value increased along with their terrestrial horizons, and also
with their attempts to impose a system upon their new outlook on
things by means of theological doctrines. In the period between
Hilduin and Saracenus, various means were employed to make an
implicit addition of beauty to the transcendentals. In the eleventh
century, for instance, Otloh of St. Emmeran attributed a fundamental feature of beauty, *consonantia,* to every creature.[39] Two centuries later, terminologies devised by thinkers such as Philip the
Chancellor made it possible to work with a more precise set of
concepts.

William of Auvergne, in his *Tractatus de Bono et Malo* (1228),
dwelt upon the beauty of virtuous behavior.[40] He argued that, since
sensible beauty is that which pleases him who sees it, interior
beauty is that which gives pleasure to the soul which grasps it "and
entices the soul to love" ("et ad amorem sui allicit"). The goodness
which we find in the human soul "is called *pulchritudo* or *decor* be-

cause of the comparison with external and visible beauty" ("hanc bonitatem vocavimus pulchritudinem seu decorem ex comparatione exterioris et visibilis pulchritudinis"). This equivalence of moral beauty and virtue (*honestum*) is clearly derived from the Stoics, from Cicero and from Augustine, and very likely from Aristotle's *Rhetoric* as well: "The beautiful is that which is desirable for its own sake, and pleasant, or that which, being good, is pleasurable because it is good."[41]

In 1242 Thomas Gallus Vercellensis completed his *Explanatio* of the Dionysian corpus. In this work he also tended to the assimilation of the good and the beautiful. And some time before 1243 Robert Grosseteste, in his commentary on Pseudo-Dionysius, attributed the name of beauty to God and added that "if everything desires the good and the beautiful together, the good and the beautiful are the same" ("si igitur omnia communiter bonum et pulchrum appetunt, idem est bonum et pulchrum").[42] He also added that, although the two names (the good and the beautiful) are united in the objects which possess them, and united also in God, whose names manifest the beneficent creative processes which proceed from him to his creatures, they are at the same time conceptually different (*diversa sunt ratione*):

> Bonum enim dicitur Deus secundum quod omnia adducit in esse et bene esse et promovet et consummat et conservat. Pulchrum autem dicitur in quantum omnia sibi ipsis et ad invicem in sui identitate facit concordia.

> God is called good because he confers being on everything, and being is good, and he increases and perfects and preserves. But he is called beautiful in that all things, both in themselves and together, produce a concordance in their identity with him.

Goodness is a name of God insofar as he is the source of existence and maintains things in being; and beauty is his name insofar as he is the "organizing cause" of the created world. It is clear that this conception of a divine formativity is of the utmost significance for aesthetics. It is worth noting also that Philip the Chancellor's distinction of the one and the true was adapted by Grosseteste in order to distinguish goodness and beauty.

Another work of fundamental importance was completed in

1245, although Grosseteste seems to have known it before then. This is the *Summa Theologica* of Alexander of Hales (*Summa Fratris Alexandri*), which was in fact the work of three Franciscan authors: John of La Rochelle, Alexander himself, and a third vaguely identified as "Brother Considerans."[43] In it we find a number of statements about beauty which were to become classic, and which throw light upon analogous remarks made by Aquinas. In the part of the work attributed to John of La Rochelle, the good is identified with being. The question is then raised "whether the good and the beautiful are the same with respect to intentionality" ("si secundum intentionem idem sunt pulchrum et bonum"). In answering this, the author uses ideas from Pseudo-Dionysius and from St. Augustine. It was in Augustine that he found the distinction between two kinds of good: virtue (*honestum*), which is sought for its own sake ("quod propter se expetendum est"), and the useful, which is referred to something else ("quod ad aliud referendum est"). Augustine also supplied a definition of virtue as "intelligible beauty" ("honestum voco intelligibilem pulchritudinem").[44] John of La Rochelle then concludes:

> Bonum, secundum quod dicitur honestum, idem est pulchro
> . . . Non sunt idem . . . differunt secundum intentionem; nam
> pulchrum dicit dispositionem boni secundum quod et placitum
> apprehensioni, bonum vero respicit dispositionem secundum
> quam delectat affectionem.

> The good, when it is considered as virtue, is the same as beauty
> . . . But they differ . . . with respect to intentionality. For
> beauty is the good when it pleases the apprehension, but good
> itself is what gives pleasure to the affections.

Here was to be found, for the first time, the simultaneous identity and difference of the good and the beautiful. Also, further on in the same work there appeared yet another distinction, namely that the beautiful has to do with formal causes, and the good with final causes. It is worth remembering in this connection that Augustine connected the word *speciosus* (beautiful) with *species,* and this in turn with "form."[45]

This is not the place to consider the senses which the term *forma* had for Augustine, for John of La Rochelle, and for Aquinas. The fact remains that it was used in formulas of this kind. Also, when we turn to the part of the *Summa Fratris Alexandri* written by Brother Considerans we find that the position adopted is substantially the same. The good, the true, and the beautiful are again said to be convertible with one another but to differ *ratione;* and again, beauty is connected with formal causes.

A contemporary reader who is familiar with the works of Aquinas may be inclined to look upon these passages as nothing out of the ordinary. He may be inclined simply to note that there is a connection, at the least a verbal connection, among them. But we must remember that in the year 1245 this kind of language was quite new. The authors of the *Summa Fratris Alexandri* were like their contemporaries in wanting to show that even monsters were beautiful, in that they are beings, because every being is beautiful and God creates nothing that is not beautiful. But John of La Rochelle and Considerans were the first to validate this view, in what we must regard as an act of speculative courage. We should not forget the caution and the prudence with which the medievals engaged in innovation. There was, after all, a traditional number of transcendentals, and it was no small thing to alter it. This was why the two authors invoked the authority of St. Augustine, using him nonetheless for their own purposes, with that interpretative ingenuity which was a characteristic of the medieval period. As Pouillon puts it, "On this matter, John of La Rochelle and Considerans were innovators. This explains the brevity and the relative modesty of what they had to say about the transcendental character of beauty."[46] The boldness of the innovation required caution in its implementation.

Turning now to Aquinas, and in particular to his *Summa Theologiae,* where the similarity to the texts we have just been looking at is most marked, we should note first that not many years separate it from the work of John of La Rochelle. Some element of caution must have remained. The *Summa Theologica* of Alexander of Hales had provided a convenient form of words which, without disturbing the classical list of transcendentals, still managed to solve the problem of beauty. There was no point in attempting a change in method, for the method then in force had become standard, and was to be found in Albertus Magnus, Thomas of York, Ulrich of Strasbourg, Robert Grosseteste, Thomas Gallus Vercellensis, and others—all in their capacity as commentators upon Pseudo-

Dionysius. When seen in this light, Aquinas's text no longer seems ambiguous. The language which he used was by then accepted; any uncertainty attached to it came from its recent introduction.

But a greater act of courage was in fact possible, and it is to be found in a little-known work of St. Bonaventure. Here, though he professes a general fidelity to the *Summa* of Alexander of Hales, he makes a notable advance upon it when he writes of "four conditions of a being, namely that it be one, true, good, and beautiful" ("quatuor conditiones entis communiter, scilicet unum, verum, bonum, pulchrum").[47] This statement is quite unequivocal, and is further clarified subsequently with the help of definitions taken from the *Summa Fratris Alexandri*. Bonaventure, however, was a rather isolated figure on this particular point; and it was not from him that Aquinas took his aesthetics. It is more relevant to note that the ideas of the *Summa Fratris Alexandri* passed on to Aquinas through the mediation of his most authoritative source, Albertus Magnus.

If we pass over his early *Summa de Bono* (1243), the work by Albertus Magnus which is of greatest relevance for us here is his *De Pulchro et Bono*. This put into writing part of his lectures on *The Divine Names* which he gave in Cologne in 1248–1252, and had a very considerable influence on Aquinas.[48] Some of its language is that of the *Summa Fratris Alexandris,* and it has a strongly Dionysian character (we should not forget that Albertus Magnus was to return to Platonist ways of thinking in his *Summa Theologiae* of 1270–1274). Also, it reflects something of the color and energy of the new, Aristotelian, cultural climate in which it was written. He says that beauty has to do with formal causes, and he defines it as "the splendor of the substantial or actual form which is found in the proportioned parts of a material thing" ("splendorem formae substantialis vel actualis supra partes materiae proportionatas").[49] This amounts to the claim that form is the objective principle of beauty—form understood in the Aristotelian sense as "act," that is, a principle of being or existential value. In this sense, beauty is identical with being, the good, and the true, even though they are all different *ratione*.[50]

Beauty is here conceived of as ontological perfection. But in his very insistence upon this basic point, Albertus Magnus differs in some respects from Aquinas. Albertus was not interested in the formal structure of consciousness during its experience of beauty. He concentrated rather upon the concrete existence which is constituted by beauty and good together. He did not differentiate beauty in terms of the fact that it "pleases when it is seen." Instead he wrote, "Virtue has a certain clarity in itself, because of which it is beautiful, *even when it is not known to anyone*" ("virtus claritatem quandam habet in se, per quam pulchra est, etiamsi a nullo cognoscatur").[51] What distinguishes beauty is not the fact that it is regarded in a certain manner, but the fact that form shines forth, a fully objective harmony, in the proportioned parts of the material.

I shall return in due course to these ideas, and we shall see how Aquinas's language suggests, within its own particular framework, quite a different perspective. For now we should note that Albertus Magnus stressed the objective character of beauty, and that in this sense he considered it to be a property coextensive with being. This is one way in which Aquinas was in his debt, as he was also with regard to the aesthetics of form. At the same time, this theoretical breakthrough by Albertus, a most effective one for all that it was unobserved, occurred within an aesthetic theory that had more to do with Pseudo-Dionysius than with Aristotle. His return to Platonism in his old age was no sudden break with his past.

Albertus related the problem of beauty to the Aristotelian concept of form, but he ignored the dialectical relation between the person who contemplates and the object contemplated. As de Bruyne puts it, Albertus considered the emotion experienced in the contemplation of beauty to be of secondary importance. His aesthetic concepts were ontological categories. He retained the Platonic vision of a pancalistic universe in all its force.

Conclusion

Aquinas's aesthetics cannot be reduced to the contents of the treatise *De Pulchro et Bono*. He did believe that beauty was a transcendental, a constant property of being. He believed that being is what *can* be seen as beautiful (for the present I shall simply stress the word *can*). He believed that all being contains the constant conditions of beauty. But does this mean that he was committed to pancalism? In a certain sense, yes. For Aquinas also the universe was the handiwork of its creator and therefore beautiful, an enormous symphony of beauty. But this did not mean a symphony of symbols, as it had for Eriugena. In this matter, Aquinas followed Albertus Magnus: the world was not a story, a bearer of messages. Eriugena's universe was a materialization descended from the Eternal, and its beauty signified the possibility of rising above matter, back to the Eternal. Aquinas's universe was a hierarchy of real existents, each of which acquired its individual value through participation, a value made concrete within definite and stable limits. In such a universe, all beauty is good, and at the root of every good is a manner of being which consists in the definite perfection associated with a certain act of existing: "unumquodque enim bonum est secundum quod est res actu" ("whatever is good, is good in that it is something actual").[52] Beauty, like the good, is grounded upon form (*super formam*), but form is the reason why something is in act, or has actuality, and so "is good for its own sake" ("est secundum se bona").[53]

And yet, as I have said, Aquinas's text is filled with uncertainties and hesitations.

Pouillon believes that these hesitations had a reason. Franciscan thinkers might have been ready to accept the concept of beauty as a transcendental found in the *Summa Fratris Alexandri*. But Albertus Magnus and Thomas Aquinas, the two Aristotelian masters, could accept such a notion only through their contact with Pseudo-Dionysius. In fact, Aquinas returned in his *Summa Theologiae* to a list of just three transcendentals, and rarely mentioned beauty. We should note, however, that he was just as cautious in his *Commentary on the Divine Names* as he was in the *Summa,* on the matter of whether beauty was a transcendental; he withdrew nothing in the latter work that he had conceded in the former. It is true that in the *Summa* he no longer used the language of the *Commentary*—the beauty of the universe, order, creating in beauty, and so on—but this was for two reasons: first, he was no longer engaged in popularizing Pseudo-Dionysius; and second, his conception of beauty was now implicit in his theoretical system as a whole. He had no further need to insist upon the transcendental character of beauty. If he was under any compulsion, it was just the opposite. As a good Aristotelian, he refrained from excessive discussion of beauty, a subject much abused by every variety of Neoplatonist, swooning at universes dissolving in visions of light.

For Grosseteste, the universe was an enormous explosion of luminous energy, which had stabilized in a mathematically ordered structure. For Pseudo-Dionysius, the universe was an inexhaustible source of beauty. Aquinas was different.[54] He tackled the themes of his *Summa* with reserve; moderation had to be reestablished.

This was not all. In a Dionysian universe, coruscating with beauty, mankind risked losing its place, of being blinded and then annulled. This is why Aquinas began in the *Summa* to deal with issues in psychology, in a way which would transform the whole question. He introduced the problem of the psychological and subjective desire for beauty, not as a secondary matter, but as part of the very essence.

The notion expressed in the words *visa placent* changed the picture. Aquinas's three formal characters of beauty—clarity, integrity, and proportion—modified it further, at least indirectly, because of their importance in his hylomorphic theory.

III

The Function and Nature of the Aesthetic *Visio*

The Problem

The metaphysical element in Aquinas's aesthetics was only part of his theory of beauty. He also dealt with the nature of the subject who is engaged in aesthetic contemplation; and it is to the role of this subject that we must now turn.

"Man," writes Aquinas, "takes pleasure in the beauty of sensible things" ("Homo delectatur in ipsa pulchritudine sensibilium").[1] There is a relation, then, between man and beauty. But is this relation constitutive of beauty? Is beauty something ontologically self-subsistent, which gives pleasure when it is apprehended? Or is it rather the case that a thing appears beautiful only when someone apprehends it in such a way as to experience a certain type of pleasure?

This problem was well known to the medievals. It appeared in Augustine, for instance:

> Si prius quaeram utrum ideo pulchra sint quia delectant; aut ideo delectent quia pulchra sunt; hic mihi sine dubitatione respondebitur, ideo delectare quia pulchra sunt.

> If I were to ask first whether things are beautiful because they give pleasure, or give pleasure because they are beautiful, I have no doubt that I will be given the answer that they give pleasure because they are beautiful.[2]

Augustine here took the objectivist position. But it cannot be said that the whole Scholastic tradition was in agreement on this matter. It might even be suggested that the medievals were persistently unsettled on the issue of beauty as a transcendental precisely because Augustine had left the theory of beauty in an unsatisfactory state.

The Scholastics were impressed by the fact that only human beings could make an aesthetic judgment. Animals, they believed, pursue their own type of good, and to some degree perceive things as they are, but they have no sense of beauty. This superior pleasure may be experienced only by rational animals.[3] And even if it is the case that beauty has objective existence, it is human beings who possess the ability to detect it.

Furthermore, there existed in the artistico-social consciousness of the Middle Ages an awareness of a type of beauty produced specifically for man and his individual and communal needs. Such artifacts did not possess value just for their own sake, but for the sake of the people who were to enjoy them and use them. As it happens, this artistico-social consciousness translated itself into rules of art which may seem irrelevant today, but which signify the awareness in question all the same. In all artistic endeavor there was the implicit belief that works of art ought to ordain a range of effects for the sake of human perception, and that only this encounter of the work with the perception of it could give birth to beauty. The rules were formulated in a technical manner, but they expressed a real feature of the artistic sensibility.[4] They made possible the birth of an aesthetico-philosophical consciousness, something that the medieval sensibility was attracted to in any case.

Medieval Texts

We saw in Chapter I that Boethius was aware of a certain accord between beautiful objects and the psychological needs of those who observe them. Even earlier than Boethius, Augustine discussed in his analysis of rhythm the correspondence between the physical and the psychological.[5] Then in his *De Ordine* he attributed aesthetic value only to visual sensations and moral qualities; in the case of hearing and the inferior senses, he said, we experience *suavitas* (pleasantness or agreeableness) rather than *pulchritudo*. In saying this, Augustine was initiating the theory that some of the human senses are *maxime cognoscitivi*—that is, most fully involved with knowledge. It was a theory which Aquinas took into his system; he considered sight and hearing to be senses of this kind. In the case of the Victorines, the joy which we experience in the perception of sensible harmony was conceived of as a natural prolongation of physical pleasure, and thus as the basis of the affective life, grounded in a correspondence between the structure of the soul and material reality.[6] Richard of St. Victor, for whom contemplation could have an aesthetic character, defined it as "a state of clear insight and detached admiration at the spectacle of wisdom" ("libera mentis perspicacia in sapientiae spectacula cum admiratione suspensa").[7] In this ecstatic moment, the soul expands and is uplifted by the beauty it perceives; it loses itself in the object.

Bonaventure also said that apprehension of the sensible world is governed by a certain rule of proportion:

> Dicitur suavitas cum virtus agens non improportionaliter excedit recipientem: quia sensus tristatur in extremis et in mediis delectatur.

> We say there is *suavitas* when an active power does not overwhelm its recipient too disproportionately; for the senses suffer from excess but delight in moderation.[8]

And elsewhere, he says that pleasure presupposes an encounter between the subject and a pleasurable object:

> Ad delectationem enim concurrit delectabile et conjunctio ejus cum eo quod delectatur.

> Delectation involved a conjunction of the delectable and a person who takes delight in it.[9]

In this relationship there is a movement of love. In fact, for Bonaventure the greatest pleasure is brought about, not by the contemplation of sensible forms, but by love. In love, the subject and the object are consciously and actively lovers.

> Ista affectio nobilissima est inter omnes, quoniam plus tenet de ratione liberalitatis . . . Unde nihil in creaturis est considerare ita deliciosum, sicut amorem mutuum; et sine amore nullae sunt deliciae.

> This affection [of love] is most honorable of all because it partakes of nobility in the highest degree . . . As far as creatures

are concerned, nothing is so delightful as mutual love, and without love there is no delight.[10]

In the works just cited, this conception of contemplation appears only briefly, as part of the epistemology of the mystical consciousness. It is found in more specific form, however, in William of Auvergne, and indeed is the reason he has been called an emotionalist.

Quemadmodum enim pulchrum visu dicimus quod natum est per seipsum placere spectantibus et delectare secundum visum.

We call a thing visually beautiful when of its own nature it gives pleasure to spectators and delight to the vision.[11]

There is, he says, an objective quality in beauty which solicits agreement with our consciousness; but the object's value is confirmed by the delighted approbation which is given to it by our sight.

Volentes quippe pulchritudinem visibilem agnoscere, visum exteriorem consulimus . . . Pulchritudinem seu decorem, quam approbat et in qua complacet sibi visus noster seu aspectus interior.

If we wish to understand visual beauty we must consider the sense of sight . . . Beauty and ornament, which our looking and our interior seeing approve [approbat] and take pleasure in.

When discussing these issues, William of Auvergne used two kinds of terms: terms pertaining to cognition (spectare, intueri, aspicere) and those pertaining to the affections (placere, delectare). His theory of the soul was that its two functions, the cognitive and the affective, were indivisibly entwined. So, if an object were simply present to some consciousness and manifested its qualities, it would provoke a sense of delight mingled with love (affectio). The subject simultaneously knows an object and reaches toward it.[12]

While these kinds of theories were being developed in speculative philosophy, similar issues were being discussed in works of a more empirical cast, in connection with the physics of vision and light. The main influence here was Arabic, in particular Alhazen's De Aspectibus or Perspectiva (c. tenth, eleventh centuries). The interests which it gave rise to were taken up in the thirteenth century, in Witelo's *De Perspectiva,* and also in a work entitled *Liber de Intelligentiis,* long attributed to Witelo but now to one Adam Pulchrae Mulieris, or Adam Belladonna.[13]

The *Liber de Intelligentiis* explained the sense of sight on the model of reflected light: a luminous object emits rays of light, and a passive potency like a mirror receives the light and reflects it. In human consciousness, however, something more occurs; the passive potency adapts itself to the active force of the stimulus, and this adaptation is experienced as pleasure, *delectatio*. It is clear that this is an aesthetic type of pleasure, which arises from the proportions which bind the human soul to the world.

Witelo analyzed more fully this interaction between the knowing subject and the object known. He distinguished two different types of apprehension or perception of visible forms.[14] One was "a grasp of visible forms . . . through intuition alone" ("comprehensio formarum visibilium . . . per solam intuitionem")—that is, the simple perception of light and color. The other was perception "through intuition together with preceding knowledge" ("per intuitionem cum scientia praecedente"). In this case, a pure and simple intuition of visible features combines with "an act of reason, which compares the different forms perceived with one another" ("actum ratiocinationis diversas formas visas ad invicem comparantem"). It is only after this complex interactive process (not dissimilar to some accounts of perception in contemporary psychology) that full knowledge of the object, grounded in the concept, comes into being.

This theory might seem to suggest that there is some element of conflict between the psychological structure of perception and the psychological structure of the intellect. But in fact the first type of perception—the immediate, intuitive kind—merely refers to the perception of data which have not yet been gathered into a perceptual "field." It does not, therefore, exclude the element of "preceding knowledge," or what contemporary psychology regards as a basic property of perception, that it is permeated with understanding and with cultural assumptions. Witelo's theory of perception, in fact, suggests that sensation combines with memory, imagination, and reason. This theory would repay further study, but here our concern is rather with the extent to which it can help us to understand analogous passages in Aquinas. We simply conclude, therefore, by noting that, for Witelo, aesthetic preception always pertained to the second type of perception.

> Formae non sunt pulchrae nisi ex intentionibus particularibus et ex conjunctione earum inter se . . . Ex conjunctione quoque plurium intentionum formarum visibilium ad invicem et non solum ex ipsis intentionibus (particularibus) visibilium, fit pulchritudo.

> Forms are not beautiful unless through the conjunction of particular observations with one another . . . Beauty arises from the conjunction of several observations of visible forms, and not from the observations alone.

It is also worth noting that Witelo discussed the objective features which warrant aesthetic apprehension. These included magnitude (so that the moon is more beautiful than the stars), pattern or design (*figura*), continuity, discontinuity (in the sense of variety and multiplicity, or variations in rhythm), the roughness (*planities*) of a body on which the light falls, and shading which alleviates the harshness of light and creates *sfumature*, as in a peacock's tail. There were also more complex features than these, which came from relations established among the simpler ones.

Witelo insisted also upon the importance of the relation between features in the object and the inclinations and *visio* in the subject. He said that every objective feature possesses a kind of suitability (*convenientia*) in respect of a subject who varies according to the time and the place. "Each person," he wrote, "makes his own estimate of beauty according to his own custom" ("sicut unicuique suus proprius mos est, sic et propria aestimatio pulchritudinis accidit unicuique"). He claimed that our evaluations of the objective features are determined by a kind of subjective focusing. Some should be viewed from a distance, so that unsightly marks, for instance, will not be seen. Others, such as book illuminations, should be looked at from close up if we want to see the details, the hidden intentions (*intentiones subtiles*), the decorum of line (*lineatio decens*), and the beautiful ordering of parts (*ordinatio partium venusta*). Aesthetic vision is based upon the play of distance and nearness; and it changes according to the axis of vision, since objects change their appearance if looked at obliquely.

If I have dwelt upon Witelo for a time it is because his *De Perspectiva* appeared in 1270, and Aquinas's *Summa,* started in 1265, appeared in 1273. It is not possible to claim that Aquinas was familiar with Witelo, nor indeed that Witelo was familiar with Aquinas, although it seems plausible that he would have known of the universally famous works of Aquinas. But in any case, they were both at work in the same period and were aware of the same community of interests, so that it seems useful to examine the one in the light of the other.

At this point we should be able to give a sharper reading of the sentence "pulchra sunt quae visa placent" ("those things are beautiful which please when they are seen"). It is no accident that it should appear as something novel, disconcerting, and unusual in the context of Scholastic language; it can undoubtedly be seen as a bold attempt to counter an excessively objectivist conception of beauty which obscured its true nature. But the fact remains that in solving one problem this expression created others. Aquinas relegated it to a *responsio* (*Summa Theologiae,* I, 5, 4 ad 1), throwing it out casually as if it were totally plausible and a foregone conclusion ("pulchra *enim* dicuntur quae visa placent"; emphasis added). But it can come to seem imprecise or profoundly allusive, or cleverly elliptical. We may even be inclined to the view that Aquinas himself gave no great weight to it and threw the remark out lightly. But even if this were so, it would acquire importance in the context of his system as a whole.

What did the term *visio* mean for Aquinas? If the word had a single meaning—if it referred just to visual perception by the eye— then the proposition at which we are looking could be simply explained in a sensationalist manner. However, let us look at what Aquinas had to say about this.

> De aliquo nomine dupliciter convenit loqui; uno modo, secundum primam eius impositionem; alio modo, secundum usum nominis. Sicut patet in nomine visionis, quod primo impositum est ad significandum actum sensus visus; sed propter dignitatem et certitudinem huius sensus extensum est hoc nomen, secundum usum loquentium, ad omnem cognitionem aliorum sensuum . . . Et ulterius etiam ad cognitionem intellectus, secundum illud Matth. 5: Beati mundo corde quoniam ipsi Deum videbunt.

> Any term may be employed in two senses: one in keeping with its original imposition, the other with common usage. This is apparent in the word *visio,* the initial reference of which was to the act of the sense of sight. This term, in view of the special nature and certitude of the sense of sight, is extended in common usage to the knowledge of all the senses . . . and it is even made to include intellectual knowledge, as in Matthew 5, 8: "Blessed are the clean of heart, for they shall 'see' God."[15]

This explanation opens up a wide range of interpretative possibilities, and so renews our original puzzlement. For we now want to know which of these meanings the aesthetic *visio* has. If the term is extended to signify every sort of sensible apprehension, can it also be taken to signify an act of the intellect? And, if so, which kind of act? An abstraction or a judgment, an intellectual intuition or an act of reason?

Aquinas's Texts

Let us now examine the whole passage in which the expression *visa placent* occurs, looking this time at some of its other aspects. The *responsio* begins with an affirmation that beauty and good are identical in the subject but differ conceptually. It then continues:

> Nam bonum proprie respicit appetitum: est enim bonum quod omnia appetunt. Et ideo habet rationem finis: nam appetitus est quasi quidam motus ad rem. Pulchrum autem respicit vim cognoscitivam; pulchra enim dicuntur quae visa placent. Unde pulchrum in debita proportione consistit, quia sensus delectatur in rebus debite proportionatis, sicut in sibi similibus; nam et sensus ratio quaedam est, et omnis virtus cognoscitiva. Et quia cognitio fit per assimilationem, similitudo autem respicit formam, pulchrum proprie pertinet ad rationem causae formalis.

> For good (being what all things desire) has properly to do with desire and so involves the idea of end (since desire is a kind of movement toward something). Beauty, on the other hand, has to do with knowledge, for those things are called beautiful which please us when they are seen. This is why beauty con-

sists in due proportion, for the senses delight in rightly proportioned things as similar to themselves, the sense faculty being a sort of proportion itself like all other knowing faculties. Now since knowing proceeds by imagining, and images have to do with form, beauty properly involves the notion of formal causes.

It has frequently been noted that *visa placent* makes the definition in the second sentence a definition in terms of the effect of beauty rather than in terms of its essence. This seems to be confirmed by the first part of the next sentence, which states that beauty "consists in"—that is, beauty is in itself—due proportion. At this point, the question of the term *visa,* and of its decisive importance, seems to be settled. But then Aquinas adds that this proportion itself consists in a relation of proportion between the human sense and an object which is rightly proportioned. In due course we shall consider whether he means "also consists in" or "mainly consists in"; but in any case, the question is here opened up again.

We should note at this point that it is once again confirmed that the perception of beauty is something cognitive, because it has to do with formal causes. Aquinas thus clears away any hint of sensationalism: we might have some doubt on this score in the case of William of Auvergne, but not here. A further point arises in connection with another passage in the *Summa,* where our pleasure or *delectatio* in beauty is described as something totally disinterested. For it arises not out of a mode of possession, but out of an act of cognition. Aesthetic pleasure has to do with the intellect, even if it does so through the mediation of the senses. It is not like the pleasure of possession or assimilation.

> Cum enim bonum sit quod omnia appetunt, de ratione boni est quod in eo quietetur appetitus; sed ad rationem pulchri pertinet quod in eius aspectu seu cognitione quietetur appetitus. Unde et illi sensus praecipue respiciunt pulchrum qui maxime cognoscitivi sunt, scilicet visus et auditus rationi deservientes; dicimus enim pulchra visibilia et pulchros sonos. In sensibilibus autem aliorum sensuum, non utimur nomine pulchritudinis; non enim dicimus pulchros sapores aut odores. Et sic patet quod pulchrum addit supra bonum quendam ordinem ad vim cognoscitivam: ita quod bonum dicatur id quod simpliciter

complacet appetitui; pulchrum autem dicatur id cuius ipsa apprehensio placet.

For the good, being what all things want, is that in which the
appetite comes to rest; whereas the beautiful is that in which
the appetite comes to rest through contemplation or knowledge. Those senses are therefore chiefly associated with beauty
which contribute most to our knowledge, namely sight and
hearing when ministering to reason; thus we speak of beautiful
sights and beautiful sounds, but not of beautiful tastes and
smells; we do not speak of beauty in reference to the other three
senses. So it is clear that beauty adds to good a reference to the
cognitive powers; "good" refers to that which simply pleases
the appetite, whereas a thing is called beautiful when the mere
apprehension of it gives us pleasure.[16]

The term *apprehensio* in this passage can be identified with *visio*
in the passage quoted earlier. It may therefore be defined as *a kind of
seeing or looking which is mediated by the senses but is of an intellectually
cognitive order, and which is both disinterested and yet produces a certain
kind of pleasure.*

We must now inquire into the nature of this type of looking, and
into its function in Aquinas's thought taken as a whole. And first,
we must ask whether it is constitutive of beauty, or simply has
something as its object to whose real character it is not essential.

The Aesthetic *Visio*

We must determine first of all whether the term *placet,* which refers
to an adjustment in the mind that follows from *visio,* is something
essential to the existence of beauty, so that we cannot call a thing
beautiful except in relation to that adjustment and that pleasure; or
whether, instead, things have within them stable and absolute conditions of beauty which *visio* singles out and which produce the
sense of pleasure.

Quite a few contemporary writers are happy to ascribe to Aquinas a degree of aesthetic subjectivism which borders upon sociological relativism. Marc de Munnynck, for instance, suggests that
for Aquinas an object is beautiful only to the extent that it is an
object of contemplation; that aesthetic knowledge is disinterested

just because the object of interest is merely an object represented in the mind of the knowing subject. In this theory, the subject and its object adjust to each other, but the only thing that the object brings to its encounter with the subject is the bare fact of its being an object, and not the real properties which it has. Aquinas's three objective conditions of beauty—clarity, integrity, and proportion—do not in fact constitute beauty. The expression *visum placet* says it all.[17] Of course, not all commentators on the subjective element in Aquinas's theory of beauty adopt such an extreme view as de Munnynck;[18] but in practice, any interpretation which takes the notion *visa placent* too narrowly runs the risk of missing Aquinas's real intentions.

As I have already remarked, the term *visa* seems to point to a definition of beauty in terms of its effect. But in fact *visa placent* has the same relation to beauty that *quod omnia appetunt* ("what all things desire") has to the good. The good is not merely what all things desire; it refers to something whose own inner structure possesses the degree of perfection which makes it desirable. Desirability does not constitute goodness, but refers rather to our attitude to goodness. It is the same with truth, for there is both an ontological truth and a formal truth. Why, then, should the same type of distinction not apply to beauty? After all, the ontological structure of the good and the true is simply the perfection of some existent, and this is why they can be the object of an appetite, or have the character of a final cause, or be the object of an intellectual judgment. It then seems natural to argue that beauty is formally constituted in a relation between a subject and a thing, but that the thing has an objective structure such that it offers itself for contemplation. And in fact Aquinas states more than once that beauty "consists in" due proportion, or that it "requires" three conditions—language which seems to refer explicitly to conditions in what is objectively real.

But until we have examined these conditions, we cannot say whether it is they, or instead the subjective aspects of seeing, that have the more important role. They might be simply the objective structure of a thing, in which case they would be its truth, not its beauty. Or they might constitute the way in which an object offers itself to *visio*, in the sense that without *visio* they could not exist. Or again, they might be genuine and specific conditions of beauty, different from those of truth and goodness. Until we have settled this, we can define neither their relation to *visio* nor their precise function. This is one of the two main reasons why we must postpone the question until after an analysis of the objective criteria of beauty.

Also, we are still not clear about the nature of the aesthetic *visio*. We know by now that it is something intellectual, but this is scarcely sufficient. It is quite clear, even without further analysis, that beauty has to do with the formal causes of things; and this connection has enabled us to recognize that the intellect has an important role in the apprehension of beauty. But nothing that we have looked at as ye⁺ will allow us to say more than this.

One interpretation of Thomist aesthetics has had great success because of its conspicuous modernity. This is the identification of the aesthetic *visio* with intuition.[19] Aquinas did in fact write about sense intuition, and suggested that its initial moment was an act of abstraction by the intellect. But the question is whether he also believed that an intuitive act *of the intellect* occurred either before or after the abstraction. On this point his interpreters have found themselves with a gap to fill. We can take Maritain as typical, not least because he exemplifies a particular approach to history and a particular kind of Thomism. Maritain knows very well that, for Aquinas, the human intellect is not intuitive in the way that angelic intellects are. But he wants to demonstrate the function of the intellect in aesthetic experience, taking beauty to mean what it did for Albertus Magnus: the brilliance of an object's form shining forth in its matter.[20] Maritain says that the intellect comes into contact with beauty only through the senses, because only the senses have the capacity for intuition that is needed for perceiving beauty. He asserts also that when the intellect is engaged in aesthetic experience it does not exercise its power of abstraction. The distinctive character of the aesthetic *visio* is that it grasps the form in the sensible and through the sensible, and it is through the apprehensions of sense that the light of being enters the intellect. Aesthetic pleasure is the repose of the intellect when it rejoices without labour or discussion; freed from its natural labor of abstraction, it "drinks the clarity of being."[21] The critical activity which properly belongs to the intellect comes afterward. The aesthetic moment is contemplative, uncritical, blessed.[22]

Another interpretation of *visio* in terms of intuition is given by de Bruyne. De Bruyne, however, does not distinguish between sensible intuition of the beautiful and intellectual knowledge, whether intuitive or abstractive, of the beautiful. He insists upon the unity of intellectual intuition, a psychological unity of intellect and sensibility, so that aesthetic apprehension is a unitary act in which it is impossible to distinguish the role of the intellect from that of the senses. He supports this interpretation of Aquinas by citing the sentence "Properly speaking, it is neither the intellect nor the sense which knows, but man, who knows through both" ("Non enim proprie loquendo sensus aut intellectus cognoscunt, sed homo per utrumque").[23]

Now, if we should claim that it is the senses which intuit, and that the intellect grasps the intelligible in the data provided by the senses, then this grasping of the intelligible would occur *before* the moment of abstraction, and we would thus be committed to accepting that there is an intellectual intuition. Aesthetic intuition would then be intellectual intuition. We must, therefore, directly face this question: is there such a thing as intellectual intuition in Aquinas?

Intellectual Intuition in Aquinas

M. D. Roland-Gosselin, in his very accurate study of this question, takes the word *intuition* in one of the senses given it in Lalande's *Vocabulaire technique e critique de la philosophie:* "a direct and immediate seeing of an object of thought which is currently present to the mind and is grasped in its individual reality" ("vue directe et immédiate d'un object de pensée actuellement présent à l'esprit et saisi dans sa réalité individuelle"). Roland-Gosselin argues that this sense of the term—which Cajetan, incidentally, rejected—entered Thomism, not from Aquinas himself, but with John of St. Thomas, and under the influence of the Franciscan school. In the course of many philosophical discussions, Thomism came to assimilate the idea. As Roland-Gosselin argues this case, it is not easily refuted.[24]

There is no need here to give detailed quotations to establish that Aquinas distinguished among various types of knowledge. One type is an immediate contact between the senses and the sensible species or nature of an object; this is an intuition of particulars, but a sensible intuition. (Aquinas, incidentally, never used the word *intueri* to signify this kind of knowledge; the word had quite a different meaning for him.) Another type is a contact between the intellect and the phantasm given to intellect by the senses. This contact instantly takes the form of an act of abstraction, through which an intelligible species is impressed upon the possible intellect and yields a concept. This whole process is so instantaneous that it appears a simple act, a *simplex apprehensio,* something natural and easy for the human intellect.[25] When the intellect is operating in this mode, it has of itself no knowledge of sensible particulars. It can acquire a certain degree of knowledge of particulars only *after* abstraction has taken place, through what is called a "reflection on the phantasm" (*reflectio ad phantasmata*); this is an act of synthesis, however, which provides only an indirect knowledge of the particular.[26] It is after all of this has taken place that the judgment can occur, and scientific knowledge can come into being.

The senses, then, give us an intuitive knowledge of the sensible; and the intellect gives us knowledge of the universal. Taking them together, we could refer to their operations as *visio,* for they provide us in some sense with a direct and immediate seeing of the species or nature of an object. However, if we are looking for a type of knowledge in which the intellect is in direct and immediate contact with the sensible, this does not exist. It would no doubt be a higher form of knowledge, and indeed it is a kind of knowing which Aquinas attributes to God and to angels, each in their own degree, but it is not within the capacity of humans.[27]

The human intellect, for Aquinas, is compelled to engage in discourse; the "lightning" of intuition in the strict sense of the term is denied to it. It is true that the sensible intuition puts us in direct contact with particulars. But even here, there is an infinity of concomitant circumstances connected with particulars—existence, place, time, to name but a few—which are not perceived intuitively. They are brought together with things, in our minds, through a complex discursive act, the act of judgment.[28]

In short, Aquinas has defined, secured, and ordered the stages of the process of cognition with such minute precision that it is impossible to disrupt their order to introduce a new element. And even if we were willing or able to do so, it is not at all evident that the best place to assign to the aesthetic *visio* is somewhere in between sensible perception and intellectual abstraction. For it is just here that Aquinas has established the various affiliations and connections with greatest clarity, in many of his works, and quite explicitly. I am using this somewhat spatialized model of Aquinas's account of cognition in order to make the point quite clear: the kind of intuition that is discussed by Maritain, de Bruyne, and many others is a modern concept which is alien to the Thomist system.

To accept Maritain's theory, in which beauty is "a lightning of the mind on a matter intelligently arranged," would entail a denial of sensible intuition. Equally, it would entail a denial of intellectual abstractive knowledge. It is simply not possible to find a place for an intellectual intuition of particulars, in which the senses play no part. Aquinas did not allow for intuition of this kind. Still less did he allow for an act of the intellect which grasps the intelligible in the sensible without the activity of abstraction. For Aquinas, there could be no such act.

The theories of aesthetic intuition found in Maritain and de Bruyne contain many things of value, but in the end they do not convince. For the moment, however, no alternative theory presents itself; and this is why we must look next at the objective conditions of beauty. When we have discovered precisely what it is in an object that the senses and the intellect apprehend, we can then go on to define the nature of the apprehension itself.

IV

The Formal Criteria of Beauty

One of the best-known parts of the Thomist aesthetic is his theory of the three formal criteria of beauty: proportion, integrity, and clarity. But the immoderate use made of these terms in the Scholastic tradition has rendered them obscure by very excess of exegesis. Once again, therefore, we must turn back to Aquinas's own words, and, by careful reading in the context of his system as a whole, attempt to flush out his meaning.

The Texts

The simplest texts are to be found in the *Summa Theologiae*. An early reference occurs in a passage already quoted in the last chapter, at I, 5, 4 ad 1, where Aquinas says that beauty has to do with knowledge (*vis cognoscitiva*), so that "those things are called beautiful which please us when they are seen." He then continues:

> Unde pulchrum in debita proportione consistit: quia sensus delectatur in rebus debite proportionatis, sicut in sibi similibus; nam et sensus ratio quaedam est, et omnis virtus cognoscitiva.

> This is why beauty consists in due proportion, for the senses delight in rightly proportioned things as similar to themselves, the sense faculty being a sort of proportion itself like all other knowing faculties.

Proportion is singled out for mention here. However, the main source for accounts of the three criteria of beauty has always been I, 39, 8c. The question posed in this article is "Whether the holy doctors have correctly assigned essential attributes to the persons [of the Trinity]." As one would expect, Aquinas's remarks on beauty in the corpus of this article acquire their significance from their context. But almost always they have been torn out of their context and handed down to us in the schematic isolation of Scholastic formulas, deprived of their original force. All the same, I shall start by looking at how they have been handed down in the Scholastic tradition, and postpone examination of the whole article for the moment. The passage, then, to which tradition has confined itself is the following:

> Ad pulchritudinem tria requiruntur. Primo quidem integritas sive perfectio: quae enim diminuta sunt, hoc ipso turpia sunt. Et debita proportio sive consonantia. Et iterum claritas; unde quae habent colorem nitidum, pulchra esse dicuntur.

> Three things are necessary for beauty: first, integrity or perfection, for things that are lacking in something are for this reason ugly; also due proportion or consonance; and again, clarity, for we call things beautiful when they are brightly colored.

Here for the first time we find the three formal criteria of beauty all together;[1] and it is only here that Aquinas provides a systematic formulation of the three.

Aquinas's first reference to two of these features, consonance and clarity, occurred in his *Commentary on the Divine Names:*

> Deus tradit pulchritudinem inquantum est causa consonantiae et claritatis in omnibus; sic enim hominem pulchrum dicimus, propter decentem proportionem in quantitate et in situ et propter hoc quod habet clarum et nitidum colorem.

> God confers beauty on things in that he is the cause of consonance and clarity in everything. So we call a man beautiful on account of his being well proportioned in his dimensions and surroundings, and because of his having a clear and bright complexion.[2]

This is much the same as what he says in the *Summa*. We should note, however, that it is not absolutely faithful to the Dionysian original. Dionysius had given the two terms a more cosmic significance, as in the following passage:

> Supersubstantiale vero pulchrum pulchritudo quidem dicitur propter traditam ab ipso omnibus existentibus iuxta proprieta-

tem uniuscuiusque pulchritudinem; et sicut universorum consonantiae et claritas causa.

That, beautiful beyond being, is said to be Beauty—for it gives beauty from itself in a manner appropriate to each; it causes the consonance and splendour of all.[3]

Aquinas's interpretation of this reduces it in scale. His is not a purely metaphysical perspective, but involves a more tangible and ascertainable kind of beauty. Consonance and clarity in Pseudo-Dionysius were highly abstract and complex in meaning, whereas in Aquinas they are concrete principles of individuation of the aesthetic object. This may be because Aquinas did not simply take them from Pseudo-Dionysius as his only source; they were already part of his language, already equipped with a more analytic and determinate significance than they had in the Areopagite.

These, then, are the main passages in which the three criteria are mentioned in connection with aesthetics. But his system in its entirety provides many other indications as to how we might clarify them further. We do not have to confine ourselves to these quotations alone.

The Concept of Form

Each of the three criteria points, either explicitly or by implication, to the concept of form. We may as well move forward and consider this notion now, though always keeping in mind its connection with the three criteria. Form, in fact, is a key concept in Aquinas's aesthetics: everything that he says about beauty indicates that it is grounded in form, and that if an object is to be experienced as beautiful it must be considered from the point of view of its formal cause. Beauty as a transcendental, for instance, is coextensive with being; but a thing has being insofar as it actualizes a rational structure that "informs" the material. This kind of theory compels us to reflect upon the concept of form. For Aquinas, aesthetic value is connected with formal causality.

However, Aquinas also occasionally refers to a triad of terms which might be called canonical—namely, *modus, species,* and *ordo* (measure or dimension, species or nature, and order). As we saw in an earlier chapter, these three constituted the Augustinian aesthetics of wisdom, based as they were upon the terms *numerus, mensura,* and *pondus* in the Book of Wisdom. In Augustine they were used to refer to the good and, sometimes, to beauty. Aquinas was content to refer them just to the notion of good. However, Aquinas also explained the three terms as constituting formal value, so that they were always part of the life of forms.

Modus, species, and *ordo* were attributed to the good, insofar as the good consists in perfection. They were thus criteria of perfection. Perfection, however, means the complete realization of form: a thing is perfect when it fully conforms to a given mode of perfection, a mode which is represented in and necessitated by form, and is realized through the realization of form. Form, for its part, establishes certain conditions and determines others,[4] and these conditions, whether primal or consequential, are precisely *modus, species,* and *ordo.* Form is determined by means of measure in its material and efficient principles (that is, its *modus*); by means of number—that is, the proportions of its constitutive elements—form is restricted to a particular *species;* and because of its inclination, or weight, it has a certain *ordo* toward its proper end.

As we shall see in due course, these three criteria are in fact various modalities of proportion. But for now at least we can conclude that they are criteria of the perfection of a thing—perfection in the sense of goodness, but also, by implication, in the sense of beauty—and that they are conditions and aspects of the substantial form of the thing. This shows yet again that the objective foundation of beauty is to be found in the formal structure of objects, which must, then, lie at the center of our inquiry.

Some questions now present themselves. When we talk about "form," about referring to it and interpreting the three criteria in connection with it and so on, in what sense are we using the term? It is a term used by Aquinas, and used in a fairly clear fashion. But when employed as a term in aesthetics it evidently acquires unpredictable overtones. The history of aesthetics shows it to possess the most divergent meanings, so that before speaking of it we are obliged to establish its signification quite clearly so as to avoid confusion with matters extraneous to our inquiries.

*   *   *

In our own culture we sometimes come across a concept of form in the sense, not of a vital principle or an immanent pattern in things, but rather of the thing itself conceived of as an "organism" structured and governed by the inner laws of its composition. Form refers here to a formed material, as a sort of ontological *quid* in the broadest sense. Thus, Adelchi Baratono writes of "a coming into being or actuality of sensible qualities . . . which present themselves [to experience] as a *de facto* unity, [so that] at every moment experience constitutes itself with a qualitative multiformity which entails some relationship among its various constituents."[5] Luigi Pareyson writes of "an organism, living its own life and endowed with internal rules . . . perfect in the harmony and unity conferred upon it by its laws of coherence, complete in the mutual proportions between the whole and its parts."[6] When form is conceived of in this way, it is synonymous with the organization and completeness of an experienceable object or a lived experience. It does not mean the rational structure within a thing. It refers, not to the relations within it, but rather to the thing itself as something organized and made what it is by those relations. It does not mean a pure structure or pattern, which can be abstracted by the mind from a complete object and imposed upon a shapeless stuff, but rather a structure or pattern which is materially at one with the object— something in virtue of which an object lives and is what it is, but which itself possesses reality and character only in virtue of being materialized in the object. It means a binding and ordering of parts which form themselves into a unity according to a rule and a finality.[7]

Form in this sense is no longer the prerogative of art alone. The whole of nature comes to be thought of as a life of forms,[8] as a form of forms, as the producing of forms. This was a conception found in the Renaissance and in Romanticism, and it is still to be found today. It has been a feature of pantheism and of mysticism, and of relationist and organicist philosophies.[9] It can be viewed both as a principle of stability and as a principle of change and metamorphosis.[10]

We do not have to interest ourselves here in whether form, conceived of in this way as an organism, is ontologically given in accordance with an a priori law of experience or is instead the product of our perceptual transactions. Our sole concern is with those concepts of form which, whatever their theoretical provenance, have some features in common.

We can now ask whether Aquinas's concept of form is in any way analogous to the one we have just looked at. At first sight the reply must be negative. Aquinas's idea of form is the same as Aristotle's "entelechy"—that is, a structural principle in things. Entelechy does not signify an object which has a structure, but is rather what combines with matter to produce an object. Form in this sense, then, means the actuality, perfection, or determinacy of a thing, although the thing consists also of matter, and matter is not reducible to form. At the same time, the form, albeit not identical with matter, cannot subsist nor have any reality if it is not individuated in matter.

A somewhat different meaning of the word *form* in Aquinas is that of "shape," or *morphē (figura)*. Form in this sense is a property, namely the quantitative boundary of a body, an external feature which can be empirically experienced. This meaning of the term, however, is only marginal in the present context, although I shall return to it later.

It would seem, then, that the Thomistic concept of form has little in common with the sense of the term examined a moment ago. However, it is well known that Aquinas used the word in yet another and broader sense, in which it means, *not the structural principle of beings, but rather those very structured beings*. By form, in this sense, he means "essence." And essence means substance conceived of as an object of understanding and of definition. Form, that is, may refer to the actualizing principle of substance, but often for Aquinas refers to substance itself.

But what is meant by "substance"? The word signifies being (*ens*) thought of as something wholly complete, something endowed with a structure which can be analyzed, and which is an ontological unity. It means the existing organism in itself. It is not something hidden beneath the structures, features, and properties of things; rather, it is the being itself of the structures, features, and properties, for these are simply modes of the being of substance. "Substance" means the focal point of the organization, the selection, and the life of substance's own multiple aspects. It means the structural constitution of a concrete thing.

If beauty, then, is the perfection of a thing and attaches to the concrete act of existing, and if it can be identified with fullness of being, so that it is transcendentally indistinguishable from being, it must follow that beauty belongs to substance. When Aquinas says that beauty is grounded in form, he means that it is grounded in the concrete substantiality of things. In Thomistic thought, the connections between form and substance are so close and so necessary that referring to one by means of the other is in certain cases quite legitimate. The natural role of a form is to assume reality by being reified in a substance; and a substance is actual only because it is actualized in a form. Outside of this relationship, form and substance are only names. A form "is" only when it combines with matter and becomes incarnate in a thing; at the same time, the ultimate perfection of the thing, such that its substance "is" existentially as well as essentially, goes beyond the form. Here we find the twofold composition of things which is basic in Aquinas's thinking: a composition of form with matter, and then a composition of essence with existence. Before the second of these two occurs, substance is merely definable and has no real existence. It would thus lack perfection, for this is a metaphysics whose highest value is not identity of essence, but fullness of existence.[11]

There is in fact a passage in the *Summa contra Gentiles* which clarifies all these concepts. Being or *esse*, Aquinas explains, is not an act either of form or of matter, but of the whole substance: "Substance itself is that which is" ("ipsa substantia est id quod est").[12] Perfection is not the prerogative of form by itself, because form is the principle of being (*principium essendi*) and is in this sense something that complements substance (*complementum substantiae*). But the proper act of a substance is to exist concretely, and so perfection— both essential and existential perfection—means the accomplishment of a process in which form is only the initial, motor constituent.

> Unde in compositis ex materia et forma nec materia nec forma potest dici ipsum quod est, nec etiam ipsum esse. Forma tamen potest dici quo est, secundum quod est essendi principium; ipsa autem tota substantia est ipsum quod est; et ipsum esse est quo substantia denominatur ens.

> Accordingly, in things composed of matter and form, neither the matter nor the form nor even being itself can be termed that

which is. Yet the form can be called "that by which it is," inasmuch as it is the principle of being; the whole substance itself, however, is "that which is." And being [*esse*] itself is that by which the substance is called a being [*ens*].[13]

Full perfection is found only in "a being" (*ens*): it is here that substance truly exists, lives, and unfolds. *Ens* signifies a concretely structured thing, an organism governed by the inner relations which give it form and so give it being, but which also goes beyond those purely abstract relations since it validates them and confers existence upon them.

When an organism is conceived of in this way, it appears to be very close to the idea of "form" which I have been trying to pinpoint. The "beings" (*entia*) which populate Aquinas's universe are not pure symbolical manifestations of the divine creativity. They are concrete realities, and they can be understood as "forms."

It should be clear by now that form in this sense is different from form in the narrow sense of entelechy. In order to distinguish these two senses, I shall henceforth indicate the first, broader sense by form (in roman type), and the second, narrower sense by the italicized *form*.

The textual evidence which we have looked at so far might justify the conclusion that, in Aquinas, the ontological reality in which beauty is grounded is form in the sense of the substantial organism. However, I propose to adopt this conclusion only as a working hypothesis. In our examination of the three formal criteria of beauty, in which they will be referred constantly to the notion of form, we shall find that form is the natural basis, both ontologically and psychologically, of the conditions that are constitutive of aesthetic value.

Proportion: The Historical Data

The first of the three criteria of beauty is proportion or consonance (*proportio sive consonantia*). One thing is in our favor, namely that the concept of proportion was the most widespread aesthetic concept in the whole of antiquity and the Middle Ages. It was the only one to be accepted universally and understood in a univocal sense, despite the richness of its various shades of meaning. An examination of its sources would be both arduous and unnecessary; so the heart of my inquiry will be an attempt to establish all the novel or important implications which this ancient idea possessed in the systematic context of Aquinas's thought.

Nonetheless, some brief historical account may be helpful. The classical definition of the beautiful was *krōma kai symmetria,* color and symmetry. This definition was repeated in various ways by both classical and Christian writers, as in these examples from Cicero and St. Augustine, respectively.

> Corporis est quaedam apta figura membrorum cum coloris quadam suavitate, eaque dicitur pulchritudo.

> In the body a certain symmetrical shape of the limbs combined with a certain charm of coloring is described as beauty.[14]

> Omnis pulchritudo est partium congruentia cum quadam suavitate coloris.

> All beauty is a harmony of parts with a certain pleasing color.[15]

But there is no point in simply gathering up definitions of this kind unless we look into their deep meaning. It is essential right at the start to emphasize two things which characterized the idea of proportion in the Greek period. One of these is that proportion did not mean just a criterion of beauty in either a mathematical and descriptive sense or a practical and operative sense; more than this, proportion was a metaphysical principle. Empedocles, for instance, wrote of, "bloody Discord, and *Harmony with her serious mien,* Beauty and Ugliness, the Speed-Nymph and the Nymph of Delay; and lovely Infallibility and dark-eyed Uncertainty,"[16] all of which were personifications of the divinity. What is involved here, in fact, is the Pythagorean theory that number is the fundamental principle of the universe. A short list of well-known quotations will serve, better than exposition, to indicate the sources of all succeeding discussion of the metaphysics of proportion.

> Everything that can be known has a Number; for it is impossible to grasp anything with the mind or to recognise it without this (*Number*).[17]

> This is how it is with Nature and Harmony: the Being of things is eternal, and Nature itself requires divine and not human in-

telligence; moreover, it would be impossible for any existing thing to be even recognised by us if there did not exist the basic Being of the things from which the universe was composed, (*namely*) both the Limiting and the Non-Limited. But since these Elements exist as unlike and unrelated, it would clearly be impossible for a universe to be created with them unless a harmony was added, in which way this (*harmony*) did come into being. Now the things which were like and related needed no harmony; but the things which were unlike and unrelated and unequally arranged are necessarily fastened together by such a harmony, through which they are destined to endure in the universe.[18]

Virtue is harmony, and so are health and all good and God himself; this is why they say that all things are constructed according to the laws of harmony.[19]

The number of worlds is neither infinite, nor one, nor five, but one hundred and eighty-three, arranged in the form of a triangle, with sixty worlds on each side. The remaining three worlds are placed one at each angle, and as the worlds turn they gently touch each other as if in a dance.[20]

Eudoxus and Archytas believed that the intervals which make up a chord could be expressed in numerical proportions. They also thought that these intervals are created by movements, and that a quick movement produces a high-pitched sound, caused by the air's being continuously and rapidly struck, while a slow movement produces a low-pitched sound, because the action is slower.[21]

They say that Lasus of Hermione, and Hippasus of Metapontum, a Pythagorean, used the principle of quickness and slowness of movement by which chords are made . . . Since he [Hippasus] believed that intervals exist in numerical proportions, he took two vases which were the same in shape and size, filled one half-full of liquid, and left the other empty. When he struck each one he obtained an octave. And again, by leaving one of the vases empty and filling the other a quarter full, he obtained a fourth; and then a fifth, by filling one vase a third full: the principle being that, in the octave, the numerical proportion was 2 to 1, in the fifth 3 to 2, and in the fourth 4 to 3.[22]

Plato and Aristotle simply took over these principles and assimilated them into broader systematic contexts.[23]

At the same time, however, proportion was also understood to be an operative principle. The earliest explicit statement of this, insofar as it can be reconstructed, was the canon of Polyclitus: "Polyclitus of Sicyon, pupil of Hagelades, made a statue of the 'Diadumenos' or Binding his Hair—a youth, but soft-looking—famous for having cost 100 talents, and also the 'Doryphoros' or Carrying a Spear—a boy, but manly-looking. He also made what artists call a 'Canon' or Model Statue, as they draw their artistic outlines from it as from a sort of standard."[24]

Polyclitus' understanding of proportion clarifies one fundamental point which we shall encounter again when looking at Aquinas; and this is, that the philosophical principle of proportion, whose basic formulation did not change for two millennia, was nonetheless actualized in artistic practice in accordance with a variety of shades of meaning. So, for instance, the Egyptian canon of proportion differed from the Greek.[25] The Egyptians used a network of equal squares which prescribed fixed and measurable quantities. Any variation involved an addition of the same basic module. For example, if the human figure was to be eighteen units in height, three units were assigned to the foot, five to the arms, and so on. In the Greek theory, however, proportion was organic, inspired we might say by the same rhetorical principle of *kairos* (fitness or measure) which applied to persuasive discourse. It was grounded in whatever was appropriate for the circumstances. The units of construction were not fixed; rather, the head related to the body and the body to the legs in a manner which depended upon the placing of the figure and the point of view. This is made clear in Galen's account of the canon of Polyclitus: "Beauty does not consist in the elements but in the harmonious proportion of the parts, the proportion of one finger to the other, of all the fingers to the rest of the hand, of the rest of the hand to the wrist, of these to the forearm, of the forearm to the whole arm, in fine, of all parts to all others, as it is written in the canon of Polyclitus."[26]

It is interesting that these variations in the understanding of proportion did not come about solely through a historical evolution of taste, but also in relation to the situation of the onlooker. It was not just a matter of how one part of an artifact related to another, but also of how the artifact, together with all its parts, related to the visual requirements of its spectators. This is quite fundamental to our understanding of those passages in Aquinas where he discusses the relation of the objective conditions of beauty to the *visio* (looking or seeing) which puts them in focus. The same point is elaborated in the following excerpt from Plato's *The Sophist*.

STRANGER: I see the likeness-making art as one part of imitation. This is met with, as a rule, whenever anyone produces the imitation by following the proportions of the original in length, breadth, and depth, and giving, besides, the appropriate colors to each part.

THEAETETUS: Yes, but do not all imitators try to do this?

STRANGER: Not those who produce some large work of sculpture or painting. For if they reproduced the true proportions of beautiful forms, the upper parts, you know, would seem smaller and the lower parts larger than they ought, because we see the former from a distance, the latter from near at hand . . . So the artists abandon the truth and give their figures not the actual proportions but those which seem to be beautiful, do they not? . . . That, then, which is other, but like, we may fairly call a likeness . . . and the part of imitation which is concerned with such things, is to be called, as we called it before, likeness-making . . . Now then, what shall we call that which appears, because it is seen from an unfavorable position, to be like the beautiful, but which would not even be likely to resemble that which claims to be like, if a person were able to see such large works adequately? Shall we not call it, since it appears, but is not like, an appearance? . . . And to the art which produces appearance, but not likeness, the most correct name we could give would be "fantastic art," would it not?[27]

This excerpt enables us to understand Vitruvius' distinction between symmetry and eurhythmy, a distinction which has been the object of much debate. Vitruvius defined symmetry as "appropriate harmony resulting from the members of the work itself, and the metrical correspondence resulting from the separate parts in relation to the aspect of the whole configuration" ("ex ipsius operis membris conveniens consensus ex partibusque separatis ad univer-

sae figurae speciem ratae partis responsus"); and he defined eurhythmy as "a pleasing appearance and a suitable aspect" ("venusta
species commodusque aspectus").[28] The latter refers to beauty
which appears beautiful to us because it is adapted to the eye. The
idea of proportion has more than one facet, but it is necessary to be
mindful of them all if we are to grasp how it spread and diversified
in the Middle Ages.

The medievals used it first of all for the purposes of metaphysical
definition. The origin of this usage was the passage in the Book of
Wisdom where God is said to order the universe according to number, weight, and measure. As we have seen, this led to the notion of
beauty as a transcendental property of being.[29] Beauty was thus
considered, not as mere ornamentation which could be produced
by means of practical rules, but as a cosmic modality which by
means of these rules, and in parallel with the rules governing the
universe, could be individuated in art. Thus, proportion was a
principle which confirmed the numerical affinity of all things with
one another.

The earliest appearance in medieval times of a Pythagorean aesthetics of proportion was in Boethius' *De Institutione Musica*.[30] Boethius begins with the discoveries which the Pythagoreans had made
about the nature of music—as recounted, for instance, in the passages from Theon of Smyrna quoted above. He tells the story of
how Pythagoras, outside a blacksmith's forge, noticed that the
pitch of the sound made by the hammers was proportional to their
weight. Boethius then defines consonance as "a unified concordance of sounds dissimilar in themselves" ("dissimilium inter se
vocum in unum redacta concordia").[31] And again, he writes that,
"Consonance, which regulates all musical modulations, cannot exist without sound" ("consonantia, quae omnem musicae modulationem regit, praeter sonum fieri non potest").[32] But consonance,
he goes on, is not simply an objective datum, for it has to do also
with a correspondence between sound and perception: "consonance is a mixture of high and low sounds striking the ear sweetly
and uniformly" ("consonantia est acuti soni gravisque mixtura
suaviter uniformiterque auribus accidens").[33] Both the body and
the soul are subject to the same laws that govern the universe, and
these are musical laws. The human soul modulates its feelings in
the manner of the musical modes, so that a drunken youth from

Taormina once moderated his frenzy when musicians who were present passed from the Phrygian to the Hypophrygian mode. Microcosm and macrocosm are related by a single mathematical rule, which is also the rule of aesthetic decorum. Psychological proportion is the same as proportion in the cosmos. The well-known Pythagorean and Boethian theory of the music of the spheres, a music produced by the rotation of the seven planets round the earth, laid it down that the further the planet was from earth the higher its tone, because it had to move more swiftly.[34]

Boethius' theory of music, then, adapted Pythagoreanism for medieval culture. Any account of the concept of proportion must keep in mind this very important influence. Two examples of the influence at work are John Scottus Eriugena and Honorius of Autun. Eriugena wrote that the beauty of creation was the result of a consonance of similars and dissimilars, and that, just as in a musical composition, the single parts are insignificant in themselves, but taken all together produce a wonderful sweetness.[35] Somewhat later, in his *Liber Duodecim Quaestionum*, Honorius of Autun devoted a chapter to explaining that "the universe is ordered like a cithera, in which there is a consonance of different kinds of things, like chords" ("quod universitas in modo citharae sit disposita, in qua diversa genera in modo chordarum sit consonantia").[36] In Aquinas we find many remarks about proportion which have been inspired by the theory and the experience of music.

Pythagorean thought also influenced Plato's *Timaeus,* a work which itself was the basis for the cosmology of the school of Chartres. As Tullio Gregory puts it, "Their universe was a development, by way of Boethius' writings on arithmetic, of the Augustinian principle that God disposes all things in accordance with order and measure—a principle which combined the classical concept of the cosmos as *consentiens conspirans continuata cognatio* [harmonious and continuous relations] with the principle of a Divinity who is life, providence, and destiny."[37] It was the *Timaeus* which reminded the medievals that "God, purposing to make it [the universe] most nearly like the every way perfect and fairest of intelligible things, fashioned one visible living creature, containing within itself all living things which are by nature of its own kind [i.e., are visible] . . . The fairest of all bonds is that which makes itself and the terms it binds together most utterly one, and this is most perfectly effected by a progression."[38]

In the metaphysics of the school of Chartres, nature was an active principle which presided at the birth and the becoming of things,[39] and whose operations and achievements involved an embellishing of the world (*exornatio mundi*)—that is, an order, an arranging of what has been created (*collectio creaturarum*). Matter is differentiated by weight and number, and so it assumes shape, figure, and color. This furnishing or fitting out of the world (*ornatus mundi*) is seen to obey laws of proportion and to result in determinate forms. It follows mathematical laws which operate from the depths of the formative energy of the life of nature—or, as William of Conches put it, "a certain force inherent in things, making similars out of similar things" ("vis quaedam rebus insita, similia de similibus operans").[40] In the metaphysics of the school of Chartres, the world was seen to be clearly ruled by number. Number, however, meant an organic principle and not an abstract mathematical rule. It was not so much that number presided over nature, as that nature was a creative force which ruled itself by number. In his *De Planctu Naturae*, Alan of Lille described nature as "a child of God, mother of creation, bond of the universe and its stable link, bright gem of those on earth, mirror for mortals, light-bearer for the world: peace, love, virtue, guide, power, order, law, end, way, leader, source, life, light, splendour, beauty, form, rule of the world."[41]

In the metaphysics of the school of Chartres, the theory of mathematical proportion took the form of an organic conception of the universe. But the medievals were influenced by another type of theory, Pythagorean and mystical, and based upon the primacy of the notion of numerical proportion. This was the metaphysics of *homo quadratus*, connected in its origins with Chalcidius and especially Macrobius, who wrote that the world was man writ large and man was the world writ small ("physici mundum magnum hominem et hominem brevem mundum esse dixerunt").[42]

The theory involved an allegorizing of human proportions, expressed in terms of mathematics. There were four cardinal points, four winds, four phases of the moon, four seasons, four letters in the name Adam, and four was the figure of Plato's tetrahedron, which corresponded to fire. Four was a macrocosmic number, and so it ruled also in the microcosm. The breadth of the human figure with arms outstretched corresponded with its height, so that it yielded the equal sides of an ideal square. There were four humors, and four stages in life. Four was also the symbol of moral perfection, so that the "tetragonal" man of Aristotle and Dante was strong and hardened. And this rule of proportion was related also to the architecture of cathedrals, so that their proportions had a human scale. As Vitruvius had taught, "No building can have a principle of construction without symmetry and proportion, and unless it has the precise order of the limbs of a well-proportioned man" ("non potest aedes nulla sine symmetria atque proportione rationem habere compositionis, nisi uti ad hominis bene figurati membrorum habuerit exactam rationem").[43]

Furthermore, the subtle analogies that connect squares with circles meant that *homo quadratus* was also "pentagonal man." What was involved here was a conception of man as circular, a conception which also went back to Vitruvius: the human figure could be inscribed in a circle whose center was the navel and whose circumference touched the ends of the fingers, the feet, and the top of the head. Thus there were five bodily extremities, as well as the five senses. Five was also a symbol of the union which propagates the species. On the macrocosmic level, five was the number of the terrestrial sphere: there were five elementary zones, and five genera of living creatures (birds, fish, plants, animals, men). On the mystical level, the pentad presided at the Creation and presided also in manifestations of God, as in the Pentateuch and the five wounds. And in mathematical mysticism, five was a circular number which, multiplied by itself, successively repeats itself: $5 \times 5 = 25; 25 \times 5 = 125; 125 \times 5 = 625 \ldots$[44]

The aesthetics of *homo quadratus* might seem a simple transposition to the theoretical level of purely practical and operative principles. But it is clear that it reflects, yet again, an underlying belief in the identity of moral and aesthetic value, in the identity of aesthetic value with a mystical and supernatural value, and, finally, in its identity with a cosmological value.[45]

Proportion as a practical and operative rule was something whose flexible variety the medievals did not succeed in capturing on the level of theory; but they did, all the same, succeed in living it. The idea of proportion was articulated in various ways—as unity in variety, or "a fitting union of different sounds" ("diversarum vocum apta coadunatio")[46]—but it is necessary always to relate these formulations to the practical activities to which they referred or with which they were contemporary. As we shall see, the concrete reality was constantly undergoing change even though its philosophical definition might remain the same.

Music provides a revealing example. For centuries the theory of music featured the term *proportion;* but what this actually signified to musicians was another matter. In the ninth century, hymns of rejoicing based upon the *alleluia* made use of tropes—that is, the various syllables were made to correspond to movements in the melody. But in the twelfth century, the polyphony of someone like Pérotin might employ a sort of pedal point, in which three or four voices would sustain the same note for sixty beats while contrapuntal structures were elaborated, like the spires of a Gothic cathedral, upon this generating base note. The definition of proportion quoted above, "diversarum vocum apta coadunatio," still applied, but clearly it had a different sense in the two musical experiences. The practical musician tended not to bother with the theory of proportion. Instead, he would write something practical such as "Whosoever wishes to compose a *conductus* must first find a canto, the most beautiful that he can. Then he must use it to construct a descant."[47] It was the practical musician who brought changes to the meaning of words such as *beautiful* or *fitting*. In the ninth century, the fifth was regarded as an imperfect consonance, but in the twelfth century the rules of descant held that the fifth was pleasing to the ear and a perfect consonance. In the thirteenth century, the third joined the consonances. What was fitting in music was subject to progressive change.

Poets and literary theorists held similar views. In the eighth century, Bede was well aware that the nature of proportion was different in the cases of syllabic meter and meter based upon quantity,[48] and later writers also accepted this fact.[49] In the thirteenth century, Geoffrey of Vinsauf's *Poetria Nova* stated that the appropriateness of literary ornament was based, not upon mathematical rules, but rather upon psychological rules and habits of sound (or, as we might put it today, a connotative code already established and known). Thus, it was fitting to describe gold as "fulvum," milk as "nitidum," and the rose as "praerubicunda."[50] It is clear that what is involved here is not a relationship based upon a universal rule of number, but rather a system of systems of literary conventions. Pursuing this line of thought, Geoffrey distinguished between a natural and an artificial way of ordering literature and gave the laws of narrative decorum belonging to each of the two orders. With this, we have left the field of aesthetics for the field of poetics.[51] Thirteenth-century writers on poetics gave detailed instructions on how to achieve an effect of symmetry in the construction of narrative, playing upon the simultaneity of events.[52] A similar kind of precept had been laid down by the younger Pliny, when he argued that the brevity of Homer's description of Achilles' shield was required by the events that followed.[53] The mathematical criterion of style gave way to a criterion of taste which pertained to rhetoric rather than to music. It owed more to the notion of *kairos* than to the mathematico-musical theory of proportion.

Similar issues arose in connection with the figurative arts.[54] It was usually the space within which a figure was inscribed that gave to it its proportions and made it acceptable—it might be in the lunette of a tympanum, or on a door column, a tondo on a façade, or an illuminated letter in a missal. Here, the rule of proportion came from the context of the image, and not from a universal canon as it had in Greek statuary. Thus, the conception of what was fit or appropriate broke up into several related concepts, with respect to which the idea of proportion acted as a "transcendental matrix"—not a medieval type of expression, perhaps, but expressing all the same an idea which we shall find in Aquinas. In somewhat plainer terms, proportion no longer signified an absolute standard of measure, but merely the general principle that measure was necessary; there could thus be an infinity of ways of making and doing things in accordance with proportion. It could mean a mystical and symbolical principle,[55] or a technical rule, or an aesthetically pleasing and objective rhythm. And there were many kinds of symbolical proportion, many ways of being effective in technique, many ways of being aesthetically pleasing. Aquinas more or less consciously assimilated these varieties of practical experience with one another and was able to explain them all as modes of proportion within his comprehensive and flexible hylomorphic theory.

The Concept of Proportion in Aquinas

An early reference to proportion, apart from its use in connection with beauty, is found in *Summa Theologiae,* I, 12, 1, which deals with the question of whether any created mind can see the essence of God. *Objectio* 4 states that there must be some proportion between the knower and the known, but that there can be no such thing as a proportion between man and God. *Responsio* 4, Aquinas's reply to this, attempts to define the concept of proportion by distinguishing between two senses of it.

> Proportio dicitur dupliciter. Uno modo certa habitudo unius quantitatis ad alteram, secundum quod duplum, triplum, et aequale sunt species proportionis. Alio modo quaelibet habitudo unius ad alterum proportio dicitur.

> When we say one thing is in proportion to another we can either mean that they are quantitatively related—in this sense double, thrice, and equal are kinds of proportion—or else we can mean just any kind of relation [*habitudo*] which one thing may have to another.

The first of these is a strictly mathematical and quantitative kind of proportion. The second, I would suggest, is a qualitative kind of proportion. It is not a narrowly mathematical relation between two things, but a "habitual" relation—there is a possibility of mutual reference or analogy, or some kind of agreement between them which subjects both to a common criterion or rule.

In the passage just quoted, the term *habitudo* is used to refer to the relation between creatures and their creator. It is a relation which arises from a basic affinity between them, and which allows us in certain circumstances to see the essence of God. But the twofold distinction of proportion has wider implications. For the idea of "habitual" proportion has various meanings in Aquinas's thought: it can on occasion be something like numerical proportion, or it can signify relations less amenable to measurement. It is necessary, therefore, to examine the different types, or at least some fundamental types, of proportion in Aquinas. In the first instance it is something which is ontologically constitutive of things, and so initially I will distinguish some of its strictly objectivist significations.

In the *Summa contra Gentiles,* where Aquinas also discusses how we see God, he again refers to proportion as *habitudo,* a relation of one thing to another. He then gives examples of such a relation: that of matter to form, or of cause to effect.[56] This shows us what direction our inquiry should take.

1. Proportion, then, can mean first of all the suitability of matter for receiving a form. Matter adapts itself to form. It consists of a simple potency in respect of the form that gives it order and actuality, in a progressive and mutual adaptation and integration of both. Matter submits to the requirements of some form or other so as to emerge from its primeval anonymity and become the matter of *this particular* form. Thus it becomes an individual and autonomous substance. In the *Summa contra Gentiles* Aquinas writes:

> Omne agens quod in agendo requirit materiam praeiacentem, habet materiam proportionatam suae actioni, ut quicquid est in virtute agentis, totum sit in potentia materiae; alias non posset in actum producere quicquid est in sua virtute activa, et sic frustra haberet virtutem ad illa.

> Every agent whose action necessitates the prior existence of matter possesses a matter proportioned to its action, so that whatever lies within the agent's power exists in its entirety in the potentiality of the matter; otherwise, the agent could not actualize all that lies within its active power, and hence, as regards the things it could not actualize, it would possess that power in vain.[57]

The chapter from which this passage comes (entitled "That God brought things into being from nothing") describes the action of any nondivine agent upon matter as a progressive movement in which matter offers itself to order and form; it is proportion conceived of as process. Later on in the same work he writes:

> Formam igitur et materiam semper oportet esse ad invicem proportionata et quasi naturaliter coaptata: quia proprius actus in propria materia fit.

> Thus, form and matter must always be mutually proportioned and, as it were, naturally adapted, because the proper act is produced in its proper matter.[58]

This statement confirms in the most unequivocal way that proportion, in the sense of an aesthetico-ontological regulative principle, refers to a complete substance. It pertains to form understood
as an organism and is not a property of *form* as act. The following
passage is quite explicit on this point.

> Quia proportio huiusmodi non est forma, sicut ipsi credebant,
> sed est dispositio materiae ad formam. Et si accipiatur proprie
> harmonia compositionis pro dispositione, bene sequitur, quod
> manente dispositione materiae ad formam manet forma, et des-
> tructa dispositione, removetur forma.

> For this kind of proportion is not form, as people used to think,
> but rather the disposition of matter to receive a form. And if it
> is then accepted that this disposition of matter is the same thing
> as a harmony in the composition [that is, the composition of
> matter with form], it follows that when the disposition of mat-
> ter to receive a form is present, then so is form; but if this dis-
> position is destroyed, then form is also taken away.[59]

It is form which produces order and design in things. But *form*
enters into several relationships of such a kind that it is subsumed
into a larger whole. One of these is, precisely, the relation of suitability which binds matter to it.

2. Another type is the proportion between essence and existence.
This is such a basic idea that it can easily be overlooked. But there
is for Aquinas a natural and necessary relation, a relation of fitness,
between a thing's essence and the energy of its act of existence. It is
the same kind of relation as the relation between potency and act.

> In quocumque enim inveniuntur aliqua duo quorum unum est
> complementum alterius, proportio unius eorum ad alterum est
> sicut proportio potentiae ad actum: nihil enim completur nisi
> per proprium actum . . . Ipsum autem esse est complementum
> substantiae existentis.

> For in whatever thing we find two, one of which is the comple-
> ment of the other, the proportion of one of them to the other is
> as the proportion of potentiality to act; for nothing is com-
> pleted except by its proper act . . . Now, being itself is the com-
> plement of the existing substance.[60]

This passage also helps to clarify the question of beauty as a transcendental. For it seems that a thing has proportion because it exists, because it "is." A thing may be said to "be" in the act of combining its essence with its existence, and this act involves a proportion, a concordance, a harmony. This proportion, furthermore, is constitutive of beauty. Thus, everything is beautiful insofar as it "is," because it "is" in virtue of a harmony of essence with existence. Something is beautiful insofar as it "is," and it "is" insofar as it is beautiful; and it has beauty in that it has proportion. This aspect of Aquinas's thinking, which has not to my knowledge been previously expounded in terms of proportion, clearly places beauty on a very rarefied metaphysical level. As we shall see in due course, people find it difficult to perceive this kind of ontological beauty—in part because of its absolute evidence and simplicity, and in part because of the depth of thought required to grasp it, possible only, perhaps, for the creative mind. But it is a type of beauty demanded by the logic of Aquinas's system.

3. Another type of proportion is sensible and basically quantitative. It is a relationship among a multitude of fixed items. Musical proportion is typical of this, and also, by extension, proportion in shape and color. It produces an immediate feeling of pleasure.

> Homo autem delectatur secundum alios sensus . . . propter convenientiam sensibilium . . . sicut cum delectatur homo in sono bene harmonizato.

> Human beings get pleasure from their senses . . . because of a suitability that things have for sensation . . . Thus, they take pleasure in nicely harmonized sound.[61]

Medieval musical theory, especially in Boethius, had made this concept of proportion a familiar one.

4. Proportion does not refer only to sensible relations. It can also mean a purely rational fit between things: logical relations, or the harmony of a sequence of thought, or the proportion of thought to the laws of thought. There is also moral proportion. This might be found in a sequence of actions, or of thoughts, when they are ordered in accordance with the moral law, or in the relation of actions

and thoughts to the practical dictates of natural reason, or the higher dictates of the divine law. Many passages in Aquinas are quite explicit about this kind of proportion.

> Et similiter pulchritudo spiritualis in hoc consistit quod conversatio hominis sive actio eius, sit bene proportionata secundum spiritualem rationis claritatem.

> So also beauty of spirit consists in conversation and actions which are well formed and suffused with intelligence.[62]

> Pulchrum in rebus humanis attenditur prout aliquid est ordinatum secundum rationem.

> In human matters beauty goes with what is well ordered according to intelligence.[63]

Statements such as these connect Aquinas with a long tradition which, whether in Cicero or in William of Auvergne, saw a relation between beauty or decorum (*pulchrum, decens*) and virtue (*honestum*). It was the Greek ideal of *kalos kagathos*. Aquinas's viewpoint, however, is distinguished by two things: first, he emphasizes the proportional, or formal, aspect of this kind of beauty; and second, he does not identify this proportional relation with beauty as such, but with only one of many types of beauty. We must note also that there is a tendency for this type to transform itself into sensible beauty; for what is at issue is the concordance between some empirical item, such as an act, a word, or a gesture, and a spiritual law.

In fact, two interpretations of moral proportion and beauty are possible, each apparently justified by Aquinas's words.

First interpretation. Beauty is found only in a concrete substance. Rational proportion is a formal relation, but it must manifest itself, or become incarnate, in a physical fact. In the case of a dance, we can perceive the correspondence between the external movements and the metrical rhythm which governs them. So, too, with the moral life: here, we can take pleasure in the correspondence between empirical behavior and the moral rhythm which governs it. This line of thought in Aquinas explains the basis of beauty in good actions and in the external dignity of the upright man.

Second interpretation. Aquinas considers the aesthetic character of a pure spiritual rhythm, which is not externalized in action. In fact, it would seem that this is the most fundamental kind of proportion, and the truest and purest beauty.

> Utrumque autem horum radicaliter in ratione invenitur . . . Et ideo in vita contemplativa, quae consistit in actu rationis, per se et essentialiter invenitur pulchritudo.

> Each of these [proportion and clarity] is rooted in the reason . . . Therefore, in the contemplative life, which consists in an activity of reason, beauty is found by the nature of the case and essentially.[64]

The exceptional importance which this conception gives to purely intellectual relations may remind us of how Boethius considered musical theory to be more excellent than music itself. And in fact we see here the intellectualism of Aquinas's aesthetics.

We can throw some light upon these two interpretations if we distinguish between the notion of beauty as a kind of principle and the definition of beauty as an experienced fact. If beauty is considered as a principle, then, according to Aquinas, it does not consist in a combination of the sensible with a spiritual rule (Maritain's "lightning of the mind on a matter intelligently arranged"). Rather, it consists essentially in the condition of organic wholeness. If beauty is understood in this way, it is not essential that form should assume a materially concrete existence—and if it did, its beauty would still be like that of a word which is thought or an act which is intended. What is essential to form is rather that it determines organic wholeness in things. I have already assimilated the Thomistic concept of form to the concept of concrete substance, because in almost all cases this is how form is realized; so that form in its simplest and, it would seem, most worthy aspect is pure organic structure. Sensuous richness, material relations, light, sound, color, sculptural values, are not essential to it. What counts is organic wholeness, and beauty consists, *per se et essentialiter,* in this.

Everything other than this essential beauty is an extra richness—items arranged proportionately and constituents of the empirical fact of beauty. However, in the last analysis these extra items increase the beauty and even determine how suitable it is for human experience. Aquinas confines himself to saying that beauty is to be found, in its most basic and essential form, in its most elementary structures, in the contemplative life. He does not claim that this type of beauty is the one that most easily and completely produces the rush of joy, the *delectatio,* the strong and total delight that attends upon aesthetic experience.

We might therefore be inclined to think that Aquinas's discussion of pure rational beauty has a merely illustrative rather than a definitive intent. But we ought not to imagine that he understood this conception of beauty in a metaphorical sense. It is distinctive of his outlook that he should concentrate upon the purely rational and value it highly; for the beauty of rational form comes nearest to the beauty of God. God is absolutely simple, so that we cannot talk about unity in multiplicity in respect of him. Proportion in God manifests itself as the harmony of his attributes with one another— his Providence with his Will, his Will with his Goodness and his Justice, his Wisdom with his Power, and so on.[65] This distinction between beauty as a principle and beauty as a fact is found throughout Aquinas and is never completely resolved. As we shall see in Chapter VIII, where I discuss the type of beauty that appeals to mankind, the whole of the Thomistic aesthetic contains an ultimate contradiction.

5. There are still other kinds of proportion. It can be understood also as the adequacy of a thing to itself—that is, its adequacy to what it is supposed to be, to the idea which its concept connotes, its adequacy to the type which its *form* calls into being. Alternatively, proportion can be understood as the fit between an object and its function. This is closely connected to the first type of adequacy, because when an object is what it ought to be it is also proportional to its function.

> Duplex est rei perfectio: prima et secunda. Prima quidem perfectio est secundum quod res in sua substantia est perfecta. Quae quidem perfectio est forma totius, quae ex integritate partium consurgit. Perfectio autem secunda est finis. Finis autem vel operatio, sicut finis citharistae est citharizare; vel est aliquid ad quod per operationem pervenitur, sicut finis aedificatoris est domus, quam aedificando facit. Prima autem perfectio est causa secundae: quia forma est principum operationis.

> There are two kinds of perfection in a thing: a first perfection and a second perfection. The first is present when the thing has

all that makes up its substance. This perfection, which is the result of integrity of parts, is the form of the whole. The second kind of perfection is the goal that the thing is to achieve. This goal is either an activity, for example playing the harp for a harpist, or it is something achieved through activity, for example the house that is the builder's goal when building. Also the first sort of perfection is the cause of the second, because form is the source of activity.[66]

Each of these two kinds of proportion, then, relates to the other turn and turn about. Each in turn is a potency to the other's act, to its perfected existence. Each becomes the stimulus for a new and deeper proportion. The first perfection is the operative principle of the second; but at the same time the second, which is the final perfection of an object, is regulative of the first, a rule and law of the *perfectio prima*.[67]

This theory, it seems to me, situates the concept of proportion beyond (or prior to) the Kantian dialectic of free beauty and adherent beauty. Whether proportion refers to the autoteleological adequacy of a thing to the requirements of its *form,* or instead to the teleological adequacy of a thing to its end or its capacity to achieve an end—in short, its functional suitability—in both cases proportion leads back to the same aesthetic ordinance.

However, the notion of beauty as something functional was very much alive in the Middle Ages. When Isidore of Seville wrote about the "seemliness" of the fingers on the hand, he put particular emphasis upon their position and function.[68] The medieval outlook was very concerned with ends, so it could not fail to be aware of this aspect of form and of the aesthetic.

6. It should be clear by now that the idea of proportion in Aquinas has a very complex intension. It often signifies, not a single type of relation between two things, but rather a dense network of relations. It can pertain to a relation between one item and another item, or between two items and a third.[69] In fact we are free to consider the relation of three, four, or an infinity of things, proportionate among themselves and proportioned also in respect of some unifying whole. This unifying whole may then be taken as one item in a new set of items unified in their turn among themselves;

and so on to infinity. In brief, what is involved is a twofold relation of parts to one another and to the whole of which they are parts.[70]

This type of pluralistic relationship is the type of order which is easiest to detect in natural and artistic organisms. Also, it can be repeated at progressively higher levels while sustaining the same proportions. It can appear in the simplest organism and be perceived in the normal fashion; or, through successive enlargements of scale (as if in a geometrical progression) it can assume a cosmic dimension. When this happens, we arrive at a conception of the universe as form: the whole of existent being as a well-proportioned organism; the macrocosm as order.

Aquinas discussed at some length this conception of the beauty of all things as an order and a proportion, particularly in his *Commentary on the Divine Names*. Here, instead of a world determined by its forms we encounter the world as a single supreme form conceived by the Supreme Maker. This is how the universe had been presented in the *Timaeus,* and how it appeared also to the school of Chartres, under the direct influence of Pseudo-Dionysius and in all probability Boethius as well. In Aquinas, however, Dionysius' cascade of passionate imagery is transformed into a rigorous description of order; and Boethius' mathematical and musical vision of things becomes more naturalistic and organic. The universe, in Aquinas, is a hyperbole of form, a gigantic metaphor for life.

The universe is a harmony of a multitude of orders. As one commentator puts it, "But the harmony of so many orders is itself an Order—a formal, dynamic unity of multiple and diverse relations of being."[71] Everything in the universe imposes boundaries on itself, staying within the confines of its form; but at the same time everything is part of an immense whole which contains them all, one within the other. As de Bruyne has felicitously expressed it, all the existents in the universal whole "s'emboîtent les uns dans les autres."[72]

All creatures have an order of congruity in respect of one another, and beyond that there is a superior order in virtue of the fact that all creation is oriented toward God. This idea of a universal order is the source of a number of central features in Aquinas's thought: his teleological conception of the created world, his conception of divine providence as an ordering force, his conception of a Supreme Good realizing itself in things. These undoubtedly constitute the heart of his metaphysical perspective. And so far as our interests here are concerned, we find that many passages in his *Commentary on the Divine Names* deal with the aesthetics of the Universal Proportion, at least in its formal aspects.

It is not an easy thing to impose a strict order upon the dazzling play of images in Pseudo-Dionysius. But for this very reason, Aquinas's phenomenology of universal proportion is a rich and exhaustive one.[73] He describes the universe as a gigantic organism which organizes its constitutive forms, all of which are in proportion to and identical with it, all engaged in a play of relationships based upon substantial compatibilities both quantitative and qualitative. There is the relationship of the whole to the substantial reality of its constitutive forms, and the mathematical relations which bind them all together. There are qualitative relations among genera and species, and a relationship which unifies contraries in genus and in matter. There is a resolution of parts into wholes, and at the same time a relationship in which they are kept distinct. These relationships, Aquinas tells us, mean that "all things lead back to the causing of beauty, because they all have to do with consonance" ("omnia ad causalitatem pulchri reducuntur, quia pertinent ad consonantiam"). Lower entities are related to higher in that they can be contained within them, and the higher can govern and order the lower. Equal entities are related by a mutual disposition of one to the other. Objects are sustained within their normal bounds, and parts are related to one another by the law of the wholes to which they belong.

> Sicut multi lapides conveniunt ad invicem ex quibus constituitur domus et similiter omnes partes universi conveniunt in ratione existendi; et hoc ideo dicit, quia non solum ex pulchro sunt mansiones rerum in seipsis, sed etiam communiones omnium in omnibus secundum proprietatem uniuscuiusque.

> Many stones fit together with one another in the building of a house; and in the same way, it is in the nature of existence that all parts of the universe fit together. The Areopagite says this because, while on account of beauty things are located within themselves, in addition all things are in communion in a manner which accords with the proporties of each.

And he adds that the various parts of things are related in mutual help and support.

> Sicut paries et tectus sustentantur ex fundamento et tectum cooperit parietem et fundamentum . . . Partibus ergo sic dispositis, sequitur earum compositio in toto, secundum quod ex omnibus partibus universi constituitur una rerum universitas.

> Just as the walls and roof are held up by foundations, and the roof covers the foundations and the wall . . . When the parts are arranged in this way, they all combine into the whole; so that out of all the parts of the universe there emerges one single wholeness of things.

The combination of things into the whole occurs in two ways: by the containment of one within the other ("per modum localis continentiae"); and by succession in time ("quantum ad temporis successionem"). And the consequence is that all things are caused by beauty ("omnia dicit ex pulchritudine causari"). The play of motion and rest which is the life and movement of the world is nothing other than its beauty, governed as it is by a supreme proportion, harmony, and rhythm.

All of this supreme order, this ordered life of a dynamic multiplicity, owes its unity to the principle of measure (*mensura*). For this reason, it generates the notion of peace, understood as the tranquillity of order (*tranquillitas ordinis*). Order is identical with life, but the order which controls life's energy is identical also with peace. There is a passage in the *De Veritate* which identifies peace with beauty, the reason being that peace is the stable perfection which exists when proportion is fully realized. "If appetite terminates in good and peace and the beautiful, this does not mean that it terminates in different goals" ("appetitum terminari ad bonum et pacem et pulchrum non est eum terminari in diversa").[74]

The Platonic conception of the world as a living creature is here presented to us in its organic wholeness. It involves a broad metaphysical perspective and a striking metaphor for the formal aspects of the real. The formal structure of every organic existent is seen in the light of the macrocosmic features of creation and is therefore revealed in its beauty. It is an ontologically immanent beauty, a beauty which is neither imposed upon things nor reducible to their pure design; rather, it lies at the heart of their existential reality. The rationale of existence is also the rationale of beauty, because it is the rationale of order and proportion.

7. Proportion has a great many ontological aspects, but it has psychological aspects as well. These also have reference to the universal order of things, but it is necessary to look at them outside this context in order to grasp their relevance to aesthetics.

All of them are connected with the psychological relationship between the senses and the objects of sense, and between the intellect and its object. One such relation is the compatibility of a given sense organ with a given objective quality—the eye with colors, for example, or the hearing with sounds. There can be an objectively rule-governed quality in sensible phenomena, as when sounds combine into a melody or several colors go together. Confronted with this, the human senses reveal a quality of connaturality, an ability to grasp and discern the rules involved in such phenomena, the rules which constitute their *ratio* or "logic"—or, to use a different term, their proportion.

We have already noted all of this in Boethius. Aquinas refers to the issue early in the *Summa Theologiae*.

> Sensus delectatur in rebus debite proportionatis, sicut in sibi similibus; nam et sensus ratio quaedam est, et omnis virtus cognoscitiva.

> The senses delight in rightly proportioned things as similar to themselves, the sense faculty being a sort of proportion like all other knowing faculties.[75]

This idea is explained more fully in his *Commentary on the De Anima*. The passage in Aristotle upon which he is commenting is:

> Si autem symphonia vox quaedam est, vox autem et auditus est sicut unum et est non sicut unum aut idem, proportio autem est symphonia, necesse est, et auditum, rationem quandam esse.

> If voice is a kind of harmony, and if the voice and the hearing of it are in one sense one and the same, though in another sense not, and if harmony always implies proportion, it follows that what is heard is a kind of *ratio*.[76]

Aquinas's commentary on this is as follows.

> Et dicit quod cum symphonia, id est vox consonans et propor-
> tionata, sit vox quaedam, et vox quodammodo sit idem quod
> auditus, et symphonia sit quaedam proportio, necesse est quod
> auditus sit quaedam proportio.

> Aristotle says that, since harmony—that is, a consonant and
> well-proportioned voice—is a kind of voice, and since voice is
> in some sense the same as what is heard, and since harmony is
> a kind of proportion, it necessarily follows that what is heard
> is a kind of proportion.[77]

Here Aquinas takes the term *ratio* in the Aristotelian text to mean
"proportion,"[78] and so it is in this sense that we should interpret
what he says in the *Summa*. Proportion thus refers in this context to
a disposition of the senses toward the sensible, in the manner of a
potency. In fact just after the quoted passage from the *Summa* Aquinas argues that the senses are corrupted by an excess of sensation;
their mutual concordance is broken. There is a proportion of the
senses such that they are fitted for sensation, and which consists in
specific quantitative and qualitative relations whose role is to connect the sense faculties of perception with the objects perceived.
Today the same web of relations is referred to as an isomorphism
between the field of perception and the structures of the mind—
part of a psychology of form which is by no means innocent of
metaphysical implications.

As well as this proportion of the senses to their object, there is a
further proportion, part of the same thing, between the intellect
and its object. Again, this is referred to early in the *Summa Theologiae*—in the article, already mentioned, in which Aquinas asks
whether a created mind can see the essence of God.[79] He says there
that a cognitive relation between the intellect and the divine essence
is made possible by a kind of proportion between them—although
at the same time he adds that the divine exceeds the intellect's capacity to such an extent that divine light is necessary for this kind
of cognition.[80]

This, together with the passages quoted from the *Commentary on
the De Anima,* suggests that in Aquinas's view there was a certain
relationship between the psychological dispositions of the perci-

pient and the nature of the act of perceiving. In general, psychological proportion would seem primarily to *allow* the aesthetic act, whereas ontological proportion is the *ground* of the causes of aesthetic pleasure. We should also note here, although this is something that we will come back to, that when we address ourselves to an object with the aim of grasping its formal connections—that is, seeing it *sub specie pulchri*—we adopt a particular type of cognitive state. This in turn implies a disposing or proportioning of oneself to the object under its formal aspects. This is why psychological proportion both permits the aesthetic act and is also its ground: without the movement to a specific type of cognition, beauty would not be actualized.

8. In all the cases we have looked at so far, proportion is based upon the vital reality of form. In this sense, it does not signify something static and crystallized in a motionless perfection, but rather a dynamic unity. It is a dynamic unity because it involves a combining of living forces which do not annul or rigidify themselves when they combine; rather, they confer life upon a type of activity whose value derives from their several vigorous and operative energies. The result is one of unity in variety, a unity which does not constrict the multiplicity of movement but merely regulates it and directs it to its end. Here is how Dewey puts it:

> There is an old formula for beauty in nature and art: Unity in variety. Everything depends upon how the preposition "in" is understood. There may be many articles in a box, many figures in a single painting, many coins in one pocket, and many documents in a safe. The unity is extraneous and the many are unrelated. The significant point is that unity and manyness are always of this sort or approximate it when the unity of the object or scene is morphological and static. The formula has meaning only when its terms are understood to concern a relation of energies. There is no fullness, no many parts, without distinctive differentiations. But they have esthetic quality, as in the richness of a musical phrase, only when distinctions depend upon reciprocal resistances. There is unity only when the resistances create a suspense that is resolved through cooperative interaction of the opposed energies. The "one" of the formula

is the realization through interacting parts of their respective energies. The "many" is the manifestation of the defined individualizations due to opposed forces that finally sustain a balance.[81]

It seems to me that formal proportion, as defined by Aquinas, has precisely these dynamic characteristics, just because it is proportion in an organism which exists, which lives. There is a dynamic tension which causes matter and form to combine in the individual, and a dynamic tension which transports essence into the excitement of existence. If we leave the plane of metaphysics, we still find a dynamic tension among the parts of things, and between subject and object in cognition. All proportion is dynamic, because it is the coefficient of perfection, the coefficient of existence.

There is a brief opusculum by Aquinas, *De Mixtione Elementorum*,[82] which is very revealing on this matter—revealing rather than conclusive, because it deals with a particular type of formal organism. However, in treating of this type, Aquinas manifests also a more general concern.

The opusculum is a discussion of "mixed bodies." A mixed body is the type of organism which results from the combination of several elementary bodies. The human body is a typical instance. Aquinas's problem is whether the simple or elementary bodies retain their substantial form within the mixed body. His answer is that they do not, and he gives lengthy refutations of the contrary view. In the mixed body, he says, there arises a new and unique substantial form. What we have, in other words, is an organism whose structure is autonomous and individual. Despite this, however, the constitutive elements within this new autonomous form are not reduced to some kind of amorphous state. The forms of the simple or elementary bodies may not remain in act, but they do subsist in a virtual manner (*in virtute*). This means that the qualities of the simple bodies—qualities which depend upon their own substantial form, which was their active principle—are turned toward and absorbed into a new quality which belongs properly to the new mixed body and is dependent upon its form. They survive as a continual alignment of the active "virtues" of the simple bodies.

The qualities under discussion here are virtues or powers, *virtutes,* dynamic energies, which subsist and remain active and through which the mixed body has life. Clearly, what is involved is less an interaction than an integration, and an integration which does not annul or render amorphous. Some quality of the simple bodies is saved: "salvatur enim virtus eorum." This is a type of formal dynamism which we shall find to be confirmed when the principle of proportion is applied to art.

In conclusion: our examination of the various types of proportion should have made it abundantly clear why proportion in Aquinas is a coefficient of beauty, why it is connected with the notion of form, and why it therefore validates the aesthetic value of every organism that exists, whether natural or artistic, spiritual or sensible.

The list of types of proportion compiled here is not exhaustive. I have indicated the principal varieties, in a factual and explanatory way, and I have indicated something of the fruitfulness of the concept in Aquinas's philosophical system. To say that the list is not exhaustive does not mean merely that we might point to other types of proportion in Aquinas, or that there is in principle an exhaustive list which it would be too time-consuming to compile. The fact is rather that proportion, because it is constitutive of beauty and thus coextensive with it, has its own transcendental character. Proportion therefore has an infinity of analogues. Every existent, beautiful in that it possesses existence, can present us with new and unsuspected types of proportion. The possible proportions are infinite in number, both in the world of nature and in art.

> Pulchritudo, sanitas, et hujusmodi, dicuntur quodammodo per respectum ad aliquid: quia aliqua contemperatio humorum facit sanitatem in puero, quae non facit in sene . . . Unde sanitas est proportio humorum in comparatione ad talem naturam. Et similiter pulchritudo consistit in proportione membrorum et colorum. Et ideo alia est pulchritudo unius, alia alterius.

> Beauty, health, and the like are defined in relation to something; for a certain mixture of the humors, which produces health in a boy, does not do the same in an old man . . . Thus, health is a proportioning of the humors in relation to some kind of nature. And in the same way, beauty consists in a proportioning of limbs and of coloring. This is why one person's beauty is different from another's.[83]

If proportion were simply a question of mathematics, there would exist a fixed rule to determine and foresee its embodiments. But proportion is a transcendental matrix which can realize itself in ever new and unsuspected ways. The idea of a new form is sufficient to ensure that the relation of matter to it will assume a totally new configuration.

> Ordo semper dicitur per comparationem ad aliquod principium. Unde sicut dicitur principium multipliciter . . . ita etiam dicitur ordo.

> Order always takes its meaning in reference to some principle. Accordingly, as the term *principle* has many senses . . . so too does the term *order.*[84]

There are no rules for the introduction of order. Order is itself a rule, but a transcendental rule, in both the Scholastic and the Kantian senses. In one perspective, in fact—namely, where the laws of intellect are also the laws of being—the a priori forms of knowledge are also the a priori forms of being insofar as they exist *in mente Dei.*

Order is not so much a model to be copied as a compulsion that must be satisfied. Proportion is a need, and proportion satisfies the need. And it is something that is known to us by way of what is at bottom a new incidence of psychological proportion: the senses have their own intelligence (*ratio quaedam est*) and will recognize the familiar harmony of things irrespective of how it may appear.

The concept of proportion is a most fruitful one and is central to the Thomist aesthetic. It is the key to a number of explanatory theories. And yet, it seems inadequate. Form, for all that it possesses proportion in itself and to itself and is proportionately related to us, may not reveal its full perfection without its other characteristics, expressive or declamatory. This is a question which we shall tackle in due course, and in particular when we look at the notion of *claritas.*

Integritas

Another characteristic of beauty, as we saw at the beginning of the chapter, is wholeness or perfection (*integritas sive perfectio*). As I have already said, *Summa Theologiae,* I, 39, 8c, is the only place where Aquinas uses the term *integritas* specifically to refer to a formal character of beauty; and for this reason, it has on occasion been overlooked or misrepresented. In some places, Aquinas means by *integritas* the size of the human body, and this has given rise to the view that it is a simple, rudimentary idea. Or it has been interpreted as a sort of breadth or power which generates pleasure of a very general kind.[85] Far more relevant, however, are those interpretations which reduce integrity to a particular type of proportion, though without, perhaps, devoting very much attention to what makes it distinctive. In listing the various types of proportion above, I mentioned the adequacy of a thing to itself, that is, to what its *form* requires it to be. Aquinas identifies integrity with perfection, and perfection means the complete realization of whatever it is that the thing is supposed to be.

> Prima quidem perfectio est, secundum quod res in sua substantia est perfecta. Quae quidem perfectio est forma totius, quae ex integritate partium consurgit.

> The first type of perfection is present when the thing has all that makes up its substance. The whole object's form is its perfection and arises out of the integrity of its parts.[86]

A thing is adequate to itself whenever none of it is missing. "Things that are lacking in something," Aquinas writes, "are for this reason ugly" ("quae enim diminuta sunt, hoc ipso turpia sunt").[87] And it is with these words that he explains the import of the concept of integrity.

Integrity, then, is a type of proportion. But it is of such importance that it has to be singled out for mention. It is a concept which reappears often in various forms in various parts of Aquinas's works; and it is an aesthetic criterion not only on the level of metaphysics but also as a concrete category of critical judgment.

> In corpore humano potest esse deformitas dupliciter; uno modo ex defectu alicuius membri, sicut mutilatos turpes dicimus; deest enim eis debita proportio ad totum.

> There are two kinds of deformity in the human body. In one, there is a defect in some limb, so that we call mutilated people

ugly. What is missing in them is a due proportion [of parts] to the whole.[88]

This passage clearly implies that a mutilated person is lacking in the most inclusive type of proportion, namely, proportion with respect to himself. And his various parts, designed as they are in relation to a form that is complete, are in some measure lacking in equilibrium; their conjunction points to something nonexistent, to a void; they are deficient in certain symmetries and correspondences.

When the concept of integrity is interpreted in this way, as something easily assimilable to proportion, it is very close to the conception of a *forma formante* in the thinking of Luigi Pareyson. "A work of art," Pareyson writes, "possesses every quality which it ought to possess, no more and no less. This is because the process which has formed the work cannot continue after its completion. It cannot be interrupted before, nor continued after, the form is realized: for if it were interrupted the form would not achieve existence and the formative process would be aborted; and if it continued, the form would extend beyond the point of its completion and would break up and disperse."[89]

Aquinas writes in his commentary on the *De Anima:*

> Manifestum est autem, quod in omnibus quae sunt secundum naturam, est certus terminus, et determinata ratio magnitudinis et augmenti . . . Non enim omnes homines sunt unius quantitatis. Sed tamen est aliqua quantitas tam magna, ultra quam species humana non porrigitur; et alia quantitas tam parva, ultra quam homo non invenitur.

> It is clear that in all things that follow their natural pattern there is a certain limit, and a determined amount of size and growth . . . Not all men are the same in size. But there is a size beyond which the human species does not go; and there is another size so small that no person falls below it.[90]

Integrity may be infringed by default or by excess. For Aquinas, the forms of things are like numbers in that any change, any addition or substraction, confounds the nature of the species and transmutes it into a different one. As Pareyson puts it, "The whole contains its parts, and follows from their indissoluble unity, only

because before it existed as something formed it decreed and ordered the parts, acting as *forma formante* in the formative process."[91]
If we apply this interpretation to the idea of natural form in Aquinas
we can see more clearly the role and the importance of integrity. So
far as artistic form is concerned, Aquinas tells us that things can be
called true in two ways: either because they are adequate to the
intellect, in which case it is logical truth; or because they are adequate to the ideas of them which preexist in the mind of God, in
which case it is ontological truth. Ontological truth, which is at the
same time existence, goodness, and beauty, is further explained as
follows:

> Unaquaeque res dicitur vera absolute, secundum ordinem ad
> intellectum a quo dependet . . . Dicitur enim domus vera, quae
> assequitur similitudinem formae quae est in mente artificis.

> Everything is said to be true in the absolute sense because of
> its relation to a mind on which it depends . . . A house, for
> instance, is true if it turns out like the plan in the architect's
> mind.[92]

Thus, in the case of man-made works there is also a form which
presides over its construction and regulates it in a law-governed
way. It is in the light of this form that we attain to an understanding
of the work. To quote Pareyson again, "The integrity of the work
is evident only to someone who knows how to grasp the whole in
the very act of giving life to its parts by constructing, promulgat-
ing, and arranging them."[93]

Aquinas's way of understanding the formative activity of form
does not coincide completely with that of Pareyson. For Pareyson,
forma formante is not so much an idea which precedes the work, as a
law of construction which arises and appears in a process of becoming which coincides with the process of forming. What is of interest to us here, however, is a point made in the course of Aquinas's
discussion of integrity. This is, that the aesthetic experience of a
thing is regulated by the concept of the thing; it involves a judgment regarding the degree of conformity between thing and concept. In the case of a mutilated person the judgment is instantaneous, because the concept of bodily integrity is so familiar to us.

We can now return to the problems raised by the notion of

beauty and integrity as bodily magnitude. As we can see, the medieval sensibility had as its physical ideal a certain size and stature in the human body—one thinks of the elongated, athletic figures in Gothic statuary. The ideal was an essential element in the concept of the body which regulated the aesthetic experience of the human figure. A person was thought to be truly beautiful if he realized what human nature demanded, and this included a sufficient degree of size and dignity. This seemingly superficial conception can therefore be traced back to its ontological roots. When we do this, the term *pulchrum* assumes its proper, ontological significance, whereas the term *formosus,* like Boethius' *formositas,* refers to external appearance only. It follows that a man who is abnormally small might have a pleasant enough external appearance but would be deficient in the deeper kind of proportion, the type required by human nature in the fullest sense.

Claritas: The Historical Data

Proportion in things, as we have seen, produces a world of appearances which are always new and unexpected. Order, after all, is a transcendental law. But how, then, are we to detect its presence? Proportion may be a reality in things, but does it possess the capacity to express itself, to declare itself to us? If order is to be an aesthetic quality, it must have the power of self-expression; it must be perceivable, and knowable as order. The question is, whether it is the attitude of the experiencing subject which produces an impression of order, or whether, instead, order is an ontological property of form. It is true that Aquinas introduced the concept of *visio* into his account of aesthetic reality; but as well as this there remains the notion of *claritas,* an objective feature of beauty, which suggests new directions of inquiry.

The term *clarity* in Aquinas's works has such a variety of meanings that we are thrown into confusion. Its meanings range from the simplest to the mystical and the metaphysical. It is employed in such a fluid manner that we become very uncertain about its exact significance.

Generally speaking, whenever Aquinas gives an illustration of what he means by clarity, he chooses something easy and superficial. We have already seen this in *Summa Theologiae*, I, 39, 8c: "et iterum claritas; unde quae habent colorem nitidum, pulchra esse dicuntur" ("and again clarity; for we call things beautiful when they are brightly colored"). Another instance is the following:

> Ad rationem pulchri sive decori concurrit et claritas et debita proportio . . . Unde pulchritudo corporis in hoc consistit, quod homo habeat membra corporis bene proportionata, cum quadam debita coloris claritate.

> Beauty or handsomeness arises when clarity and due proportion run together . . . So, beauty of body consists in this, that a person has well-proportioned limbs, together with a certain requisite clarity of color.[94]

This conception, of beauty as color appropriately arranged, is found in all the classical sources, from the Stoics to Plotinus, and is always accompanied by the idea of proportion. If we limit ourselves to this sense of *claritas,* it denotes such things as a nice complexion, the warm hue of a sculpture, or the brilliant green of a meadow. When set off against the notion of symmetry, clarity seems identical with *chrōma,* a term which Bosanquet, who does not seek any deeper ontological significance, defines as "brightness of color."[95] In this sense it is neither ontological nor metaphysical, but physical only—*claritas* as an effect of light. It is a conception which points to Aristotle's physics of light and color, a theory which explains the mechanics of luminous phenomena and the corresponding sensations, but is of no interest to us here.

It is true that Aquinas writes in one place, "The beauty of the heavenly bodies consists mainly in light" ("pulchritudo autem coelestium corporum praecipue consistit in luce").[96] Light and color undoubtedly contribute to beauty. But if we go back to Aquinas's theory of the origin of these two phenomena, we find nothing of relevance to aesthetics. Thus, he tells us that light is neither a body nor a substance, but a quality in a body that is luminous of itself. This quality does not pass over into an opaque body when it is lit up; rather, it generates in the body its own luminosity and color, brings its own intrinsic potency (its "diaphaneity") into act. In this way, the colors and every kind of brightness are brought into being.[97] But the question still remains why we find color pleasing, what it is in brightness that evokes and solicits aesthetic pleasure. Are we bound always and everywhere to interpret *claritas* in this purely physical sense?

What is at first disconcerting for the interpreter is that elsewhere *claritas* has quite a different meaning. Sometimes it signifies *lumen rationis,* the light of reason. For instance, Aquinas condemns the sin of intemperance because of the aesthetic disvalue which it countenances: immoderate and intemperate pleasure, he says, "dulls the light of reason, from which comes all the clarity and beauty of virtue" ("minus apparet de lumine rationis, ex qua est tota claritas et pulchritudo virtutis").[98] Elsewhere, speaking about beauty and proportion in the rational and moral life, he says that clarity, along with proportion, is "rooted in the reason" ("radicaliter in ratione"), because one of the elements in reason is "a light which shows things forth" ("lumen manifestans").[99] Again, in the passage quoted above where Aquinas refers to color as an example of clarity, he immediately goes on to define spiritual beauty as any discourse or action which is "well proportioned in accordance with the spiritual clarity of reason" ("bene proportionata secundum spiritualem rationis claritatem").[100] And in this same article, *objectio* 2 and its corresponding *responsio* introduce yet another sense of *claritas.* It is connected etymologically with the word *clarus,* understood as meaning "famous" or "esteemed." It refers thus to a renown in which some individual is metaphorically clothed, a renown which flows from his virtue. In this sense, a virtuous person is beautiful partly because of his manifest splendor in the estimation of others.

There are still other passages in Aquinas which refer to the *claritas* of the bodies of the saints, of Christ's transfigured body, of the things of this world at the end of time, and so on. This mystical-eschatological sense of the term refers to a particular type of clarity which cannot be experienced on earth.

In Aquinas, then, the term *claritas* does not have a univocal sense. Its various connotations become manifest on different ontological levels. I have distinguished four types of clarity: (1) light and physical color; (2) the light of reason that makes things known, *lumen manifestans;* (3) the shining forth of earthly renown; (4) the celestial glory of the glorified bodies of the blessed, Christ's transfigured body, and objects when they are renewed at the end of time. This diverse range of meaning is justified by the fact that the concept of clarity was very ancient, as ancient as that of proportion. Its diffusion throughout the classical and medieval tradition conferred upon it a multiplicity of senses. It did not even possess the kind of univocal element found in the idea of proportion. Thus, Aquinas was using a traditional term in a number of senses which were already well known. What we must now consider is whether they all led back to some kind of common denominator. Therefore, we must rapidly survey the ways in which the concept manifested itself during the Middle Ages.

The concept of light is a contradictory one in Aquinas, just because it was contradictory in the whole medieval tradition. The medieval alertness to qualities of proportion was firmly grounded in a theoretical base which gave it sustenance, but the medieval awareness of light and color seemed rather an unreflective expression of ordinary taste. The medievals took pleasure in anything luminous, colored, or brilliant, and their love of color was characterized by immediacy and simplicity. We have only to think of medieval illuminations to see that the artists always employed elementary colors, simple juxtapositions, straightforward color patterns in which *sfumatura* is unknown. It is no platitude to refer to them as heraldic colors, for, as in heraldry, these painters avoided *chiaroscuro* and took pleasure in using colors in which there was no ambiguity. We find the same thing in medieval poets, who were also unambiguous in their references to color: grass was green, blood was red, and milk white. Color never faded into shadow. Here, for instance, is a passage which could equally well be called a heraldic document, a poetic description, or a pictorial rendering translated into words. It is from Chrétien de Troyes's *Erec et Enide*, and it testifies to the medieval ideal where color was concerned.

> The one who went at her behest came bringing to her the mantle and the tunic, which was lined with white ermine even to the sleeves. At the wrists and on the neck-band there was in truth more than half a mark's weight of beaten gold, and everywhere set in the gold there were precious stones of divers colours, indigo and green, blue and dark brown . . . In the tassels there was more than an ounce of gold; on one a hyacinth, and on the other a ruby flashed more bright than burning candle. The fur lining was of white ermine; never was finer seen or

found. The cloth was skilfully embroidered with little crosses, all different, indigo, vermilion, dark blue, white, green, blue and yellow.[101]

And once again, it is worth recalling Dante's "dolce colore di oriental zaffiro" and Guinizelli's "visio di neve colorato in grana."[102] In the *Chanson de Roland* we read of Durandal, *clère et blanche,* shining and flaming against the sun. Such examples are endless.[103] It was no accident that the medievals should develop a figurative technique in which, to an unsurpassed degree, the brilliance of simple colors was married to the brilliance of light passing through them: the stained glasswork in Gothic cathedrals. But the love of color was evident outside the sphere of art, in everyday life and habits, in clothing, ornament, and weapons. One of the best accounts of the medieval sensitivity to color is found in Huizinga. It refers to late medieval Burgundy but can be extended to the High Middle Ages in general. Huizinga records the enthusiasm of Froissart for the way in which the sun's rays played upon helmets and cuirasses, pennants and banners. We find the same kind of thing in Joinville's *Histoire de St. Louis*. Again, Huizinga tells of the advice given, in *Le blason des couleurs,* to use combinations of pale yellow and blue, of orange and white, orange and pink, pink and white, and black and white. And there is a passage in Olivier de la Marche which describes a young woman dressed "in violet-coloured silk on a hackney covered with a housing of blue silk, led by three men in vermilion-tinted silk and in hoods of green silk."[104]

Philosophers displayed the same preference for simple colors. Hugh of St. Victor and William of Auvergne both praised the color green as the loveliest of all, and William even tried to explain why. He did so in terms of psychological relations, claiming that green lay between white, which dilates the eye, and black, which makes it contract.[105] We begin to see that when Aquinas says, "Things are called beautiful when they are brightly colored,"[106] he is not being naïve and trite. A whole sweep of culture provided its justificaïion. Our task is merely that of seeing how a fact of everyday taste was fitted into his philosophical system.

So far, I have been discussing color. But color is born of light. The problem of light is the foundation of the problem of color. And in fact a mysticism of light, a love of light, and a poetics of light were constants in medieval culture. The whole of its literature exalted the flashing and glittering of light and flame. In Chapter I we saw how Suger responded to light falling through the stained-glass windows of his church; his feelings were born of a neo-Platonic aesthetics of light.[107] Dante's *Paradiso* made use of a complete repertoire of metaphors and Patristic conventions to render theological realities in terms of light.[108] The writings of the mystics unhesitatingly identified the immediate experience of divinity with an experience of light. St. Hildegard speaks of Lucifer (before his fall) as being as bright as a sky full of stars, throwing light upon the universe.[109]

God, then, appeared to the medievals preeminently as light—we have seen this already in Eriugena and Pseudo-Dionysius. However, the medievals did not develop this conception independently. There was a large Eastern tradition which had passed into Latin culture during the late Roman Empire. This tradition extended back to the Egyptian Ra and the Persian Ahura Mazda, was mediated by the neo-Platonists (who revived the Platonic concept of the Good, the "sun" of the Ideas), and passed by way of St. Augustine into Pseudo-Dionysius, with his metaphors of God as *lumen*, fire, a fountain of light.[110] And at the same time the Arab tradition, as it was assimilated into the Latin West, passed on its pantheistic visions of glittering light from the works of Avempace and ibn-Tufail.[111]

Thus, whenever medieval theology and philosophy encountered everyday medieval taste, they found common ground, and it would be difficult to say whether the taste or the corresponding theories had the stronger influence on the other. What can be said, however, is that as theory was progressively refined it revealed a problem arising from the encounter. This will become clear in the texts which I consider next.

Medieval literature, painting, and customs all display a rich sensitivity to color. But on the level of theory, the attempt to give systematic expression to this sensibility produced a contradiction. It is a contradiction which appeared, perhaps for the first time, certainly with exemplary clarity, in a passage in St. Augustine's *De Quantitate Animae*. Here, Augustine describes beauty as geometrical regularity. He says that an equilateral triangle is more beautiful than a scalene triangle because it has more *aequalitas,* or evenness. A square is more beautiful still; and a circle is most beautiful of all, for in a circle there is no angle to interrupt the continuity of the circumference. But then, the force of these deductions compels Augustine to claim that the point is even more beautiful again, for it is one, indivisible, the center, beginning, and end of itself, the generating point of the circle with its beauty.[112] In this way, a theory which begins with an explanation of geometrical beauty in terms of measurable relations among quantifiable entities—an aesthetics of proportion, in other words—turns into a qualitative aesthetics. If beauty is born from a system of relations, whence comes the beauty of the point, which is absolutely without relations?

This contrast between the quantitative and the qualitative, the measurable and the intuitable, defines the contrast between proportion and clarity. Thus, beauty comes to have two attributes, neither of which has any bearing on the other. It was a contradiction which medieval taste and artistic practices were able to cope with, relying upon a kind of principle of complementarity which was lived but not expressed in theory. Philosophy, however, was unable to achieve this kind of compromise, and the medievals were unable to devise a theoretical principle of complementarity in the sense found in contemporary physics. They had to find either a unitary explanation of the world or none at all. Thus, the contradiction between number and light put them to the test.

Scholasticism provided two kinds of solution to this problem. One was marked by a physico-aesthetic cosmology and can be found in Robert Grosseteste and St. Bonaventure. The other, characterized by an ontology of form, was devised by Albertus Magnus and Thomas Aquinas.

There was a set of common preoccupations at the roots of both types of theory. I have already referred to the polemical struggle against Manichaeism, which provoked an attempt to unify the positive features of the universe and to discover their common origin. Another influence was that of the research into optics which flourished in the thirteenth century, and which we have looked at in connection with the problem of vision. Roger Bacon proclaimed optics as the new science which was destined to solve all problems. In the *Roman de la rose,* Jean de Meun made Nature speak of the wonders of the rainbow, and of the marvels of curved mirrors, in which giants and dwarfs were inverted in size. And there was Witelo's *De Perspectiva,* which developed from Alhazen's earlier *De Aspectibus.* The psychology of aesthetic seeing was established autonomously, but it would be a mistake to study it separately from developments in the metaphysics of light. It was Robert Grosseteste who gave to light metaphysics a systematic form, and combined it with the metaphysics of proportion.

Grosseteste succeeded in showing that light and proportion were not different types of reality. (One thinks here of the modern contrast between the analogue and the digital in theories of perception and communication theory.) For in the first place, if beauty is grounded in proportion, light is proportion par excellence.

> Haec per se pulchra est, quia ejus natura simplex est, sibique omnia simul. Quapropter maxime unita et ad se per aequalitatem concordissime proportionata, proportionum autem concordia pulchritudo est.

> [Light] is beautiful in itself, for its nature is simple and all of it is there at once. Wherefore it is integrated in the highest degree and most harmoniously proportioned and equal to itself, for beauty is a harmony of proportions.[113]

Looked at in this way, God is beautiful because "he is simple in the highest degree, and in the highest concordance and harmony with himself" ("Deus autem summe simplex est sui ad se summa concordia et convenientia").[114] However, it seems reasonable to suggest that Grosseteste is here engaging in wordplay, notwithstanding Augustine's praise for this type of theory. If we are to find Grosseteste's assimilation of light with proportion we must look elsewhere, not at his aesthetics but at his cosmology of light.

In his treatise *De Luce,* Grosseteste's neo–Platonism appears in his conception of light as a creative potency. As light diffuses, it materializes depending upon the resistances which it encounters in matter. In a kind of anticipation of Henri Bergson, Grosseteste pictures light as a vital impulse which meets with material obstacles and assumes particularity in accordance with mathematical relationships. Proportion is the form which light, when it takes on material existence, confers upon the bodies which it generates.

> Lux per se in omnem partem se ipsam diffundit, ita ut a puncto lucis sphera lucis quamvis magna generetur, nisi obsistat ombrosum . . . Corporeitas ergo aut est ipsa lux aut est dictum opus faciens et in materiam dimensiones inducens, in quantum participat ipsam lucem et agit per virtutem ipsius lucis.

> Light of its very nature diffuses itself in every direction in such a way that a point of light will produce instantaneously a sphere of light of any size whatsoever, unless some opaque object stands in the way . . . Corporeity [sic], therefore, is either light itself or the agent which performs the aforementioned operation and introduces dimensions into matter in virtue of its participation in light, and acts through the power of this same light.[115]

Grosseteste's work is of great importance for our purposes here, because he showed that it was possible to bring the concepts of clarity and proportion together. But if we are on the track of Aquinas's theory on this subject, Grosseteste takes us in the wrong direction. In fact, Grosseteste effects his amalgamation of the two values by making one of them a cause and the other an effect; proportion is generated by clarity.[116]

In Aquinas, the two are combined against a background of hylomorphism, with not a trace of emanationist philosophy. However, it is worth looking briefly at the way in which Platonism and Aristotelianism combined in Bonaventure's solution to this problem.

For Bonaventure, light embodies the divine energy of participation. But it also belongs to bodies, for it is their substantial form.

> Lux est natura communis reperta in omnibus corporibus tam coelestibus quam terrestribus.

> Light is common by nature to all bodies, both celestial and terrestrial.[117]

> Lux est forma substantialis corporum, secundum cujus maiorem et minorem partecipationem corpora habent verius et dignius esse in genere entium.

> Light is the substantial form of bodies; by their greater or lesser participation in light, bodies acquire the truth and dignity of their being.[118]

For Bonaventure, as for Grosseteste, light freely diffuses itself and is the source of motion. It penetrates to the bowels of the earth, forming its minerals and the seeds of its life, for it possesses the energy of the celestial bodies (*virtus stellarum*). But for Bonaventure, light is also substantial form, though a substantial form which descends from above to instill its energy into material bodies. Light can also exist in a mode which he refers to as *lumen*. In this form it is carried through space by transparent media, and when it strikes against opaque bodies it is reflected as *color* or *splendor*. In these circumstances, light becomes an accidental form—a theory, this, which is correctly Aristotelian.

We find a similar type of theory in Aquinas, though only when he is talking about light as physical light, or *lumen*. This he defines as "an active quality deriving from the substantial form of the sun" ("qualitas activa consequens formam substantialem solis").[119] This encounters a capacity in transparent bodies to receive and retransmit light, and "this participation or effect of *lux* in a transparent object is called *lumen*" ("ipsa participatio vel affectus lucis in diaphano vocatur lumen").[120] Light in this sense was an accident. But when Aquinas referred to light in a metaphysical sense, he meant, as we shall see, something like *form* in Aristotle's philosophy—a part of material organisms, and indeed part of their essence. Like any other vital principle, it was undoubtedly an effect of divine participation, but it was not conferred on bodies by way of emanation. It was not something extracorporeal which became concrete in bodies by taking on its existence from theirs.

There are relatively few passages in Aquinas which deal with *claritas,* and they tend to occur in comparatively unimportant contexts. So, if we are to arrive at the truth of the matter we must look at them very closely. It was of course impossible for Aquinas to overlook the metaphysical implications of the term, to take it in a purely superficial and obvious way. But we must ask whether he accepted without reservation the neo-Platonic, more or less emanationist, interpretations of it. We cannot ignore the fact that in Aquinas the term *claritas* occurs only in connection with beauty. In thirteenth-century light metaphysics, clarity was not just an aesthetic concept, but a constitutive principle of reality. For Aquinas, by contrast, clarity had nothing to do with the objective structure of being or with creation; he restricted its significance to the problem of beauty. So it was necessary for Aquinas, even while accepting and assimilating the imposing wealth of meaning which the term traditionally held, to seek to ground it upon different premises.

The only work which provides any help on this issue is Albertus Magnus's treatise *De Pulchro et Bono*. Here, the whole matter is dealt with systematically, and with a clarity not to be found anywhere else, not even in Aquinas. Albertus Magnus was the first to use the term *claritas* in a context of Aristotelian hylomorphism and to reduce the whole question to one of *form*, along the lines indicated in the *Summa* of Alexander of Hales. He subjected the whole issue to a most remarkable alteration. Before him, *claritas* or *splendor* had been a metaphysical principle, a transcendent reality immersed in bodies by way of a process of emanation. Or, as an alternative to this, *claritas* had been a simple physical property of bodies. With Albertus Magnus, however, it became an ontological principle, immanent in things. Accordingly, he defined beauty as "the splendor of substantial or actual form in the proportioned and bounded parts of matter" ("splendorem formae substantialis vel actualis supra partes materiae proportionatas et terminatas").[121] An even better account of beauty is the following.

> Ratio pulchri in universali consistit in resplendentia formae supra partes materiae proportionatas vel super diversas vires vel actiones.

> The nature of the beautiful consists in general in a resplendence of form, whether in the duly ordered parts of material objects, or in men, or in actions.

As we shall see, the term *resplendentia* can be identified with *claritas*. Beauty, according to Albertus, "adds a certain resplendence and clarity to anything that has proportion" ("addit resplendentiam et claritatem quandam super quaedam proportionata"). He therefore took the view that the essence of beauty, the *ratio pulchri*, was precisely this resplendence. There was no question here of three or more formal criteria; resplendence of form was all that mattered.

> Pulchritudo non consistit in componentibus, sicut in materialibus, sed in resplendentia formae, sicut in formali.

> Beauty consists, not in the components of a thing, that is, in its matter, but rather in the resplendence of its form, that is, in its formal aspects.

Proportion also had a part to play in this theory, as order in multiplicity. But it was essential that *form,* the instrument of order, should stamp proportion with its luminous presence. As de Bruyne remarks, *convenientia* in Albertus's aesthetics was a kind of substratum of beauty, its necessary condition but subordinate nonetheless.[122] The truly distinctive mark of beauty was *resplendentia.* Also, Albertus was very clear in his view that resplendence was rooted in *form,* conceived of as a principle of organization. We must not forget that *De Pulchro et Bono* was a commentary on Dionysius the Areopagite, so that its author was always tempted by the notion that clarity had a transcendental significance. Dionysius, we recall, wrote that what was beautiful beyond being "causes the consonance and splendour [*claritas*] of all; it flashes forth upon all, after the manner of light, the beauty producing gifts of its flowing ray" ("consonantiae et claritatis causa, ad similitudinem luminis, cum fulgore immittens universis pulchrificas fontani radii ipsius traditiones").[123] Albertus Magnus, however, wrote:

> Sicut vocare ad se, convenit pulchritudini in quantum est finis et bonum, sic etiam congregare convenit sibi in quantum est forma; et secundum hoc non convenit lumini.

> Beauty calls things to it because it is an end and a good. In the same way, it gathers things together [that is, connects them with one another because they all participate in beauty] because it is form. But this does not apply to light.

Form, which "gathers things together," is the source of resplendence: "as it shines forth in the material parts of things, so it is beauty, whose nature it is to gather things together" ("secundum autem quod resplendet super partes materiae sic est pulchrum habens rationem congregandi").

Throughout this discussion, Albertus was referring to metaphysical beauty (beauty *in universali*). Human and concrete beauty appeared only by way of comparison. By staying on this abstract level he avoided the danger of trivializing the concept of *resplenden-*

tia formae. Thus, his conception of beauty quite clearly refers to an ordered multiplicity in which there shines forth an ordering design, an existential idea, the *form* which gathers things together.

It is very important, however, to take care over the precise meaning of "resplendence." De Bruyne and Pouillon, two writers who have examined the text with scientific thoroughness, refusing the frivolity or convenience of attributing it to Aquinas, have both noted that resplendence must be understood in a sense that is strictly ontological and objectivist. It does not refer to the knowing subject. Resplendence is not the expressiveness of an object with respect to someone or something else. It is, rather, a clarity which belongs to the order which the object possesses; it can be identified as the property through which being manifests itself. This interpretation fits in with the objectivism of Albertus's aesthetics, and it must be kept in mind when we pass on to Aquinas. The problem of *claritas* reached Aquinas already solved, at least in the way indicated here. The treatise *De Pulchro et Bono,* which Aquinas transcribed with his own hand, which he studied at Cologne, probably the first work to set the problem of beauty before him in a worthwhile manner, interpreted the idea of clarity in terms of hylomorphism. It was the only interpretation which he would have found acceptable.

Claritas in Aquinas

It is inconceivable that, after the lessons he received from his teacher, Aquinas could have withdrawn again to traditional ideas quite out of keeping with their guiding spirit. It would be equally strange if he had given aesthetic value a basis in form, defining it by means of two strictly ontological criteria (proportion and integrity), and then added a third criterion which had nothing to do with the first two, a criterion which would keep beauty on the phenomenal level.

And even if the Thomistic texts which we have already looked at might be capable of misleading us, Aquinas's commentary on Pseudo-Dionysius is much clearer—though not as clear, we should note, as the corresponding passages in Albertus Magnus.

The terms *claritas* and *consonantia* occur in chapter IV of *The Di-*

vine Names (for instance, in the passage quoted above). Dionysius explains that God is the cause of clarity because he imparts to all creation a certain splendor "after the manner of light" ("ad similitudinem luminis"). Aquinas's gloss upon this is that the "gifts" (*traditiones*) of divine light to which Dionysius refers are to be understood as a rhetorical figure for participation.[124] In this way Aquinas gives conceptual form to Dionysius' image and converts it into a metaphysics of participation.

This move on Aquinas's part necessitates a new and deeper interpretation of *claritas,* which he provides a little further on in his *Commentary.* Dionysius had written that supersubstantial beauty conferred being upon all existing things, and that clarity was an aspect of beauty. In Aquinas's view, this meant that *form,* through which things take possession of being, is a participation in the divine light.

> Omnis autem forma, per quam res habet esse, est participatio quaedam divinae claritatis; et hoc est quod subdit, quod singula sunt pulchra secundum propriam rationem, idest secundum propriam formam.
>
> All form, through which things have being, is a certain participation in the divine clarity. And this is what [Dionysius] adds, that particulars are beautiful because of their own nature—that is, because of their form.[125]

Here, the causes of beauty are connected with the *form* of things. Aquinas's language may not be as open as that of Albertus, but he leaves no room for doubt either. In this passage clarity is connected with the notion of participation, and it thus becomes a property of form, an ontological property involving participation in life and being. And if clarity is interpreted as participation of form in being, this shows, without the necessity of further explanation, that Aquinas understands it in the spirit of Albertus Magnus.

We may wish to inquire, however, why Aquinas was not more generous in providing explanations of this point, either here or in his other works. The answer lies in the fact that he never took a specific interest in the problems of beauty for their own sake. He never wrote a treatise, or even an article, about it. He never felt the need to put his ideas on aesthetics into systematic form. He always mentioned the problem of beauty as if by chance, and his remarks about it were always parenthetic. But this was not because he had no interest in aesthetics. The reason was rather the opposite: it came naturally to him to see the world in terms of its beauty; it was something spontaneous, effortless, and habitual. It showed itself in his writing as a dominant tonality. It was an effective and religious coloring, rather than a theological question formulated as a problem and demanding arguments and solutions. It was not in the least like the problem of universals or the problem of divine foreknowledge.

It was a natural and everyday fact of life that the world was conceived of aesthetically. All that it needed in the way of systematic expression was something very general, and there were plenty of traditional formulas which did that. At the same time, however, as Aquinas's system took form the traditional formulas incorporated within it changed in their significance and importance. The aesthetic system could grow stronger and deeper only by falling into line with the imperatives of a general metaphysical system.

It has been claimed, by a neo-Thomist metaphysician, that aesthetics is an independent variable of metaphysics. But the truth is that, in metaphysics, aesthetics is strictly dependent upon the system in general. Aquinas could well have employed the term *proportio* in the way that was customary up to his own time; but in fact it acquired in Aquinas's works a breadth of philosophical implication which cannot be gainsaid. He also used the term *claritas,* and if we wished we could assume, gratuitously, that he meant it in the most banal of senses. But in fact it necessarily became something more— an aspect of the life of forms, an ontological principle. The absurdity would be if Aquinas had rejected these consequences, if he had failed to be aware of the metamorphosis which the concept of clarity underwent in his hands. But of course this did not happen, and indeed the clear example of Albertus Magnus would have prevented it. We must look again with care at the relevant short passages in the *Summa Theologiae,* and we shall find that Albertus's principles are implicit in them. Thus, Aquinas says that intemperate behavior is ugly, because it does not possess the light of reason which would make it beautiful. We do not find, shining forth in the action, a rational design, an ideal *form,* which is harmonious and complete. An intemperate action is not an organism with a structure, in which the structural principle clearly manifests itself and shows itself by extending its rule over the whole. Elsewhere Aquinas says that spiritual beauty consists in the fact that human discourse and action are proportioned in accordance with a resplendence of the reason. And we find similar ideas in the other passages about moral and rational beauty.

Claritas is explained to be physical color only whenever the term is being used in this precise sense. It might be useful here to refer to a theory which was very widespread in medieval times, an Aristotelian theory but one which was already to be found in Isidore of Seville. It stated that the soul presided over the mixing of the humors and the composition of the blood. It thus was the cause of skin color, which became in turn an external manifestation of an internal physiological balance. Consequently, external beauty or *suavitas coloris* derived from the soul, which is the substantial *form* of the body. (Isidore thought that the word *formosus* came from *formo,* the humor of the blood.) The surface *claritas* of color became a sign and expression of a principle of organization, and so "resplendence of form" referred to something physical.

Let us turn next to the beauty of the celestial bodies. As we have seen, their beauty consists of light; and light, Aquinas writes, "is an active quality deriving from the substantial form of the sun, or of any other body that is self-illuminating" ("lux est qualitas activa consequens formam substantialem solis, vel cujuscumque alterius corporis a se lucentis").[126] This means that there is the same relationship between the light of a celestial body and its substantial *form* as between the color of the human body and the soul. Here again, resplendence of form is something physical.

The whole of question 85 in the *Supplement* to the *Summa Theologiae* deals with *claritas* in the glorified bodies of the blessed. It is explained as the spiritual clarity of the soul in its glory flowing over into the body. Elsewhere in the *Summa,* Aquinas writes that "the clarity of the risen body will correspond to the degree of grace and glory in the mind" ("qualitatem mentis, quantum ad quantitatem gratiae et gloriae, repraesentabit claritas corporis").[127]

Still elsewhere Aquinas gives a similar explanation of the *claritas* of Christ's transfigured body: "for splendor flows from the soul into the glorified body, by way of a permanent quality affecting the body" ("nam ad corpus glorificatum redundat claritas ab anima, sicut qualitas quaedam permanens corpus afficiens").[128]

In all of these cases, it is invariably the substantial *form* of the body which imposes the required order upon it, and which manifests itself as the body's organizing principle. Aquinas knew very well that the term *claritas* was in this way acquiring a new dimension. But he placed no stress upon the metamorphosis, for the simple reason that it was of no specific interest to him.

This minor terminological transformation came about in the same way as all the great evolutions and revolutions in medieval philosophy—that is, under cover of silence and indifference. What mattered was to stay within the tradition, not to innovate. Innovation might occur, but without show. This was one of the most widespread and implicit of the methodological criteria of Scholasticism.

We, however, do not have to leave the Thomistic transformation of *claritas* in this implicit state. If we wish to capture the essence of his aesthetics, we must not be afraid to make inferences even from what he may have left in embryo, provided we do not end up with anachronisms. And in fact, if we strive to pinpoint the exact sense of *claritas* in Aquinas we find that it has a different meaning from that which it had for Albertus Magnus, even though the latter's *De Pulchro et Bono* was one of its sources.

In Albertus Magnus, resplendence was the essence of beauty, *ratio pulchri,* a quality specific to beauty. In Aquinas, however, while it is true that clarity is one of the three criteria of beauty, the *ratio pulchri* resides in the fact that beauty has to do with cognition, that things are called beautiful "which please us when they are seen." There can be no doubt about this contrast. In Albertus there is no reference to the knowing subject. "Virtue," he says in *De Pulchro et Bono,* "has a certain clarity because of which it is beautiful even if it is not known by anyone" ("virtus claritatem quandam habet in se per qua pulchra est, etiamsi a nullo cognoscatur"). But in Aquinas a reference to the knowing subject is constitutive of beauty; and since this is so, the meaning of *claritas* changes.

Let us take stock. The beauty of an object is identified, in Aquinas, with its perfection, its fullness of being. It is the coefficient of this perfection that the object be subject to the transcendental law of proportion, because of which it is an organism with a structure, and the structure conforms to a particular order. In its purely formal aspect—the aspect which is of interest in aesthetics—a perfect object is an object which has integrity and proportion, and nothing more is required. Its form is complete, ontologically ready to be judged beautiful. To speak of the "resplendence" of the form is simply a figure of speech for referring yet again to integrity and proportion, the wholeness which saturates and coordinates the constituent parts.

The object is ontologically ready to be judged beautiful. However, if this judgment is to actually take place, it is necessary that a seeing or looking (*visio*) should be focused upon the thing. And it is therefore necessary that there should be a new and essential type of proportion, this time between the knowing subject and the object. Only then can the subject isolate and contemplate the object in its formal structure. At this point the perfect organism, the form, "expresses" itself, declares itself. It is closed within itself and does not refer to anything outside itself. But it does signify itself; it signifies itself to a subject. Or, better, it is the subject who makes the ontological structure—which in itself is operative only, an essential principle of life and of subsistence—significative and expressive. The object's definability, or essence—which is also its existential consistency, or substance, and also its functional principle, or nature—presents itself to us as its form. Proportion presents itself as clarity. Proportion *is* its own clarity. It is fullness of form, therefore fullness of rationality, therefore the fullness of knowability; but it is a knowability which becomes actual only in relation to the knowing eye.

If, then, we faithfully adhere to the spirit of the Thomist system and draw out his principles to their logical conclusion, we necessarily arrive at the following definition. *Clarity is the fundamental communicability of form, which is made actual in relation to someone's looking at or seeing of the object.* The rationality that belongs to every form is the "light" which manifests itself to aesthetic seeing.[129]

For this reason, I am not inclined to accept those interpretations which take clarity to be a formal element, as opposed to a material element, in an object, and to be governed by proportion. In the first place, it belongs to an outlook which is distinctive of and specific to Albertus Magnus. And in the second place, it smacks of the dialectic of form and matter, or form and content, which Aquinas here superseded. Also, I look upon as reductionist those interpretations which confine the notion of clarity to art alone, which take it to mean the manifestation of the ideal through sensible relations of sounds and shapes or volumes; or, again, the view that clarity is the shining forth of the universal in the particular work of art. No doubt clarity does refer to these things; but it does not mean *only* these.

My own interpretation is fully consistent with the Thomistic concept of form. It is possible, of course, that I have exaggerated the importance of something comparatively trivial; but it is legitimate to try to wrest as much as possible from Aquinas's ideas. And in any case, the sparseness of reference to clarity in his writings was a product of habit rather than lack of interest. The medievals took it for granted that things were intelligible and knowable. Thus, the fact that a structure should have the capacity to signify itself to formal contemplation was quite evident and did not have to be insisted upon. If an objectively existing proportion offered itself to *visio,* clarity was a necessary corollary. This is why Aquinas paid scant attention to the ontological and formal aspect of clarity and relied upon definitions that were more natural and accessible. Even Albertus's theory of clarity, which has an implicit presence in Aquinas, did not call for further explanation. It was something already included in the idea of proportion and order.

With regard to the question of *claritas* in Aquinas, it is fair to say that the historical data, and the texts to which I have referred, have made it rather difficult to arrive at a conclusion. It would have been quicker to look for an answer solely by way of logical inference. It is perhaps for this very reason that most commentators, starting from only the best-known passages in Aquinas, have quickly concluded that *claritas* has an ontological significance, without experiencing any doubts on the matter. But their very certainty has often led them to exaggerate the significance of their views.[130]

Conclusion

This analysis of the three formal criteria of beauty has led us to perceive beauty as something objective and to identify its objectivity with the formal aspect of things. When the formal aspect is an object of aesthetic contemplation, it reveals itself for what it is and acquires from the encounter its aesthetic quality. It makes beauty concrete.

These conclusions can clearly be drawn even if we consider form only in terms of its integrity and proportion and in relation to the aesthetic *visio* (which, it will be recalled, attends to its object *sub ratione causa formalis*). The notion of clarity automatically follows from this encounter of *visio* with form. Even if Aquinas himself had understood the word *claritas* in some other way, all the arguments I have expounded here would still be valid. When one attends to an object with a view to discerning its formal structure, it declares itself to the vision and defines itself in all its properties as an organism endowed with proportion.

However, once it is accepted that form is the cause and origin of the aesthetic, it becomes superfluous to engage in too minute an analysis of the three formal criteria, too exact a definition of their meaning, or too careful an examination of their individual roles. Proportion, integrity, and clarity are three ways in which form can be considered *as a whole*. Form is proportion with integrity which manifests itself as such; form is the totality of a relation as it manifests itself; form is the self-signifying proportion of some whole. The three criteria are reciprocally implicative, each continually referring to the other, and no description of any one of them can be allowed to obscure the reality of the other two. The reality of form is the permanent substratum of this interplay of references.

V

Concrete Problems and Applications

In the preceding chapter we looked at the aesthetic significance of the concept of form and at the three formal criteria of beauty. We are now in a position to seek further verification of the conclusions arrived at there. In particular, I wish to discuss whether Aquinas used the three criteria, and his aesthetic theory as a whole, in the concrete analysis of individual instances of beauty. It will be useful to see whether he ever defined the issues of aesthetics in this concrete manner; and also, whether he did so explicitly or otherwise, and indeed whether he did so consciously or not.

So, under the general rubric of the applications of Aquinas's principles to particular cases, I am going to look at the following issues: the beauty of Christ, as the Second Person of the Trinity; the beauty of mankind; symbols; allegory and poetic beauty in general; and the educative role of music.

The Beauty of the Son of God

First among these questions is that of the beauty of Christ as the Second Person of the Trinity. It is for obvious reasons the paramount question, and not just one among many others. It was no accident that Aquinas's fullest account of the three criteria of beauty (*Summa Theologiae*, I, 39, 8c) should occur in the question in the *Summa* which deals with beauty in its highest form, the beauty of God. God is beauty in a preeminent sense of the term, and the attribute known as "species" belongs especially to the Son of God. Beauty therefore attains its most complete realization in the Second Person and possesses in him a preeminent and paradigmatic existence.

This conception of the Son of God, as beauty and arising out of beauty, had come down to Aquinas from various sources. The school of Chartres had devised a theory of the Trinity in which the Son of God was said to be the formal cause of things, the creator, that is, of the forms of existing things. Aquinas, however, never referred to the school of Chartres; the idea came to him rather from the Patristic tradition, and in particular, as we can see by his quotations, from St. Hilary and St. Augustine.

The problem, as Aquinas put it, was whether the qualities attributed to the persons of the Trinity by the doctors of the church were accurate. Among these attributes were three which had been given by St. Hilary: eternity, species (*species* means both "species" and "comeliness"), and enjoyment (*usus*).[1] St. Hilary attributed species to the son of God and equated this with image, *imago*. Aquinas agreed that the son was an "image," for reasons connected with the traditional explanation of how the Second and Third Persons proceed from the Father.[2] He added that an image is something that represents something else, and represents it because of a likeness to it. And an image can be called a species because an image comes about through the derivation of a form from something else.

> Species prout ponitur ab Hilario in definitione imaginis importat formam deductam in aliquo ab alio. Hoc enim modo imago dicitur esse species alicujus, sicuti id quod assimilatur alicui dicitur forma ejus inquantum habet formam illi similem.
>
> The term *species,* as Hillary put it into the definition of image, connotes a form derived in one thing from another. In such a usage an image means the species of something, in the way that anything made like another is said to be in the form of the other, namely by having a like form.[3]

An exact image of a thing can be referred to as the *form* of the thing, and so its image is also its species. The definitive point is that the concept of an image is connected with that of *form*—that an image is a kind of duplicate of *form*.[4] So when we are speaking of images, species means *form*.[5] And in the question which we are looking at here (*Summa Theologiae,* I, 39), it is also said to mean beauty.

Two points stand out very clearly in all of this. One is that the idea of the beautiful is referred yet again to that of *form*, to such an extent in fact that the term *species* is used to signify both ideas. The other point is that beauty is ascribed to images, that is, to reproductions of *form;* and that this is possible, not because an image is an imitation of some beautiful form (we shall see this in a moment), but rather because the new form—the form in the image—has a harmonious relation of conformity with the original form.

This second point is very valuable in connection with the thorny problem of how the medievals regarded the aesthetic value of works of art. I will look at this question in due course; but in the meantime it would seem fair to say that there was at least one type of man-made object which possessed the character of beauty, namely, imitations of already existing forms. For the moment, I confine myself to these alone. It is in this connection that the beauty of the Son of God, considered as an image of the Father, is most significant. For it has to do with the Image par excellence, and so with all images.

But now let us return to *Summa Theologiae,* I, 39, 8. Aquinas discusses there the three attributes given by St. Hilary—eternity, species or beauty, and enjoyment—and adds some others, all of them in connection with the Trinity. He considers the nature of God in the light of the four ways in which we are wont to think of creatures, for our knowledge of creatures is related by analogy to our knowledge of God. A created thing can be thought of, first, simply as a thing; second, as it is one thing; third, as it is the subject of activity; and fourth, as it stands in a relationship to its effects. The first of these is thinking of something "as it is a certain being" ("inquantum est ens quoddam"); and, if the Trinity is thought of in this way, as "God himself in terms of his own being" ("absolute Deus secundum esse suum"), it is possible to apply to it the attributes of eternity, species, and enjoyment.

Thus, if we think of God in terms of his own being, we can predicate beauty of the Son of God. "Species or beauty," Aquinas writes, "bears a resemblance to the properties of the Son" ("Species autem sive pulchritudo habet similitudinem cum propriis Filii"). And so, the three formal criteria of beauty are predicable of him also. He possesses integrity because he possesses the nature of the Father truly and perfectly within himself. He possesses rightness (*convenientia*) in the highest degree because he is a clear image of the Father (*imago expressa Patris*)—and in fact the beauty of an image derives from this capacity for agreement with the object imitated, the form reproduced. As Aquinas writes, "We notice that an image is called beautiful if it represents a thing, even an ugly thing, faithfully" ("Unde videmus quod aliqua imago dicitur esse pulchra, si perfecte repraesentat rem, quamvis turpem").[6] Finally, the Son possesses clarity in that he is the Word, "the light and splendour of the mind, in John Damascene's description" ("quod quidem lux est et splendor intellectus, ut Damascenus dicit"). The Son of God, then, is a perfect image, an entity adequate to his own nature, harmoniously in accord with the Father, and resplendent with an expressive life—for he is the Word—which is profoundly rational, a *splendor intellectus*.

The Beauty of Mankind

On every occasion that Aquinas decides to give a concrete example of beauty, or of what is meant by proportion and clarity, he invariably has recourse to the human body. For Aquinas, man is one of the most perfect and complete of organisms, in which spiritual and material elements combine, grounded in a wide range of proportional relations. The structural order which man possesses is an exact image of proportion in the macrocosm. He is, therefore, the most noble among terrestrial forms; he is form par excellence.

It is the medieval conception of man that we find in Aquinas, although he has endowed it with conceptual rigor and expressed it in the fullest and most orderly way. It is a conception in which we find a rigid hierarchy of values that stemmed from the theocentric character of medieval humanism. But it is also dominated by a sense of human grandeur and dignity. We will find this sense in the passages that I am going to examine now, even though they may deal only with the human body. Aquinas did not, in fact, discuss the theory of *homo quadratus,* nor the conception of man as microcosm: he absorbed these ideas, but they were superseded by his own thinking, which centered upon the organic conception of form.

Article 3 of *Summa Theologiae,* I, 91, deals with the question "Whether man's body has a suitable constitution" ("utrum corpus hominis habuerit convenientiam dispositionem"). Aquinas's answer to this begins by specifying that things are given their constitution in relation to their end: form is structured in accordance with its finality. This is a reference to the proportion which obtains between things and their functions, and which is one of the principal types of concordance. When something is disposed toward an end, it means that certain of its parts are subordinated to others, that there is an inclination toward a harmony of the whole even at the expense of the parts. If one dwells upon the part, caring for its beauty to a point where harmony in the whole is damaged, the result is a failed enterprise and a deformed, unbalanced object. Thus, a craftsman who manufactures a saw will not make it out of glass, even though glass is more noble and beautiful than metal, because a glass saw is not suitable for its function. "Its beauty," Aquinas says, "would be an obstacle to its end" ("quia talis pulchritudo esset impedimentum finis"). Aquinas does not mean, however, that beauty should be subordinated to more pressing functional requirements. He is emphasizing, rather, that true beauty consists in suitability for an end.

It follows that God's creatures are subject to the same criteria, and Aquinas goes on to consider them in this light. He says that the end of the human body, the end in respect of which its matter must be suitably arranged, is the rational soul and its activities. "Matter subserves form, and instruments subserve the actions of the agents using them" ("materia enim est propter formam, et instrumenta propter actiones agentis"). God therefore has created the human body so that it has a wonderful concordance with its substantial *form*.

> Dico ergo quod Deus instituit corpus humanum in optima dispositione secundum convenientiam ad talem formam et ad tales operationes.

> So what I say is that God has established the human body with the best possible constitution to fit it for this kind of form and this kind of activity.

The human body is an organism whose structure corresponds to the requirements of its *form*, which is its immediate end and its substantial act. Thus, every part of it reveals the ordering activity of its *form* and expresses the order that governs it. In this connection we can usefully refer to a passage in the *Summa contra Gentiles*, which also deals, in a rather more abstract fashion, with the soul conceived of as the substantial *form* of the body.

> Anima est forma totius corporis quod etiam est forma singularium partium . . . Si igitur anima est actus singularium partium, actus autem est in eo cuius est actus: relinquitur quod sit secundum suam essentiam in qualibet parte corporis . . . In qualibet forma apparet quod est tota in toto et tota in qualibet parte eius.

> The soul is the form of the whole body in such fashion as to be also the form of each part . . . Consequently, if the soul is the act of each part, and an act is in the thing whose act it is, it follows that the soul is by its essence in each part of the body . . . It is clear that the whole of every form is in the whole subject, and the whole of it in each part.[7]

The law-giving quality of *form* shines forth in the structured parts of a thing and reveals it to be a unifying and life-giving order. Beauty in an organism consists in this perfect adequacy to its *form,* this proportioning of its parts in accordance with the requirements of *form,* the self-revelation of *form* in each of the ordered parts. Thus it is with the human body; its beauty arises from the fact that all of its parts answer to the requirements of human nature.

> Si vero accipiantur membra, ut manus et pes et huiusmodi, earum dispositio naturae conveniens, est pulchritudo.

> If the members of the body, such as the hand and foot, are in a state which accords with nature, we have the disposition of beauty.[8]

Each part of the body is beautiful insofar as it reveals its proper functional character; and the whole body is beautiful in virtue of the concurrence of all of its parts, in such a way that even those parts which appear to be imperfect reveal themselves to be limitations which are wisely arranged for the harmony of the whole.

Human beauty, then, arises from this substantial unity of body and soul, which is one of the key points in Aquinas's anthropology.

> Ex anima enim et corpore dicitur esse homo, sicut ex duabus rebus quaedam res tertia constituta, quae neutra illarum est.

What we call man comes from a soul and a body, just as out of two things a third may be constituted, which is neither of them.[9]

This harmonious union gives birth to a finely calibrated form in which the play of sensation and intellect, of understanding and will, and of all the essential powers of the soul, is set out in accordance with a law of order.

> Sciendum est, quod secundum naturae ordinem, propter colligantiam virium animae in una essentia, et animae et corporis in uno esse compositi, vires superiores et inferiores, et etiam corpus invicem in se effluunt quod in aliquo eorum superabundat . . . Anima enim coniuncta corpori, eius complexiones imitatur secundum amentiam vel docilitatem, et alia hujusmodi . . . Similiter ex viribus superioribus fit redundantia in inferiores; cum ad motum voluntatis intensum sequitur passio in sensuali appetitu, et ex intensa contemplatione retrahuntur vel impediuntur vires animales a suis actibus.

> It should be borne in mind that, in conformity with the order of nature, because of the conjunction of the powers of the soul in one essence and of the soul and body in the one existence of the composite, the higher powers and the lower, and even the body and the soul, let flow from one to the other whatever superabounds in any one of them . . . For a soul joined to a body imitates its makeup in point of insanity or docility and the like . . . In the same way too there occurs an overflow from the higher powers into the lower, as when a passion in sense appetite follows upon an intense movement of the will, and the animal powers are withdrawn or barred from their acts by intense contemplation.[10]

But let us return to the details of the human body, continuing with *Summa Theologiae,* I, 91, 3. In the *responsiones* of this article, Aquinas considers the senses, stature, and other attributes of the body, in the light of the principle set forth in the *corpus.* One thing peculiar to man, he says, is a very refined sense of touch, superior to that of any other animal. This is because touch is the basis of all the other senses. But in the case of the outer senses, man is inferior to other animals. However, these apparent deficiencies in man are in fact made necessary by his superior harmony. Thus, the weakness of his sense of smell is caused by the size of his brain: an organ of this size (and its size is itself necessitated by specific factors which Aquinas lists elsewhere) is very moist, in order to temper and balance the heat radiated by the heart—and moistness is a hindrance to smell, which requires dryness. As can be seen, a traditional explanation of the body is here connected with the conception of form. So the parts of the body which would seem inferior if considered in isolation, or as expendable for the sake of the whole, come instead to acquire a dignity and a rational character.

Similar arguments are used by Aquinas to explain the weakness of man's sight and hearing, and his moderate swiftness is explained as a requirement of his composition (*complexio*). Again, man is ill equipped with claws, horns, fur and feathers, since these originate in the terrestrial element which predominates in animals. In man, this element is combined proportionately with the other three elements, so that it cannot produce an excess of its characteristic products. To compensate, man is equipped with hands, most noble of the bodily organs, the *organum organorum*,[11] which make up for what he lacks and enable him to engage in manufacture. With these remarks, Aquinas verifies the suitability of the bodily members and of the sensible faculties. They represent an adoption of the "scientific" opinion which was to be found in a great many of the traditional authors.

He adopts a more literary tone when he turns to the reasons for man's erect posture. His discussion of this attribute, which expresses man's dignity best of all, produces a touch of aesthetic emotion in his dry Latin. There are four reasons, he says, why man has an erect posture, three of them strictly physiological. One is that the sensitive inner powers, whose center of control and coordination is the brain ("in quo quoddammodo perficiuntur"), should not be hindered in their activity by a prone or lowered position of the head. A second is that the hands should not have to function as forefeet, but should be free for their proper tasks. A third is that, since man does not use his hands as forefeet, he need not use his mouth for gathering food; consequently, his tongue and lips are not hardened by use and are suited for speech. There is a fourth reason, however, which Aquinas puts first of all. This is that the senses are given to man, not just for his preservation, but for the purposes of knowledge. Animals' senses are directed down to the earth, like their faces, directed to food and immediate necessities. The human senses are seated in an upright face, especially the sense of sight, the most subtle of the sensory faculties; this is so that man may be capable of knowing sensible objects, both celestial and terrestrial, in such a way as to make inferences to intelligible truth.

> Homo vero habet faciem erectam, ut per sensus, et praecipue per visum, qui est subtilior et plures differentias rerum osten-dit, libere possit ex omni parte sensibilia cognoscere, et coeles-tia et terrena, ut ex omnibus intelligibilem colligat veritatem.

> Man has his face on top, in order that his senses, and especially the sense of sight, which is finer than the others and shows him more distinctions between things, may be free to become aware of sense objects in every direction, on the earth and in the heav-ens, so that from them all he may gather intelligible truth. [12]

Human beauty is thus a noble beauty, which is in turn an expres-sion and a cause of the capacity for aesthetic experience which dis-tinguishes mankind. In fact, it is just in this context that Aquinas feels the need to emphasize the dignity of man by referring to his capacity for aesthetic pleasure. Man differs from animals in using his senses for knowledge; and so, while the animals employ their senses exclusively for carnal satisfactions, "only man takes pleasure in the beauty of sense objects for its own sake" ("solus homo delec-tatur in ipsa pulchritudine sensibilium secundum seipsam"). Man's erect posture, his holding his head upright, are signs of his great dignity; and in order to articulate a sense of this dignity, Aquinas feels he must make reference to the aesthetic attitude, as to one of the most noble of the human faculties. [13]

The Beauty of Music

In the next chapter I shall discuss in detail the relation between the philosophy of beauty and the theory of art. Here, by way of intro-duction, I wish to bring together some of the few passages in which Aquinas exhibits his aesthetic taste, and his spontaneous reactions to certain empirical issues connected with various arts.

Music appears in Aquinas to be the art most intimately and specifically connected with the aesthetic, and with pleasure. Boethius had given the concept of proportion a musical sense in addition to its established sense; and when the Scholastics transferred it further to the realms of psychology and ontology, they were conscious of the translation of meaning involved.

> Constat quod harmonia proprie dicta est consonantia in sonis; sed isti transumpserunt istud nomen ad omnem debitam proportionem.

> It is well known that harmony, properly so-called, means consonance in sounds. But [Empedocles and Democritus] transferred that name to every just proportion.[14]

There is therefore a kind of musicality underlying all beauty, because of its proportion.

> Universum . . . non potest esse melius propter decentissimum ordinem his rebus attributum a Deo in quo bonum universi consistit. Quorum si unum aliquod esset melius corrumperetur proportio ordinis; sicut si una chorda plus debito intenderetur, corrumperetur citharae melodia.

> The universe cannot be better than it is; its good consists in the world order, most handsome it is and bestowed by God. For one part to be improved out of recognition would spoil the proportions of the whole design; overstretch one lute string and the melody is lost.[15]

Aquinas's interest in music was stimulated in part by the cultural training which had made him familiar with Boethius's *De Institutione Musica* and St. Augustine's *De Musica*. In part, also, it came from his direct experience of sacred music. The latter issue is dealt with specifically in a question in the *Summa Theologiae* where he discusses whether it is appropriate to praise God by means of sacred music (II–II, 91).

If he is taken in a strict theoretical sense, Aquinas's treatment of this matter might seem very utilitarian, very concerned with didactic values and very little with the artistic. To the question put in article 1, whether God should be praised vocally, he replies in the affirmative. This is not so that we may reveal to God our interior disposition, for this is something which he already knows; rather, it is to excite a state of affection within us, through the act of praise, and to make that feeling more intense.

> Et ideo necessaria est laus oris, non quidem propter Deum, sed propter ipsum laudantem, cuius affectus excitatur in Deum ex laude ipsius.
>
> Vocal praise of God is necessary, therefore, not for his sake but for our own, since by praising him our devotion is aroused. [16]

The harmonies of those who give praise create an atmosphere of piety and move the bystanders to an interior disposition of adoration and love.

> Valet tamen exterior laus ad excitandum interiorem affectum laudantis, et ad provocandos alios ad Dei laudem.
>
> Vocal praise arouses the interior affection of the one praising and prompts others to praise God. [17]

Music is necessary in this public act of praise, because it is extremely useful in producing the desired effect. The human soul is moved in various ways by different kinds of music, so that a musical rendition makes prayer suited to eliciting the requisite feeling of devotion.

> Et ideo salubriter fuit institutum ut in divinas laudes cantus assumerentur, ut animi infirmorum magis provocarentur ad devotionem.
>
> Wisely, therefore, song has been used in praising God, so that the minds of the fainthearted may be incited to devotion. [18]

However, we ought to guard against the imputation of utilitarianism to Aquinas's views. These views are grounded in the science of music and are connected very clearly with his fundamental criteria of the aesthetic. In fact, his belief that rhythm and melody had a significant influence on body and mind can be traced back to the Greek theory of music, a theory which the medievals accepted in its fundamental aspects.

Its main elements were as follows. Music can arouse a Bacchic delirium, releasing unconscious forces which were hitherto repressed; and it can also halt and prevent emotional outbursts, and lead people back to a state of tranquillity. Or again, it can produce fresh emotions which persuade us to perform certain actions and not others. A certain psychic state corresponds to each of the musical modes. Thus, the Ionian and Mixed Lydian modes bring relaxation; the Dorian mode produces virility and courage; the Phrygian mode causes us to be calm and workmanlike; the Mixed Lydian mode cannot be considered for respectable women. These matters were discussed by Plato in *The Republic,* and by Aristotle in his *Politics.*[19] Aristotle distinguished ethical melody from practical melody and melody which arouses; the first kind should be used in education, and the other two for theatrical performances. In general, we may say that the Greek theory of music conceived of it in this "psychagogic" manner.

These beliefs came down in a body to the Middle Ages. Boethius' *De Institutione Musica* contains many references to the various properties of the modes and of melodies. He tells of how Pythagoras calmed a drunken youth of Taormina, who had been excited by the Phrygian mode, by making him listen to a melody in spondaic rhythm in the Hypophrygian mode. He goes on:

> Pythagorici, cum diurnas in somno resolverent curas, quibusdam cantilenis uterentur, ut eis lenis et quietus sopor inreperet. Itaque experrecti aliis quibusdam modis stuporem somni confusionemque purgabant, id nimirum scientes quod tota nostrae animae corporisque compago musica coaptatione conjuncta sit . . . Quia non potest dubitari, quin nostrae animae et corporis status eisdem quodammodo proportionibus videatur esse compositus, quibus armonicas modulationes posterior disputatio conjungi copularique monstrabit.

> The Pythagoreans, when dissolving their daily cares in sleep, employed certain tunes to induce a gentle and quiet drowsiness. So also when arising they got rid of the stupefaction of sleep with the help of certain other modes, knowing for a certainty that the union of our soul with our body is held together by the binding force of music . . . For it cannot be denied that the condition of our soul and body seems composed of certain proportions, and subsequent argument will show that these proportions combine and join together harmonic measures.[20]

This kind of passage in Boethius brought Greek musical theory to the Middle Ages under the rubric of "proportion"; and it was in this light that Aquinas took it over.

> Manifestum est autem quod secundum diversas melodias sonorum, animi hominum diversimode disponuntur, ut patet per Philosophum et per Boetium.

> Clearly, the human soul is moved in various ways by different sounds of music, as Aristotle and Boethius recognized.[21]

Even without reference to Aquinas's sources, it is clear that he conceives of the psychagogic efficacy of music as a relationship between sensible proportion and a psychological state. Thus, the application of this theory to sacred music is in harmony with a traditional theory and is grounded in considerations of form.

Aquinas's words, then, indicate his awareness of the emotive value of music. But in addition they suggest his acceptance of a purely contemplative attitude to it. As we saw in an earlier chapter, he gives a justification of the disinterested contemplation of music, independent of music's effects or its function. He explicitly refers to pleasure in music as an example of the pure pleasures which pose no problems of temperance or of intemperance.[22] There is a kind of pleasure, simultaneously sensible and intellectual, to be got from harmony in sound; not only is it not sinful, but it is one of those prerogatives which make human beings superior. In St. Augustine's discussion of sacred music there was a recurrent theme, namely, his fear that he would concentrate on the music without reference to its religious function, his fear of losing himself in vain contemplation. Aquinas, who always has Augustine in mind and quotes from him repeatedly, seems unaffected by this fear and solves the problem in a different manner: he recognizes the psychagogic function of sacred music and puts the pleasure experienced in music on a different level. He says that it is correct to speak against those who sing in church "in a theatrical manner" ("more theatrico"), just because sacred music is one thing and theatrical music another. It is only in this sense that we should understand Augustine's penitence at following the beauty of song rather than its religious significance. What happened was that Augustine brought to a religious service a state of mind which was legitimate only in quite a different kind of context.[23]

This is also how we should interpret Aquinas's rejection of instrumental accompaniment to sacred music. He has been accused
of conservatism on this account, but in fact his rejection was firmly
rooted in medieval culture. There was a close link in people's minds
between instrumental music and paganism; it might evoke the
memory, for instance, of St. Jerome saying that a Christian girl
should not even know what a flute is. Aquinas himself remarked
that the church did not use instruments such as the harp and the
lyre "for fear of imitating the Jews" ("ne videatur judaizare").[24] Instruments, he goes on, should not be used for sacred music just
because they produce an aesthetic pleasure so strong that the soul is
diverted from its original intent, which is religious rather than aesthetic.

> Huiusmodi enim musica instrumenta magis animum movent
> ad delectationem quam per ea formetur interius bona dispo-
> sitio.
>
> Musical instruments usually move the soul to pleasure rather
> than creating a good disposition in it.[25]

Aquinas's rejection of instrumental music is inspired, not by a dis-
dain for aesthetic experience, but by an acknowledgment of it. He
has no thought of forbidding its use on other occasions. He accepts
a strictly aesthetic role for music, in addition to its power to stimulate immediate emotion. And he does not exclude the possibility
that music may have an educative function which is effected precisely in the course of aesthetic contemplation; the idea here is that
an experience of proportion in a beautiful object can induce within
us a state of order and harmony. This view is implied in a number
of passages in Aquinas.[26]

In the case of sacred music, however, aesthetic intentions are of
no account. Its only function is to edify us by its effect upon our
psychology. To the objection that when we are singing we understand the words less easily, Aquinas replies that the words are of
secondary importance to the surge of religious feeling which arises
in singers and listeners.

> Et eadem etiam est ratio de audientibus, in quibus, etsi aliqui
> non intelligant quae cantantur, intelligunt tamen propter quid

cantantur, scilicet ad laudem Dei; et hoc sufficit ad devotionem excitandam.

The same is true of the hearers, for even if they do not understand what is sung, they understand why it is sung, namely, for God's honor, and this is enough to arouse their devotion.[27]

Play and Playful Verse

Medieval culture provides another notable example of artistic expression which had no direct function and which was the object of disinterested contemplation. This was the composition of light verse, which poets and even scholars, both lay and ecclesiastical, often put to melodies, taken from well-known liturgical Sequences.

These little compositions were held in a certain regard. They were learned by the young men in the *scholae cantorum,* and somewhat later they even became part of Scholastic culture in the guise of grammatical and stylistic exercises.[28] Still later, this secular verse expanded into a larger enterprise through the activities of minstrels and troubadours—persons who are usually referred to generically as *histriones* by ecclesiastical writers. This was a realm of music and poetry devoted simply to pleasure, to gaiety, to a pastime.

In the *Summa Theologiae,* Aquinas discusses in one place (II–II, 168) whether there is a justification for simple verbal, musical, and dramatic amusements. He takes the view that play (*ludus*) and wordplay (*iocus*) are acts whose finality is within themselves;[29] they have no educative role, but are acceptable because of their capacity to lighten the labors of the intellect. The pleasure which they give is directed to the recreation of the mind, and so they are in a sense their own end. His arguments have to do in the main with a problematic which is both ethical and pedagogical, but we can also infer that there is a certain aesthetic quality in play. He does not discuss whether *iocus* is endowed with any kind of formal proportion, but he does insist upon a proportion between play and the needs of the subject. Play, he says, is sufficient and complete only when it is in harmony with the requirements and the capacities for recreation which people possess.

Operationes sunt delectabiles, inquantum sunt proportionatae et connaturales operanti . . . Otium et ludus et alia quae ad requiem pertinent delectabilia sunt, inquantum auferunt tristitiam quae est ex labore.

An activity gives pleasure insofar as it is congenial to the agent's natural capacities and inclinations . . . Leisure, play, and other things that go with rest, give pleasure; they relieve us of the distress that comes from overwork.[30]

The pleasure given by play is thus conditional upon a proportion, an agreement with stable order. In fact this agreement constitutes the perfection of play, since its end is just the pleasure which it should be able to bring. We should note that even here, in establishing the rationale of a form of free play, Aquinas cannot avoid a finalistic, hierarchical perspective. Even when something is free and unconnected with any particular enterprise, it still possesses an order which is fixed and determined by an end.

The Symbolical Attitude

Music and play are, so to speak, simple forms of communication. We turn next to Aquinas's attitude toward more complex forms, which in the Middle Ages were exemplified in allegorical poetry, and in symbolism in painting, sculpture, and architecture. In the next chapter I shall conduct a theoretical examination of an aesthetic problem which is posed by artifacts that possess a number of levels of symbolism. This arises because it is necessary to define the nature of a complex artistic form, whose individual constituents are not just material items as in a material form, nor emotive stimuli as in music, but elements with meaning—each of which, furthermore, brings into the formal structure of the work the particular universe to which it refers. It is easy to see, therefore, that the application of Aquinas's aesthetic criteria to this type of artifact is a significant testing ground for his aesthetic theory.

In many ways, medieval symbol and allegory seem very alien to Aquinas's thinking, based as it is upon the concrete perspective of hylomorphism, and thus upon a world of objects rather than of symbols. For this reason, we must take a look at the features and proclivities of this universe of symbol and allegory, in order to discover how Aquinas responded to it.[31]

There is no doubt that medieval people inhabited a world populated by supersensible and supernatural meanings. Nature spoke to them in a heraldic language, so that, as the verses attributed to Alan of Lille put it,

> Omnis mundi creatura
> quasi liber et pictura
> nobis est in speculum;
> nostrae vitae, nostrae mortis,
> nostri status, nostrae sortis,
> fidele signaculum.

> Every creature of this earth is like a picture or a book: it is a mirror of ourselves. It is a faithful mark of our life and of our death, of our condition and our fate.[32]

This kind of thing has given rise to talk about a primitive mentality in the medievals, such that they were incapable of differentiating things from one another. Nowadays, of course, what we have learned about the primitive mentality and its methods of classification makes us very cautious about drawing such comparisons. However, Lewis Mumford has also described the medieval stance as neurotic; and in fact it would not be difficult to attribute their symbolical outlook to the flight from the real which, in a different way, caused the exaggerated attachment to theory of Boethius. This is something we have seen already in his theory of music. Medieval culture was formed in an era of dissolution and ruin. The Roman Empire was fragmenting, and the individual suffered from a sense of insecurity.[33] New types of community were as yet unable to provide an adequate guarantee of cohesion and mutual protection. It might seem natural, therefore, in the face of a hostile reality, to look for some kind of anchorage by ascribing a different and ulterior meaning to events, something beyond their immediate significance. A lion, wolf, and lynx were in an immediate sense dangerous; but they could be incorporated in a more orderly scheme of things if they were understood as signs in the universal lexicon with which God spoke to men through nature—directing them, sign following sign, toward eternal happiness.[34]

However, it would take us too far afield if we were to look into the social and psychological causes of the medieval symbolical outlook. We must look instead at how this tradition came down to Aquinas, and how he dealt with it.

First of all, then, we should distinguish three types of attitude which are thought of and referred to as medieval symbolism. They have many points of contact, and they cannot always be distinguished within the writings of the same author; but they have differing cultural roots, and, as it were, different machinery for their transmission. They are (1) metaphysical symbolism, (2) universal allegory, and (3) the poetics of allegory. These three are often confused with one another. For convenience, therefore, I shall present them as three abstract models of the symbolical mentality.

Metaphysical symbolism had very ancient roots, and we have come across it already in authors such as Pseudo-Dionysius. Another kind of source was the late Roman author Macrobius. In his *In Somnium Scipionis,* the medievals read that all things are like so many mirrors, which reflect in their beauty the unique visage of God.[35] And if everything reflects the face of God, this does not mean merely that there are partial, heraldic types of correspondence between the supernatural realm and objects which are in some way out of the ordinary. It suggests, rather, that we must learn to read and continually decipher the book of the universe.

In this kind of outlook, *everything* speaks of something else. It is a symbolical vision which engages the whole of nature. "All bodies," said Richard of St. Victor, "have a likeness to good things which are invisible."[36] At the very outset of medieval speculative thinking, John Scottus Eriugena set the tone with his openly symbolical *Weltanschauung.* "In my judgment," he wrote, "there is nothing among visible and corporeal things which does not signify something incorporeal and intelligible" ("Nihil enim visibilium rerum, corporaliumque est, ut arbitror, quod non incorporale quid et intelligibile significat").[37] Huizinga puts it as follows. "Of no great truth was the medieval mind more conscious than of St. Paul's phrase: *Videmus nunc per speculum in aenigmate, tunc autem facie ad faciem.* The Middle Ages never forgot that all things would be absurd, if their meaning were exhausted in their function and their place in the phenomenal world, if by their essence they did not reach into a world beyond this."[38] We have to recover the profoundly genetic character of medieval thought, the sense of logical causality which translated itself into diagrammatic schemes, in which things diverge and ramify and link up in chains. To quote Huizinga again, "From the causal point of view, symbolism appears as a sort of short-circuit of thought . . . Embracing all nature and all history, symbolism gave a conception of the world, of a still more rigorous unity than that which modern science can offer . . . About each idea other ideas group themselves, forming symmetrical figures, as in a kaleidoscope." [39]

Through this kind of polyphonic concordance, the medievals had a special ability to discover the supernatural reality hidden in things. They knew how to penetrate within them. As Gilson has remarked, the medieval sense of symbolical meaning in things became so powerful that they forgot to verify their existence: the Arabian phoenix, with all the mystical grandeur of its significations, had more reality than many objects which had been experienced concretely. Even when something was existentially present and manifest, the medievals were always intrigued most of all by its higher meaning. Thus, Adam of St. Victor could use even a simple nut as an image of Christ: its hull was Christ's flesh, its shell the wood of the Cross, and the precious kernel, man's nourishment, was Christ's hidden divinity. Objects were seen as essentially created by God, and thus as the word of God become object, God's message become nature, intimations of God become everyday things. The world seemed a storehouse of symbols, ruled by a Providence which would not leave man unprovided for but surrounded him with trustworthy signs.

If we turn to the thirteenth century, however, and search the works of Aquinas for traces of this major element in the medieval sensibility, we find ourselves disconcerted. This world of Baudelairean *correspondances* is totally foreign to Aquinas. It was not that the symbolical outlook had vanished by his time. It continued to pervade the whole of medieval life. It was to be found in the writings of the mystics, and the encyclopedists, who were for long to continue their dissertations upon the most exquisitely fine meanings in flowers, precious stones, and beasts. But in Aquinas—that is, in the person who gave most complete expression to the philosophical and theological thinking of the age—all of this has vanished. This is a development, however, which is susceptible of explanation, and an explanation which yields valuable insights. Gilson, again, has remarked that the characteristically symbolical outlook of the twelfth century meant that it was a century unable to observe nature accurately. Nature indeed was celebrated, but no one thought to observe it. Objects were felt to possess their own particular reality in the degree to which they served for everyday use; but as soon as there was any attempt to explain objects, they lost this reality. The reason was that explanation amounted to the disclosure that the thing being explained was a sign, together with a disclosure of what it was a sign of. In the bestiaries and lapidaries of the time, the substance of the beasts and stones was reduced to their symbolical meaning; the material out of which they were composed did not matter. There was something missing in the twelfth century, and in the symbolical mentality as a whole, which caused this absorption of concrete reality into a universe of symbols. What was lacking was any conception, however slight, that nature had a structure of itself and was intelligible in itself. This was a conception that entered the Middle Ages only with Aristotelian physics.[40]

When the medievals began to discover the ontological and formal reality of things—when they began, we might say, to scrutinize them with a living and passionate attention—the symbolical universe lost something of its substance. The new outlook was also a religious one, something to which the Thomist system is a majestic witness, but it had a different basis. Providence was no longer regarded as the marshaling of signs, but rather as the reifying of forms. The symbolical vision turned into a naturalistic vision, which aspired to study causal connections with critical acuity. The only remaining trace of the mentality which had gone was, perhaps, the concept of analogy—the only conscious trace, at any rate, an inheritance voluntarily accepted, although one which changed its nature and appearance when transplanted into a new soil. And even analogy appears in Aquinas as yet another aspect of proportion, a proportion between an effect and its cause. It was a concept which he employed with such caution that it seems less a metaphysical reality than a methodological criterion.[41]

Universal Allegory

The model of universal allegory differs from that of metaphysical symbolism. In the symbolical outlook, all things refer in the first instance to the supernatural simply because they exist. It follows that the mere fact of possessing being manifests itself to us as a sign. In so doing, however, it may happen that something has the character of a complex sign. In the language of semiotics, we might say that it is a sign with a large connotative potential, actualized through rhetorical processes.

Let us return to Adam of St. Victor and his interpretation of a nut. The model of universal symbolism determines that a nut is like every other created thing on the earth, a sign of God's creative power. More accurately, we might say that God himself, in creating the nut, creates it also as a sign which directly denotes his power to give it existence. However, when Adam of St. Victor uses the hull, shell, and kernel as metaphors of particular supernatural realities, in that instant the sign begins to be used in a connotative manner. It is in this fashion that an existent becomes a metaphor—not every existent, but those which lend themselves to metaphorical use because of their iconic features. And in constructing such metaphors, the medieval mentality seems to renege upon its most characteristic intellectual process, inference by way of chains of causes and effects. In universal symbolism, the relation between an object and a supernatural reality was a relation of cause and effect; but here, by contrast, the object and the supernatural are related by what Huizinga calls "a sort of short-circuit of thought." Thus, the ostrich becomes a symbol of justice because its feathers, equal in size, evoke the idea of equality and unity. The pelican becomes a symbol of Christ because the legend that she feeds her children with her own flesh makes her a metaphor of the Eucharist. At this point, however, we might feel like asking whether the pelican legend is the primary significatum, upon which the eucharistic metaphor is based, or whether instead the need for a eucharistic metaphor brought about the requisite element in the legend—so that, paradoxically, the historical and supernatural Christ would be the vehicle for a pelican metaphor.

As I have said, this is a kind of poetic operation which seems alien to the deductive spirit of the medievals. At the very least it seems alien to the late Middle Ages. Yet this was the very period in which, far from being rejected, we find allegory legitimized as a communicative rubric. And in fact what happened was that allegory received its stamp of authority from a certain principle of concordance.

Huizinga explains the ascendancy of the symbol in medieval thought in the following way. The mind abstracts from two different entities certain similar properties and then puts these properties side by side.[42] To put it in contemporary language, it creates a structural model. Thus, virgins and martyrs shine forth amidst their persecutors just as white and red roses shine forth amidst thorns; what both these classes of beings have in common is their color (the color of rose petals and of blood) and their relation to a situation of duress. It should be noted that, if an abstraction of this sort of homologous model is to occur, the "short-circuit" must already have taken place. The short-circuit, the identification of things through their essences, is invariably grounded in a relation of compatibility; and this relation is a form of analogy, in the least metaphysical sense of the term: the rose is to its thorns as the martyr is to his persecutors.

A rose is different, of course, from a martyr. But the pleasure which we take in bringing a beautiful metaphor to light—and allegory is simply a chain of codified metaphors which are deduced one from the other—is caused by what Pseudo-Dionysius noted as the incongruity of a symbol with respect to the object symbolized.[43] There is an incongruity, first, because if there was not, there would be an identity instead, and then there could be no relation of proportion between the two (that is, the relation $x : y :: y : z$); and, second, as Dionysius says, because it is incongruity which gives birth to the pleasure of interpretation. This in fact points us to another "artistic" element in universal allegory, namely, that the understanding of allegory involves the understanding of a relation of compatibility, and also an aesthetic enjoyment of this relation which is due in part to the effort of interpretation.

This element of enigma in medieval poetry is the aspect which seems most alien to the modern aesthetic sensibility—though not to our contemporaries: one thinks of Pound, Eliot, Joyce, and today's avant-garde in general. But of course it would be totally antihistorical to deny that interpretation could be an aesthetic experience, just because it did not seem to be assimilable to the modern idea that our perception of beauty is something immediate and natural. One of the specific and fundamental aesthetic values, for the medievals, lay in the kind of difficult reading of a text which brought to light some unexpected element of proportion. It was something which they sought out and which, as we have seen and shall see below, they sought to justify on the theoretical level. In the medieval cultural model, allegory was a modality which was both artistic and aesthetic, and wholly legitimate.

Scriptural and Poetic Allegory

The problem, then, is not this, but one that brings us to Aquinas. In the twelfth century, universal allegory was still indistinguishable from metaphysical symbolism; it was a modality of interpretation of a universe still conceived of as written by God in metaphorical characters. So our problem is to see how universal allegory gradually transformed itself and established itself, in the thirteenth century, as a poetics of allegory.

The practice of universal allegory compelled medieval philosophers to make an important distinction. For, as it happened, the allegorical world view was taking, often at the same time and in the same author, three different forms. There was, first, an allegorical interpretation of any item in the real world; this was known as allegory *in factis*. Second, there was an allegorical interpretation of metaphors and allegories in poetry, known as allegory *in verbis*. Finally, allegorical interpretations of scripture could be allegory both *in factis* and *in verbis*.[44] The complexity of the issue arose from the fact that the allegorical interpretation of the world was a consequence, historically speaking, of the allegorical interpretation of the Bible.

In the early centuries of Christianity, Gnosticism inclined to the view that truth was to be found only in the New Testament. Origen, however, desired to preserve both Testaments, each continuous with the other. He therefore had to determine how it was that they were saying the same thing, the same truth, since to all appearances they spoke differently. His solution was that they should be read in parallel. The Old Testament was the signifier, or the letter, of which the New Testament was the signified, or the spirit. But at the same time, the New Testament also was a letter, whose spirit had to do with salvation and moral duty. The semiotic process was thus rather complicated. There was a first book which spoke allegorically of a second book, and the second book spoke through parables of something else. Moreover, in this beautiful example of unlimited semiosis, there was a puzzling identification of the sender (the divine Logos), the signifying message (words, Logoi), the content (the divine message, Logos), and the referent (Christ, the Logos)—a web of identities and differences, complicated by the fact that Christ, as Logos, insofar as he was the ensemble of all the divine archetypes, was fundamentally polysemous. Thus, both Testaments spoke at the same time of their sender, their content, and their referent, and their meaning was a nebula of all possible archetypes. The scriptures were in the position of saying everything. Everything, though, was rather too much for interpreters interested in truth.

The symbolical nature of sacred scripture had therefore to be tamed. Potentially, the scriptures had every possible meaning; so the reading of them had to be governed by a code. This is why the church fathers devised the theory of the allegorical senses. At first, there were said to be three such senses in the Bible: the literal, the moral, and the mystical or pneumatic. Then these became four: literal, allegorical, moral, and anagogical. According to the well-known verses attributed to Nicholas of Lyre,

> Littera gesta docet, quid credat allegoria,
> moralis quid agas, quo tendas anagogia.

> The literal sense tells us of events; the allegorical teaches our faith; the moral tells us what to do; the anagogical shows us where we are going.

The theory of the four senses provided a kind of guarantee of the correct decoding of the scriptures. Still, the Patristic and Scholastic minds could never avoid the sense of an inexhaustible profundity in the Bible, which they frequently compared to a forest or an ocean. For St. Jerome, the scriptures were "an infinite forest of meanings" ("infinitam sensuum sylvam").[45] Origen wrote of "a most enormous forest of Scripture" ("latissimam Scripturae sylvam")[46] and "a mysterious ocean of the divinity, or, so to speak, a labyrinth" ("oceanum mysterium Dei, ut sic loquar, labyrinthum"): if we should enter this ocean in a small boat, our minds are seized by fear and we are submerged by its whirlpools.[47] Gilbert of Stanford compared the scriptures to a fast river which, as it flows, keeps producing new meanings.[48] These are like waves and currents, coming one after the other, yet none of them annuls any of the others, but combines with them to enrich progressively the immense store of divine wisdom. Everyone can get something from this inexhaustible store of meanings, each in accordance with his intellectual ability.

The church fathers and the medievals had two problems, then. One was the problem of how to reconcile the infinity of interpretations with the specific and limited truth of the message—how to discover in the Bible, not ever-new things, but the same everlasting truth expressed in ever-new ways: *non nova sed nove,* as they put it. The second problem was that of deciding when a passage in scripture should be taken as a figure of something else, when it should be understood allegorically rather than literally.

St. Augustine, in *De Doctrina Christiana,* was the first to provide rules for determining when a fact or event in scripture was to be understood figuratively rather than literally.[49] It was easy enough to know when verbal tropes such as metaphor were being used; for, if they were taken literally, the text would look mendacious. But what was one to do in those cases in which the reported events made literal sense, and yet could be interpreted symbolically? Augustine replied that we are entitled to suspect a figurative meaning whenever the scriptures say something which, though literally intelligible, is contrary to faith and morals. For instance, Jesus consented to be honored and anointed by a courtesan. However, it is impossible to accept that he would really have encouraged such a lascivious ritual. Therefore, the story must stand for something else. Similarly, we should suspect an ulterior meaning in scripture whenever it contains things which are apparently and inexplicably superfluous, or again, whenever we come across expressions which have very little meaning when taken literally, such as proper names or series of numbers.

St. Augustine, then, looked for allegory in the Bible, not just in the case of verbal expressions, but also in the case of apparently trivial incidents—though of course it is presupposed that the incidents are recounted verbally. In fact he gave priority to allegory *in factis* over allegory *in verbis.* Thus the Psalms could be understood as having an ulterior meaning, and not just because of the frequent use of rhetorical devices. What was essential was the series of "historical" events which could be read beyond the letter. God had planned the Bible story; it was a book written by his own hand, *liber scriptus digito suo*. Therefore, the characters in the Old Testament were constrained to act as they did in order to announce the characters and events in the New Testament. The very facts recounted in the Bible story were to be understood as signs.

Augustine had received from the classical tradition the rules of rhetoric which guided him in decoding allegory *in verbis*. But he had no precise rules for decoding allegory *in factis;* and, as I have already said, he could not allow the facts recounted in the Bible to be completely open to any interpretation at all. Therefore, if he was to understand and interpret these facts properly, it was necessary that he be familiar with the meaning of the things, the objects, which the Bible mentioned.

This explains why medieval civilization took to compiling various types of encyclopedias. Extrapolating from the Hellenistic *Physiologos** and from Pliny the Elder's *Historia naturalis,* they constructed bestiaries, herbaries, lapidaries, and *imagines mundi,*[50] in which allegorical meanings were assigned to everything in the "real" world. We find in these encyclopedias that the same object or creature can have contrasting meanings, so that the lion can be both a figure of Christ and a figure of Satan. Part of the work of medieval commentators was to formulate the rules for determining which was the correct meaning in a given text. An elephant, a unicorn, a jewel, a stone, or a flower could have a number of meanings, but in a particular context these had to be reduced to one.

It was in this way that the emergence of a scriptural hermeneutics brought about the emergence of universal allegory. Just as scripture was permeated with signs, so, too, was the real world. And the natural consequence of such a world view was the widespread use of allegory and metaphor in poetry. This secular employment of allegory *in verbis* was a product of the widespread belief that the world was itself an allegory *in factis*.

Now that we have traced back the three types of allegory to their

*A collection of Christian allegories based upon the marvels and peculiarities of the animal world. It first appeared in Alexandria toward the end of the second century and was widely translated and read in the Middle Ages.

origin, we are in a better position to appreciate the originality of Aquinas's treatment of the issue.

Aquinas's Theory of Allegory

Aquinas's definitions of the poetic realm always have reference to the problems of biblical exegesis. They occur whenever he distinguishes between sacred and profane writings, and between the different relationships which, in the two cases, govern the way in which the signs refer to their objects. In the very first question of the *Summa Theologiae,* where he discusses the nature of Christian Theology, Aquinas asks whether it is appropriate that metaphors should be used in the Bible, and whether, in consequence, the stories told in it should be interpreted metaphorically.[51] The first *objectio* which he gives (in article 9) is that sacred knowledge should not proceed by way of similitudes, because they are characteristic of poetic knowledge, which is "inferior teaching or knowledge," *infima doctrina.* Two things emerge from this: first, Aquinas asserts that the use of similitudes, of metaphors, is distinctive of poetry (*poetry* is a term which he employs in a broad sense); second, however, he apparently denigrates poetry as *infima doctrina.*

This definition of the *modus poeticus* is reinforced in other passages, for instance when he writes, "Human reason fails to grasp the import of poetical utterance on account of its deficiency in truth" ("poetica non capiuntur a ratione humana propter defectum veritatis qui est in eis").[52] This quotation has been used by some commentators to present Aquinas as a precursor of modern aesthetics—as if he were marketing the notion of a *perceptio confusa* and upholding the view that poetry gives us an embryonic, magical, grasp of being. Here again we must guard against excess and defect alike, and avoid above all the temptation of facile translation. Why does Aquinas use the expression *infima doctrina?* The reasons are obvious. In the first place, he conceives of poetic art as a *ratio factibilium*—a way of making something. Thus, poetry involves knowledge, on the one hand (because it is an invention and exposition of facts and events, feelings and thoughts), and, on the other hand, work or labor. When it is compared with pure thinking, therefore, it has to take an inferior place. In addition, our knowledge of the laws of the composition of poetry is something separate from the poetry itself. We recall Boethius saying this as well: someone who composes verse intuitively is inferior to someone who knows the laws of music and of meter. And again, in this passage at the beginning of the *Summa* poetic knowledge is being compared with sacred knowledge, and it can only suffer by the comparison. So it seems reasonable to conclude that, in a tradition which ordered man's activities in a hierarchy, according to its connection with the supernatural (whether revealed, investigated, or sought after), Aquinas's conception of the worth of the *modus poeticus* arose simply from a classification of values. It did not indicate contempt.

In the case of the definition of poetry as something essentially "deficient in truth," the explanation is not immediately evident. What we can deny is that it has anything to do with *perceptio confusa*: Aquinas would have been exceedingly put out by any such conception as this. The most plausible interpretation is as follows. The objects which are referred to in poetry are imagined, invented objects; for it is important to note that when Aquinas refers in these passages to the "poetic," he is not talking about a committed art such as the didactic art of the cathedrals, but rather of the creation of fictions, and to narratives designed to give pleasure. "Poetry," as he puts it, "employs metaphors for the sake of representation, in which we are born to take delight" ("poetica utitur metaphoris propter repraesentationem, repraesentatio enim naturaliter homini delectabilis est").[53] In this kind of enterprise, the poet seeks to present his reader with something unknown, unknown because nonexistent or never envisaged, and something inconceivable because conceptually without definition. This does not mean that the poet's object is some reality which in itself evades conceptualization, but only that the conceptual knowledge of something involves defining it by way of its genus and its species. The poet, then, makes manifest a reality of this kind—a reality which has in itself, or at least has for us, a "deficiency in truth"—by means of representation; and representation can come about only by way of a similitude. We might recall here what we have seen already about Aquinas's theory of imagination, as the transposition and recreation of *form*. If we cannot accurately grasp the *form* of something—either because it does not exist, or because we are unable to adopt a cognitive attitude toward it—then we can only reproduce the *form* of something else, already known to us, and seek to use this to give some account of the original thing which interests us. Thus, the "deficiency in truth" of a poetic similitude refers to its theoretical limit, not some kind of intuitive profundity. It certainly does not detract from its value.

This clears up something that might have been a stumbling-block. Aquinas's descriptions of poetry, as *infima doctrina* and deficient in truth, were not definitive. They emerged only in the context of a comparison. As we have seen, he was seeking to justify the necessity for representing the mysteries of religion through metaphor and allegory. What he said in effect was: these mysteries exceed our faculties of understanding, and we are therefore compelled to represent them by means of similitudes; it is the same as for the poet, who uses metaphors to indicate those things which, because of their unreality, we can grasp only when translated and allegorized in this way.

When dealing with allegorical language in the Bible, Aquinas tries above all to establish whether and why the scriptures have several meanings, and to determine also what those meanings are. "Holy Scripture," he writes, "fittingly delivers divine and spiritual realities under bodily guises" ("conveniens est sacrae scripturae divina et spiritualia sub similitudine corporalium tradere").[54] The reason for this is that all human knowledge begins in the senses; so when the divine mysteries are presented in a form that is corporeal, sensible, and comprehensible, they become more evident. In themselves they exceed human reason; but when presented in the form of familiar events and figures, they lead the intellect easily and smoothly to the threshold of the truth.[55] The issue, then, is how one should proceed in the reading of the scriptures. And the first and most elementary of the ways of understanding them is in the historical or literal sense.[56]

The historical sense is a foundation for other senses, which Aquinas groups together as the "spiritual sense."

> Illa vero significatio qua res significatae per voces, iterum res alias significant, dicitur sensus spiritualis; qui super litteralem fundatur, et eum supponit.

> That meaning, however, whereby the things signified by the words in their turn also signify other things, is called the spiritual sense; it is based on and presupposes the literal sense.[57]

The literal sense signifies and can be identified with the events told of in the sacred history. Thus, when we say that the literal sense is the foundation of the spiritual sense, this means that the incidents and persons of the sacred history have the value of a *sign*—that as well as their historical truth and reality they also have a symbolical reality. Aquinas explicitly states that the events of this history have been ordered by God, the only one who could so order them, in such a way that they have a significance.

> Deus adhibet ad significationem aliquorum ipsum cursum rerum suae providentiae subiectarum.
>
> God establishes the meaning of the course of events subject to his providence.[58]

Does this mean that Aquinas accepts the idea of universal allegory? The answer is yes, but *only insofar as sacred history is concerned*. In the whole sweep of the Incarnation and the salvation of mankind, God has, once and once only, made use of people, objects, and history as expressions in his own language. It is the only enterprise of this kind which Aquinas ascribes to providence. Therefore, the sacred history is marked by a character which is quite unique in comparison with other human events. The medieval world of allegory was confined to the affairs of the Hebrews. The events recounted in the Bible were ordered as a vast message, expressed through its literal sense but pointing toward a spiritual meaning. The spiritual meaning had various aspects. It was *allegorical* whenever the persons and events of the Old Law prefigured those of the New Law; it was *moral* whenever the actions of Christ indicated how we should live; and it was *anagogical* when it referred to the things of heaven. The Old Law was a figure of the New, and the New Law was both a figure of future glory and a rule of action. The truth of the scriptures was directed toward both faith and morals, *ad recte credendum* and *ad recte operandum*.

On several occasions, however, Aquinas stresses that these three senses, particularly the allegorical sense, are not a matter of grammar and style, but depend directly upon *things* which *in themselves* signify something else.

> Sensus spiritualis . . . accipitur vel consistit in hoc quod quaedam res per figuram aliarum rerum exprimuntur.

> The spiritual sense, it is understood, consists in this, that certain things are expressed by means of a figure involving other things.[59]

Also, Aquinas's way of justifying biblical allegory is such that it acquires an aesthetic value: for there is a proportion between historical facts and their supernatural meaning; and again, there is a proportion between verbal expressions and the historical facts which they convey. "It is quite clear," Aquinas says, "that words signify things, and that one thing can be a figure of another" ("inquantum scilicet verba significant res, et una res potest esse figura alterius").[60]

Up to this point, it might seem that Aquinas was not particularly original when compared with previous tradition. However, he makes two important claims.

1. There is a spiritual sense only in the story told in scripture. It is only in sacred history that God has so acted upon mundane events that they have come to signify something else. There is no spiritual sense in secular history, nor in the individuals and events of the natural world. There is no mystical significance in what has happened since the Redemption. Human history is a history of facts, not of signs.

> Unde in nulla scientia, humana industria inventa, proprie loquendo, potest inveniri nisi litteralis sensus.
>
> Strictly speaking, every science which has been invented by human industry yields a literal meaning only.[61]

Universal allegory is thus liquidated. Mundane events are returned to their natural status. If they have a meaning, they have it only in the eyes of a philosopher, who sees them as natural proofs of God's existence, but not as symbolic messages. With Aquinas, we witness a kind of secularization of postbiblical history and the natural world.

2. There is a spiritual sense in scripture, where facts refer to something else; but there is no spiritual sense in secular poetry. Poetry, in Aquinas's view, is a semiotic phenomenon—"Poetic fictions," he writes, "have no other end than to have meaning" ("fictiones poeticae non sunt ad aliud ordinatae nisi ad significandum")[62]—but its meaning is literal only. This claim inevitably

strikes us as too crude and radical. Aquinas, himself a poet, knew very well that poets employ rhetorical figures and allegory. But the poetical second sense is a subspecies of the literal sense, and Aquinas calls it "parabolic." And this sense, which is found in tropes and allegory, "does not go beyond the literal sense" ("non supergreditur modum litteralis sensus").[63]

The same thing applies whenever the scriptures make use of poetic devices of allegory *in verbis*. Thus, if they should represent Christ by the image of a goat, this goat is not something that symbolizes future events, but only a verbal or pictorial simile which parabolically—that is, literally—stands for the name Christ.[64]

It might be thought that Aquinas is here playing with words, that he is calling "parabolic" the sense which previous authors were wont to call allegorical, that he has not changed anything. However, he is in fact proposing a radically different approach to poetic language. For allegorical meaning is the meaning of an object and is learned by an investigation of the object. Parabolic sense, by contrast, is the meaning of a verbal or pictorial image which is so appropriate and so well proportioned to its sense that it proclaims itself to be at one with it.

> Per voces significatur aliquid proprie, et aliquid figurative; nec est litteralis sensus ipsa figura, sed id quod est figuratum.

> Words can signify something properly and something figuratively; in the latter case the literal sense is not the figure of speech itself, but the object it figures.[65]

In what manner, we must ask, does the notion of parabolic sense differ from that of the spiritual senses found in scripture? In order to answer this, it must be noted first that what Aquinas meant by "literal sense" was "the sense which the author intends" ("sensus litteralis est quem auctor intendit").[66] In contemporary language, we could say that for Aquinas the literal sense is not just the meaning of a *sentence,* but also the meaning of its *utterance.* What a verbal expression can convey is not just the sum of the conventional meaning of its lexical components, but also the intentions of the person who utters it at a certain time and in a certain context. When Christ is referred to by the image of a goat, the meaning of the word *goat,* or of the image, is determined by the fact that the author, in that specific context, intended to mean "scapegoat." Thus, it seems that for Aquinas both sentence-meaning and utterance-meaning belong to the literal sense, since both represent what the utterer of the sentence had in mind. We can therefore understand why the sense conveyed by tropes and allegories can be assimilated into literal sense: it represents exactly what the author wants to say.

But why should it be that the spiritual senses found in scripture are not equally literal? The answer is that the biblical authors were not aware that their historical accounts possessed the senses in question. Scripture had these senses in the mind of God, and would have them later for those readers who sought in the Old Testament for a prefiguring of the New. But the authors themselves wrote under divine inspiration; they did not know what they were really saying. Poets, by contrast, know what they want to say and what they are saying. Poets therefore speak literally, even when they use rhetorical figures.

Aquinas seems to move away from current medieval opinion, according to which the pleasure of poetry arises out of a subtle play of the intellect when it grasps a network of mystical correspondences. He seems to suggest that the correspondence is so exact that the pleasure consists in a sort of instantaneous understanding. But such an interpretation would be, once again, a modern reading of his words. Aquinas, who was a trained and skillful medieval poet, believed that we are able to grasp parabolic sense by virtue of established and accepted rhetorical conventions. The reader understands immediately that a goat stands for Christ, because there is a "code" of poetic allegories. It is because this code exists and is largely employed by poets (including the biblical authors) that allegory *in verbis* is immediately understood as if it were a literal expression.

This act of "decoding" poetic allegory is so easy that the interpreter understands, effortlessly, the proportion between words and their literal meaning, and between literal and parabolic meaning. Thus, the pleasure of this immediate understanding, this radiance of the intended meaning within and alongside the literal meaning, can be explained again in terms of proportion, integrity, and clarity. The very discussion of the beauty of the image reminds us of this.

Didactic Parabolism

We can now inquire whether this parabolic language is usable only for pleasure, in poetic narrative, or whether it can also be used for didactic purposes—in religious sculpture, for instance. When Aquinas writes about parabolic meaning he does so in connection with poetry, and in so doing he refers to a taste for representations which are sought purely for pleasure. But whenever he wants to provide an example of a parabolic expression, he uses that of a goat as an image of Christ in the Bible and in other literary works. This is clearly a didactic use.

Aquinas also devotes a lengthy portion of the *Summa Theologiae* to an analysis of the causes, reasons, structures, values, and topicality of the ceremonial precepts of the Old Law.[67] This is one of the rare occasions on which he seems to indulge in the taste of the period. He takes time to explain the spiritual meanings of the Temple, its parts, and its instruments of worship, clearly looking on these as signs and metaphors. His interest was fully justified, of course, because at issue was the interpretation of the Bible, and not the subtle allegorizing of everyday facts and objects which exercised the encyclopedists of the time.

In Aquinas's view, the ceremonial rites and instruments, required by the precepts of the Old Law, symbolized the future events of the New Law and probably had an allegorical sense (allegory *in factis*). Their prophetic meaning was not "intended" by their authors. In contrast, the precepts of the Christian liturgy were introduced by the church with the conscious intention of signifying the joys of the life to come;[68] thus they were certainly endowed with a merely parabolic meaning.[69]

Aquinas says that the ceremonial precepts "have a mystical and figurative character" ("habent rationes figurales et mysticas").[70] But the word *figurative* does not refer to some new type of sense; it refers rather to a normal parabolic sense based upon convention. Doing something figurative, Aquinas says, means "doing something in order to represent something else" ("facere aliqua facta ad alia repraesentanda")[71]—and this he identifies with a theatrical or poetical activity.[72] However, the poet uses figurative expressions "because of a deficiency in truth" ("propter defectum veritatis"), whereas a religious ceremony presents the divine through images "because of an excess of truth" ("propter excedentem veritatem").[73] In both cases there is an act, expression, or object which, on the basis of widespread convention, acquires a specific meaning and is a figure of something else.

The reason for all of this is that human beings cannot easily grasp the highest truth, but must approach it by way of sensible representations.

> Et ideo utilius fuit ut sub quodam figurarum velamine divina mysteria rudi populo traderentur, ut sic saltem ea implicite cognoscerent, dum illis figuris deservirent ad honorem Dei.

> It was, therefore, better for the divine mysteries to be conveyed to an uncultured people as it were veiled by means of figures, so that at least they should have an implicit knowledge of them in using these figures for the honor of God.[74]

This kind of argument coincides almost word for word with the argument advanced by those—Suger foremost among them— who aimed to promote and defend religious art as something allegorical and didactic. And there is a remarkable resemblance to a pronouncement of the Synod of Arras in 1025:

> Illiterati, quod per scripturam non possunt intueri, hoc per quaedam picturae lineamenta contemplantur.

> Unlettered people, who cannot appreciate this through reading scripture, can grasp it in the contemplation of pictures.[75]

By way of illustration, let us take the portals of a Gothic cathedral. We note first of all that each column in the portal houses a statue of a human figure; in this way, the sculptural and the figurative are combined. The human figure is stylized and usually portrays a particular human type. It is stylized, in fact, because it imitates a *form;* that is, it is stylized because it represents a type (representation, it will be recalled, means the construction of an image through the reproduction of a *form*). Insofar as the statue is a representation, its function is to give pleasure. But in addition, it acquires a significative value through its parabolic sense: the sculptured figures are equipped with certain characteristic signs—a particular kind of headgear, for instance—which are incomprehensible to us, but with which the medievals were fully familiar. Popular tradition, the representation of the mysteries of religion, and the whole cultural iconography of the time had accustomed them to understanding these signs as characteristics of the Jews in general, and of biblical characters in particular. These statues in cathedral portals, bearing royal insignia (they were long mistaken for Merovingian kings) and distinguished by particular items of clothing, appeared to the medieval observer quite unambiguously as kings mentioned in the Bible and as Old Testament personages. Where further specification was necessary, other signs were added to designate with greater precision which person was being depicted. Thus, a female figure on the portal of St. Bénigne in Dijon has one foot shaped like that of a goose; this *Regina Piedoca* is none other than the Queen of Sheba, portrayed in accordance with a widespread iconographical convention. And Aquinas, for his part, would have spoken of parabolism in connection with cathedral statuary.

These figures have a significative as well as a sculptural character. They are not just human figures, but images of biblical royalty—images, often, of this or that particular king or queen. But we do not pass from their sculptural character to their meaning; instead, they appear as figures and as significative of certain individuals in the very same instant.

> Per voces significatur aliquid proprie et aliquid figurative; nec est litteralis sensus ipsa figura, sed id quod est figuratum.

> Words [and, we can add, images] can signify something properly and something figuratively; in the latter case the literal sense is not the figure of speech itself, but the object it figures.[76]

The literal sense of the statue-columns consists in their being biblical monarchs, Solomon or the Queen of Sheba. But to this first, parabolic sense there is added another. This consists no longer in the joint meaningfulness of sculptural shape and historical reference, but rather in the joint meaningfulness of architectural location and mystical reference. As I have said already, these biblical characters indicate how the Old Law is an entrance and anteroom to the New. The chosen people, who awaited for centuries the coming of

Christ, sit upon the threshold of the Temple and receive the faithful. After them comes the mystery of the New Covenant. In the darkness of the cathedral, watched over by kings and prophets, we find the tabernacle and the presence of the living Christ.[77]

This is the crucial and didactic point in the achievements of medieval sculpture. And yet the formal mechanism which governs this play of correspondences is always the same: in the medieval tradition, the Queen of Sheba signified the pagan world before Christ and prefigured the Magi; and it was enough to recognise her statue on a portal column to enter immediately upon this play of figurative references. We must now interpret this aspect of medieval art in terms of the Thomistic aesthetic, and this can be done as follows. In a statue-column, there is a relation of proportion between the architectural and the sculptural, and also between the sculptural and a representational goal. The representational aspect is in turn proportionate to its figurative meaning; and its figurative character is precisely proportionate to its mystical significance. In other words, the column is at one and the same time a *statue*, a *human image* embodying the features of the human species, an *image of a biblical character*, and, finally, an instruction in and pointer to the mystical and the religious—thus, an *anteroom* to the mysteries of the Christian faith. This organism of stone expresses meaning simultaneously in all of these ways; it is just as much a mystical message as an image of man. The harmonious, rule-governed nature of the sculptural endeavor is adapted to the requirements of historical signification, and this in turn is adapted to the necessities of instruction in the supernatural. The whole thing is then adapted to the possible ways of understanding possessed by the medieval people to whom it was directed. There is, therefore, a proportion between the structure of the object and the capacity for understanding possessed by the observer.

To conclude. This organism of stone, which is intended to give instruction, which is constructed for speaking to the masses—this organism did in fact speak effectively to them. Thus, it was adequate to its ultimate perfection, its functional perfection. It was an art form characterized by proportion in its features and in its functions, by an integrated concordance with its own essence, and by clarity in both its sculptural and its associative structures. To know this triple harmony was to know its beauty. It was architecturally functional because it was a column. It edified the masses, for it was a page of the catechism written in stone. It gave pleasure to the observer and to the faithful and beautified the house of God, lucent in its colors and harmonious in its lines. It inspired a sense of reverence and of prayer and expressed a hieratic majesty which made ready the Christian soul for religious ceremonies. But it was beautiful above all because it realized all of this in accordance with the canons of integrity, clarity, and proportion.

A Thomist Poetics

I shall conclude this survey of Aquinas's critical remarks and observations by speculating on the form which a Thomistic poetics might take, if it existed. It would most likely conform with the principles of his aesthetics, converted into rules governing concrete artistic labors. Aquinas's poetics would be a classical poetics, a poetics of precision, in which beauty consists in being adapted to an end, in the ability to express well whatever it is that has to be said. It is a poetics which is evident in Aquinas's own compositions, where musical values combine with theological subtleties and emotional content in a single clear, condensed, turn of phrase. We can look again at a stanza, referred to in an earlier chapter, from the hymn *Verbum supernum prodiens*.

> Se nascens dedit socium,
> Convescens in edulium,
> Se moriens in pretium,
> Se regnans dat in praemium.

> In birth he gave himself as our fellow man;
> In eating with us he gave himself as our food;
> In dying he took upon himself our debt;
> In reigning he gives himself as our reward.

Here, the whole mystery of the Redemption is expressed in a terse and brilliant rhetorical manoeuver. The same thing can be found in some of Aquinas's prayers.

> Et praecor te, ut haec Sancta Communio non sit mihi reatus ad poenam, sed intercessio salutaris ad veniam. Sit mihi armatura

fidei, et scutum bonae voluntatis. Sit vitiorum meorum evacu-
atio, concupiscientiae et libidinis exterminatio, charitatis et pa-
tientiae, humilitatis et obedientiae, omniumque virtutum aug-
mentatio; contra insidias inimicorum meorum, tam visibilium
quam invisibilium, firma defensio; motuum meorum, tam car-
nalium quam spiritualium, perfecta quietatio; in te uno ac vero
Deo firma adhaesio, atque mei finis felix consummatio.

I pray that this Holy Communion should not be, for me, an
accusation leading to my punishment, but an intervention
bringing salvation and pardon. May it be to me an armor of
faith and a shield of goodwill. May it bring a release of my sins,
an extinguishing of my desires and wantonness, an increase in
my love and patience, humility and obedience, and in all my
virtues; against the hostile approaches of my enemies, visible
and invisible, may it be a firm defense; may all carnal and spiritual feelings be in perfect peace; to you, the one and true God,
may I firmly cleave, and may my end be a happy consumma-
tion.

This illustrates how the three criteria of proportion, integrity, and
clarity have been turned into the rules of medieval prose.[78]

Aquinas and Dante

It is interesting to note that Aquinas's assimilation of allegory *in
verbis* to parabolic sense—that is, to a subspecies of literal sense—
had no influence upon the poets of his time. Dante provides very
strong evidence of this in his letter to Can Grande della Scala, in
which he expounds the theoretical principles involved in an allegorical reading of his *Divine Comedy*.

Early on, Dante makes it clear that his poem must be read as a
"polysemous" work, one which has several senses. He then illustrates the meaning of polysemy with his celebrated example from
Psalms 113:1–2: "When Israel went out of Egypt, the house of Ja-
cob from a barbarous people, Judea was made his sanctuary, Israel
his dominion." Dante's comment on this is as follows.

If we look at the letter alone, what is signified to us is the departure of the sons of Israel from Egypt during the time of Moses;
if at the allegory, what is signified to us is our redemption
through Christ; if at the moral sense, what is signified to us is

the conversion of the soul from the sorrow and misery of sin to the state of grace; if at the anagogical, what is signified to us is the departure of the sanctified soul from bondage to the corruption of this world into the freedom of eternal glory.[79]

There seems to be nothing in this which is at variance with the tradition of biblical interpretation. But many commentators have felt uneasy, because Dante is here using an example of biblical interpretation to illustrate how we should read his own, secular, poem. One way around this, and one which has been suggested by some, is that the letter is a forgery. It "should" be a forgery, because Dante was supposed to be a good Thomist, and the letter contradicts Aquinas's view that secular poetry has only a literal sense. However, even if the letter were a forgery, it would be a forgery which from the beginning was taken to be authentic, and this means that it said nothing repugnant to Dante's contemporaries. Moreover, Dante's *Il convivio* is certainly not a forgery, and in this treatise he also provides suggestions for reading his poems allegorically. Here, however, he does maintain a distinction, ignored in the letter, between the allegory of poets and the allegory of theologians.

In *Il convivio*, Dante explains what meaning he intended his poems to have. In this sense, therefore, we could say that he aligns himself with the Thomistic view: the allegorical sense of his poems is still parabolic, because it represents what Dante intended to mean. In the letter, by contrast, his illustrations seem quite evidently to be instances of allegory *in factis*. And elsewhere in the letter he writes that the manner of treatment (*modus tractandis*) employed in the *Divine Comedy* is "poetic, fictive, descriptive, digressive, and transumptive." These were traditional features of poetic discourse; but he then adds, "and it also consists in definition, division, proof, refutation, and the giving of examples"[80]—and these are features of theological and philosophical discourse. Furthermore, we know that Dante always read mythological tales, and the works of the classical poets, as if they were allegories *in factis*. It is in such terms that he writes of these poets in his *De Vulgari Eloquentia;* and in the *Divine Comedy* he refers to the poet Statius as

> . . . come quei che va di notte,
> che porta il lume dietro e sè non giova,
> ma dopo sè fa le persone dotte.

> . . . as one who proceeds in the night, and carries a light behind
> him—not for himself, but for those who follow him.
> (*Purgatorio*, XXII, 67–69)

Here, Statius is conceived of as a seer; for his poetry, and pagan
poetry in general, conveyed spiritual meaning of which the authors
were not aware.

For Dante, therefore, poets continue the work of the scriptures,
and his own poem is a new instance of prophetical writing; it is
endowed with spiritual senses just as the scriptures are. The poet,
moreover, is divinely inspired. He writes what love inspires him to,
and his work can sustain the same kind of allegorical reading as the
scriptures. The poet is justified in inviting his reader to guess what
is hidden "sotto il velame delli versi strani" ("under the veil of curious verse").

So, just as Aquinas was devaluing the *modus poeticus,* the poets
themselves evaded his intellectual influence; they initiated a new,
mystical approach to poetic texts, a new way of reading which,
through various avatars, was to survive down to our own time.

What keeps Dante in sympathy with Aquinas's approach is the
fact that he does not ascribe an infinite or an indefinite number of
meanings to poetry. He seems to confine the spiritual senses to
four, which are encoded and decoded on the basis of rhetorical convention and the "code" provided by medieval encyclopedias. But
of course this code could continue to operate only so long as allegory *in verbis* was based upon the conventions embodied in the encyclopedias, conventions which governed universal allegory as a
unified world view. This world view collapsed, however, under the
influence of Aquinas and of the new Aristotelian secularization of
the natural world.

What was to happen to poets, after the world was emptied of its
mystical significance, and when it became uncertain under whose
inspiration—God? Love? Something else?—the poet uncon-
sciously spoke? It can be seen that when Aquinas implemented a
theological secularization of the natural world, he set free the mystical drives within poetic activity.

VI

The Theory of Art

The preceding chapter has demonstrated that Aquinas employed his own aesthetic criteria, instinctively as it were, whenever he was engaged in defining the concrete artistic situation. This critical habit, however, is no evidence of a conscious philosophical definition of the relations between art and beauty. It was a critical practice which could well have been a happy accident. We must therefore look to see whether Aquinas's general system permitted a connection between the artistic and the aesthetic. We have already seen how the aesthetic characteristics of form were defined; now we must ask whether these characteristics can be applied also to artistic forms—whether, that is, the medieval philosophy of beauty was bound up with the medieval theory of art. Did the medievals believe that art gave rise to forms, and that these forms could possess beauty? Also, did they believe, as we do now, that art is inventive or "creative"?

The five sections which follow attempt to answer these five questions:

1. What are the relations between art and nature? And thus, to what extent does art "invent" or "create"?
2. What is the character of artistic form in relation to natural form?
3. Can beauty be predicated of artistic form? And if so, in what manner and for what reason?
4. Is there a place in Aquinas's system for the category of "fine art," specifiable within art in general and designed particularly for aesthetic ends?
5. Does the Thomistic system contain the notion of art's autonomy in the modern sense of that term?

Art and Invention

If we search Aquinas's works for the passages where he mentions art, we will find that his thinking seems in no way different from that of the cultural tradition to which he belonged. He defines art as *recta ratio factibilium*[1]—that is, right judgment concerning things to be made, and that is to say a perfect knowledge of the rules of manufacture. Art means "knowing how to make." The ideas about art which we find in medieval philosophers, artists, and writers of treatises about art, were closely connected with the classical and intellectualistic theory of human making. Definitions such as "ars est recta ratio factibilium" or the similar "ars est principium faciendi et cogitandi quae sunt facienda" ("art consists in the principles for making and judging whatever is to be made")[2] had no definite paternity. From the Carolingians to Duns Scotus, the medievals simply repeated them and reformulated them in various guises. Aristotle was the starting point, but they took their formulas from the whole Greek tradition, from Cicero, the Stoics, Marius Victorinus, Isidore of Seville, Cassiodorus.

The medieval notion of art contained two elements: one was cognitive (*ratio, cogitatio*); the other was productive (*faciendi, factibilium*). Art was a knowledge of the rules by means of which things can be produced. It was a knowledge of given and objective rules: Cassiodorus, liberal as always in etymology, said that art was so called because it delimits or circumscribes (*arctat*),[3] and John of Salisbury repeated this centuries later.[4] But it was also called *ars* from the Greek *aretē* (excellence), according to both Cassiodorus and Isidore of Seville,[5] because it was a power of the practical intellect, a *virtus operativa*. Art belonged to the realm of making, not of doing. Doing pertained to morality and was subject to the regulative virtue of prudence (*recta ratio agibilium*). There was something of an analogy between art and prudence; but prudence governed the practical judgment in contingent situations, and sought the good of mankind, whereas art regulated operations on physical materials, as in sculpture, or upon mental materials, as in logic and rhetoric. Its aim was a goodness of the work (*bonum operis*). The important thing for the craftsman was that he should make a good sword, for example, and it was not his concern whether it was used for good or evil purposes.[6] Art was a "science" (*ars sine scientia nihil est*), which produced objects endowed with their own laws, constructed objects. Art was not expression, but construction, an operation aiming at a certain result. The word *artifex* applied alike to blacksmiths, orators, poets, painters, and sheepshearers. *Ars* was a very broad concept, which extended to what we think of today as technology and craft. The theory of art was in the first instance a theory of craftsmanship. The craftsman or *artifex* produced something which completed, integrated, or prolonged nature. Man was an artist because he possessed so little: he was born naked, without tusks or claws, unable to run fast or to shelter within a shell or a natural armor. But he could observe the works of nature and imitate them. He saw how water ran down the side of a hill without accumulating on the top or sinking in, and invented a roof for his house.[7] "Every work is either the work of the Creator, or a work of Nature, or the work of an artificer imitating nature" ("omne enim opus est vel opus Creatoris, vel opus Naturae, vel opus artificis imitantis naturam").[8]

But if art imitated nature, this did not involve a servile copying of natural models. Artistic imitation involved invention and reworking. It joined together what was separate and separated what was joined; it prolonged the operations of nature; it was productive like nature and continued nature's creative labors. It was true, as Aquinas said, that "art imitates nature"—but "in its manner of operation" ("ars imitatur naturam in sua operatione").[9] The last phrase in this is an important element in a formula which is often thought to be more banal than it really is. The medieval theory of art is interesting precisely for this reason, that it was a theory of human technology seen as an extension of nature.

Art produced objects in a more economical way than nature did; and nature for her part encouraged the mind's genius—defined by John of Salisbury as "a certain power infused into the soul by nature, and effective in itself" ("vis quaedam animo naturaliter insita, per se valens")[10]—for perceiving and memorizing objects, for examining and systematizing them. Looked at in this way, art and technology were a constructive ability which operated upon the things provided by nature, giving them new forms, in a sort of continual tinkering which copied the operative laws of nature.

But this type of theory created a problem. How exactly did art succeed in copying the processes of nature and in individuating new forms? What models did it have? The problem here was that of the "exemplary idea" which was the basis for the artist's work—a problem, thus, of inspiration on the one hand and of creativity on the other. We are familiar with the way in which modern thought developed these two notions in the Mannerist theories of Idea and Genius;[11] but we are also conscious of how alien Mannerism is to an Aristotelian theory of art.[12]

The view that art involves a new type of knowledge, that it is a method of discovery, even a method of creation, did not arrive in the Middle Ages until the appearance of proto-humanists such as Albertino Mussato.[13] It was only in this kind of setting that there could emerge the notion of the "poet theologian," and that, as Garin puts it, there could be "a tendency to assign to poetry a revelatory function, making it central to human experience, and its supreme moment . . . the point at which humanity sees right to the foundations of its condition."[14]

The view that poetry is an expression of feeling was perhaps to be found among the poets, but not among the theorists. At most it appeared in various forms among the mystics, who provided the seeds of something which, in quite a different guise, might be called an aesthetics of feeling and of intuition. It would be interesting to follow up the Franciscan discussions on the primacy of will and of love, and St. Bonaventure's discussion of the rules of the "harmonious smoothness" ("aequalitas numerosa"—clearly an aesthetic rule) which exists in the depths of the soul. It would be worth looking at certain Judeo-Arabic views on poetry as insight;[15] at Avicenna's treatise on the imagination, which is referred explicitly to poetry;[16] at a theme recurrent in medieval literature, the divine madness of the poet;[17] and at the conception of illumination in grace, through which, according to Meister Eckhart, we conceive an image of anything whose exemplary idea exists in the mind of God.[18]

But all of these, as I have said, lie outside the theory of art of which Aquinas makes use. It is not that Aquinas does not look at the problem of exemplary ideas, or fails to recognize the existence of a faculty of imagination. But if we are to avoid serious misunderstanding of these conceptions, we must now quickly review what he says about them. What he says is in fact of little use in discovering his theory of invention and creation, but it will put us on the road to discovering the possible connections, within his system, between art and the aesthetic.

Aquinas studies the nature of the artificer's productive operations on several occasions, in relation to the question of those ideas in God's mind which are exemplary causes of things. In this context, the word *idea* is decisively linked with the concept of *form*, understood precisely as exemplary cause.

> Omnes creaturae sunt in mente divina sicut arca in mente artificis. Sed arca in mente artificis est per suam similitudinem et ideam.
>
> All creatures are in the divine mind, just as a piece of furniture is in the mind of its maker. But a piece of furniture is in its maker's mind because of its idea and its likeness.[19]

This "likeness" is the product of a certain connection between a quality in the idea and the thing whose exemplar it is. The idea is therefore

> forma exemplaris ad cujus imitationem aliquid constituitur . . . Dicimus enim formam artis in artifice esse exemplar vel ideam artificiati.
>
> an exemplary form in imitation of which something is made . . . For we say that the form of art in the artist is the exemplar or idea of the artistic product.[20]

The idea, as an exemplary *form,* is not the *form* as an object of perception, but rather the *form* of the object as it is taken by the artificer for the purpose of producing an imitation of it.

> Et tunc intellectus operativus, praeconcipiens formam operati, habet ut ideam ipsam formam rei imitatae, prout est illius rei imitatae.
>
> The operative intellect, when preconceiving the form of what is made, possesses as an idea the very form of the thing imitated, precisely as the form of the thing made.[21]

The formation of something in accordance with an exemplary form is, therefore, a formation by way of imitation. But, imitation of what? Strictly speaking, it is imitation of the exemplary *forms* themselves. And an exemplary *form*, we should note, is not exemplary simply of substantial *form*, but of a *form* which is connected with matter and which, together with matter, is formative of a concrete particular.

> Unde proprie idea non respondet materiae tantum, nec formae tantum; sed toti composito respondet una idea, quae est factiva totius et quantum ad formam et quantum ad materiam.

> Hence, properly speaking, there is no idea corresponding merely to matter or merely to form; but one idea corresponds to the entire composite—an idea that causes the whole, both its form and its matter.[22]

This is an important passage, for it ties in with the conception of aesthetic form as a whole substance—a substance in all its concreteness as an ordered and existing entity—which we have found to be typical of the Thomistic aesthetic. And it is in keeping with this conception that Aquinas should say that only one exemplary *form* is involved in the production of an object.

> Unde, cum idea, proprie loquendo, sit forma rei operabilis inquantum hujusmodi, non erit talium accidentium idea distincta, sed subjecti cum omnibus accidentibus ejus erit una idea; sicut aedificator unam formam habet de domo et omnibus quae domui accidunt inquantum hujusmodi, per quam domum cum omnibus talibus suis accidentibus simul in esse producit, cujusmodi accidens est quadratura ipsius, et alia hujusmodi.

> Consequently, since an idea, properly speaking, is a form of something that can be made, considered precisely under this aspect, there will not be distinct ideas of such accidents. There will be only one idea, that of the subject with all its accidents—just as an architect has one form of a house and of all the accidents that pertain to a house as such, and by means of this one form brings into being the house and all its accidents, such as its square shape and the like.[23]

This applies, of course, to those accidental properties which are connected strictly with the nature of the object being made—in the case of the house, its square shape. But in the case of the accidental properties which it may acquire over and above, after it has been made, the artificer conceives extra exemplary ideas. Aquinas's example is of paintings added to a house after it has been built in all its essentials. This distinction is important, because it is connected with the functionalist conception of artistic form—that is, that whatever makes something useful and workable in the appropriate context also makes it beautiful. Ornaments and other additions are not superfluous; they are an ulterior artistic act, produced on the basis of different exemplary forms.[24]

Thus, as the artificer proceeds with his constructive endeavors, he has in his mind an idea of the object he is making. An architect, says Aquinas, "intends to make the house to the pattern of the form which he has conceived in his mind" ("artifex intendit domum assimilare formae quam mente concepit").[25] And the beauty of the house does not consist only in its correspondence with the objective canons of proportion; it consists also (and we saw this already in discussing Aquinas's theory of the image) in its proportionate correspondence with its exemplary form. Aquinas writes that "the form of a house in the mind of the architect is something understood by him, to the likeness of which he produces the form of a house in the matter" ("forma enim domus in mente aedificatoris est aliquid ab eo intellectum, ad cujus similitudinem domum in materia format").[26] But the question then is: *where did he get the idea of the house he wanted to build?* It is easy to talk about imitating exemplary forms whenever the forms exist in nature, as when the artist imitates an animal or the human figure. But in such cases a serious problem arises, the solution to which is constantly in danger of Platonism, since it was unthinkable in medieval philosophy that the human spirit could engage in creation. For where, then, does the artificer get the idea of an artificial object which he wants to make? In Augustinian thought the answer to this was easy: the idea of a house, or of a ship, is given to us by God, as an innate deposit of knowledge. The artificer discovers within his own mind an idea of the thing to be made, and his constructive labors proceed through a kind of illumination.

But the Aristotelian and Thomistic conception of an immanent form in things provides, in contrast, no appreciable solution to the problem of creativity. So much is this so that Aquinas actually risks adopting a Platonist solution, at least by implication; for he states that all things, in that they have being, imitate the divine idea "in different ways, each one according to its own proper manner" ("diversimode ipsam imitantur, et unaquaeque secundum proprium modum suum").[27] Here, the word *idea* means essence; God, seeing and foreseeing all the varying degrees in which things imitate his essence, conceives the exemplary ideas of artificial things also. In this sense, the idea of a house exists inchoately in the divine exemplar and becomes determinate in the intellect of the artist who conceives it.

However, Aquinas also noted that God could have foreknowledge of all our future actions, without the human will's losing its autonomy. In the same way, the inchoate divine exemplars, and God's foreknowledge of the objects of which they were exemplars, did not annul the autonomy and novelty of human actions. In fact we must look for a satisfactory solution to the problem in Aquinas's theory of the imagination (*phantasia*), although it is a confused and disappointing theory.[28]

Phantasia, in Aquinas, is one of the four internal powers of the sensitive part of man, and can be identified as the imagination. The other three powers are the common sense, the estimative power (which in human beings is cognitive), and memory. Imagination is "a kind of storehouse of forms received by sense" ("quasi thesaurus quidam formarum per sensum acceptarum").[29] Its role in the act of simple apprehension is clear: once an object has been perceived by the senses, imagination features as a passive faculty upon which the phantasm is imprinted. It is by means of the phantasm that the agent intellect individuates a universal form for the possible intellect. The phantasm is an image of a thing, and the imagination is thus a receptacle for images—and thus also the only way for the intellect to know things in their individuality, whenever the act of simple apprehension is succeeded by a reflection on the phantasm.

However, imagination is not a purely receptive faculty. It does gather up images, but it is then able in some way to modify and combine them. Imaginative consciousness is therefore most appropriate in sleep, in madmen, or to those in the grip of passion. It is found also in the normal way of things, whenever I have before my eyes, as if they actually existed, the forms of things remembered or forms engendered by the collecting and arranging of several remembered things.[30] The latter type of process is characteristic of the imagination, and Aquinas stresses this in particular because he is opposed to Avicenna's view that there is a fifth power of the internal sense.

> Avicenna vero ponit quintam potentiam, mediam inter aesti-mativam et imaginationem, quae componit et dividit formas imaginatas; ut patet cum ex forma imaginata auri et forma im-aginata montis componimus unam formam montis aurei, quem nunquam vidimus. Sed ista operatio non apparet in aliis animalibus ab homine, in quo ad hoc sufficit virtus imagina-tiva.

> Avicenna did indeed maintain a fifth power, somewhere be-tween instinct and imagination, a power which composes and divides imagined forms, as when from the image of gold and the image of mountain we compose the single form of a golden mountain which we have never seen. But this activity is not found in animals other than man, in whom the power of imag-ination suffices to account for it.[31]

For Aquinas, then, imagination is a cognitive power which "from likenesses first conceived can form others" ("ex speciebus primo conceptis alias formare possunt").[32] In this it is a bit like the intellect, since "from genus and difference we can form the notion of a species" ("ex praeconceptis speciebus generis et differentiae format rationem speciei").[33] However, the way of arranging things in the imagination is not the same as that of the intellect. "Imagi-nation," Aquinas stresses, "does not combine nor divide" ("phan-tasia autem non componit neque dividit").[34] This does not contra-dict what has just been said about the imagination. For this way of arranging things (*compositio*), by combining and dividing them, is characteristic of the intellectual labors performed in the act of judg-ment; and that is, the act of determining the reality or otherwise of an object, and whether it is the object of an appetite or not. By contrast, the kind of *compositio* found in the imagination involves simply a free rearranging of the elements in experience.

> Est quaedam operatio animae in homine quae dividendo et componendo format diversas rerum imagines, etiam quae non sunt a sensibus acceptae.

> There is an activity in the soul of man which, by separating and joining, forms different images of things, even of things not received from the senses.[35]

Thus, the idea of a house can be conceived by way of this process of rearranging. The architect or builder does not extract the idea from some internal store of ideas, by means of divine illumination or from a hyperuranic source. Instead, his experience enables him to conceive of the possibility of something not given in nature, but which can be realized through the use of natural objects and through constructional activities analogous to those of nature. Art imitates nature, we recall again, *in sua operatione*.

Art is here seen as the activity of combining things; and in fact Aquinas says no more than this. But we should note that the activity involves a dividing and a rearranging. Dividing things results in a variety of elements, and rearranging them restores them to unity in accordance with a rule of proportion. Here, then, is a connection with proportion; we find yet again that artistic endeavors always result in a form endowed with proportion.

Nowhere does Aquinas state that the construction of a ship or the formulation of a syllogism—both products of art—has an aesthetic end. But he cannot deny either that the product, once completed, can be an object of aesthetic experience. As we have seen, he had no difficulty in talking about the aesthetic values of poetry and music. And yet, there is something surprising about this: it has been claimed, and with some justification, that on the theoretical level there was no connection in Aquinas between the realms of art and beauty. However, we have seen that on the practical level there was such a connection. And if we look at the theoretical implications of his analysis of the artistic process, we will find that, even though the theoretical connection was never made explicit, it existed just to the extent that it justified the practical connection. Thus we find him saying that "no one takes the trouble to make an effigy or representation unless for its beauty" ("nullus curat effigiare vel repraesentare nisi ad pulchrum").[36] He often remarks upon the beauty of architecture and uses the example of architecture to explain the nature of proportion.[37]

The Ontology of Artistic Form

Romantic and Idealist aesthetics identified the aesthetic with the artistic. Croce even went so far as to say that "natural beauty is simply a stimulus to aesthetic reproduction, which presupposes previous production," and that "each refers the natural fact to the expression in his mind."[38] Here he subordinated natural beauty to the only type of beauty which he accepted as genuine, lyrical intuition; it was therefore artistic also, since art was lyrical intuition. In this way, a great deal of modern aesthetics considers artistic form to possess an ontological value superior to that of natural forms, just because it is a product of the human spirit. This view is quite different from the Thomistic conception of art. For Aquinas, artistic form is ontologically dependent; it possesses its own value, but it has no metaphysical autonomy, nor can it rival divine creation.

We cannot introduce this issue by repeating what Aquinas says about art's imitating nature *in sua operatione*. For elsewhere he also writes that art imitates nature "insofar as it is able to" ("ars imitatur naturam in quantum potest").[39] This is a limitation on the possibilities of art, arising from the fact that "art operates upon the material which nature provides" ("ars enim operatur ex materia quam natura ministrat").[40] Art always starts with a material which precedes it. As St. Bonaventure put it, "the soul can make new compositions, but it cannot make new things" ("anima enim facit novas compositiones, licet non faciat novas res").[41]

To compose is not to create: this is the point. This was an indispensable principle in the medieval theory of art; and it is expressed in terms of hylomorphic theory in the following passage from Aquinas, a passage which I shall take as a guide.

> Ars autem deficit ab operatione naturae; quia natura dat formam substantialem, quod ars facere non potest; sed omnes formae artificiales sunt accidentales.

> Art is deficient when compared with the operations of nature. For nature bestows substantial form, which art cannot do. Rather, all artificial forms are accidental.[42]

The statement that all artificial forms are accidental is one that is frequently repeated by Aquinas. It amounts to saying that artistic form is not substantial but accidental *form*.

Aquinas's opusculum *De Principiis Naturae* gives the clearest and most thorough account of this theory. In the first chapter he explains the distinction—not a new one—between a potency to substantial being and a potency to accidental being. For example, a sperm is in potency to the substantial being of a man, and a man is in potency to the accidental property of whiteness. Matter which is in potency to substantial being is called matter *ex qua,* whereas matter which is in potency to accidental being is matter *in qua.* Or, better, the former of these is, speaking strictly, true and genuine matter, whereas the latter should rather be referred to as "subject." In other words, a subject is a substance; it is already the product of the combining of matter with substantial *form*—matter which, before the combining took place, was in potency to that *form.* It is the substance, however, to which accidental forms become attached. Matter becomes actual through its meeting with substantial *form;* but the subject does not acquire being from the accidental form, for the accidental form merely actuates a potency in the subject. In fact it is just the opposite: accidental form acquires being from its subject.

> Subiectum enim dat esse accidenti, scilicet existendi, quia accidens non habet esse nisi per subiectum; unde dicitur quod accidentia sunt in subiecto, non autem dicitur quod forma substantialis sit in subiecto. Et secundum hoc differt materia a subiecto, quia subiectum est quod non habet esse ex eo quod advenit, sed per se habet completum esse, sicut homo non habet esse ab albedine; sed materia habet esse ex eo quod sibi advenit, quia de se habet esse incompletum.

> The subject gives being or existence to an accident, because an accident has no being unless through a subject. Thus, we say that accidents are in a subject, but we do not say that substantial form is in a subject. For this reason, we distinguish between matter and subject. For a subject does not acquire being from whatever happens to it, but has its whole being in itself—so that a man, for instance, does not acquire being from the fact that he is white. Matter, however, does acquire being from what happens to it, for in itself its being is incomplete.[43]

In both cases there is a form which brings a potency to act. But in the case of a subject and its accidents, the act is not a substantial act (that is, one which confers being upon the whole), but an accidental act (that is, which confers being upon the accident, in virtue of its being a part of the whole). In both cases there is an act of generation, namely a "movement toward form" (*motus ad formam*). But in the case of substantial *form* it is a simple generation (*generatio simpliciter*), whereas in the case of accidents it is a generation with respect to something (*generatio secundum quid*). That is, matter is made actual by a substantial *form* fully and completely; but when a subject is actuated by an accident it is actuated as white, or actuated as warm, and so on.

In chapter 3 of *De Principiis Naturae*, Aquinas refers to works of art by way of illustration. Three things are necessary, he says, for the generating of a reality: matter in potency, a privation of being, and an actuating form. Take a certain quantity of metal. If it is to become a statue, it must be the case that it is not already the statue; but as well as this, it must potentially be what it is going to become.

> Sicut quando ex cupro fit idolum, cuprum quod est potentia ad formam idoli est materia; hoc autem quod est infiguratum sive indispositum est privatio formae. Illud a qua dicitur idolum est forma, non autem substantialis, quia cuprum ante adventum illius formae habet esse in actu, et eius esse non dependet ab illa figura, sed est forma accidentalis. Omnes enim formae artificiales sunt accidentales; ars enim non operatur nisi supra id quod iam constitutum est in esse a natura.

> When an idol is made out of copper, the copper, which is in potency to the form of the idol, is the matter. And this matter, which is without shape or order, is lacking in form. The idol is so called because of its form; but this is not substantial form, for before the copper acquires this form it already has actual being, and its being is not dependent upon the shape that it will acquire. Rather, it is accidental form. For all artificial forms are accidental forms; art can operate only upon something which is already naturally in being.

The language of this passage is unequivocal. Artistic forms are ontologically dependent because they are introduced into a material substratum whose substantial nature is not altered. Artistic form does give reality to the values of proportion and integrity, but it can do so only because of the concrete existence which belongs to the subject. Artistic form is like a mark made upon a solid block of stone: the mark may well be most elaborate and harmonious, but we cannot ignore the fact that it exists in and with the block of stone, and that it can exist there only because the block had the potency to be marked, and to be marked in that particular manner. A. Silva-Tarouca puts it as follows.

> In an architectural work, for instance, or in any other human construction, anything which is altered must always be something which already exists. The operative plan and the final intention—for example, those of an architect—can in practice exert a profound influence upon the mode of being of the material from which the work is made. But no matter how great the influence, the stone and the timber, the tiles and the colors, and so on are always something given to the architect. They are not called into existence for the first time by the fact that the architect is building a house. They already existed, with the mode of existence of stones, trees, and the like. This, their original mode of existence, was not included essentially and initially in the plan of construction, in the ordering principle "house." It is not as if pine trees would not have existed if the architect had not decided to use them in his construction.[44]

But now that this is clear, we can reasonably ask whether we are entitled to define artistic form as form in the first place. And to this Aquinas gives the answer that artistic form, when understood in this way, can be regarded as what he calls *figura*—that is, shape; and that is also a quality of the fourth species.

Let us look at the explanation of this. In *Summa Theologiae*, I–II, 3 ob. 3, Aquinas distinguishes four species of quality: (1) a habit or disposition ("habitus vel dispositio"), (2) a natural potency or lack of it ("potentia vel impotentia naturalis") (3) an affection or the quality of being affected ("passio vel passibilis qualitas"), and (4) the form and shape surrounding something ("forma et circa aliquid constans figura"). Regarding qualities of the first species, Aquinas quotes Aristotle's definition of *habitus* or *dispositio*.

> Habitus dicitur dispositio secundum quam bene aut male disponitur dispositum, et aut secundum se aut ad aliud.

> A habit is a disposition which is either good or bad for its possessor, either absolutely [*secundum se*] or relatively [*ad aliud*].[45]

A disposition *secundum se* has to do with a *form* rather than an activity. It refers to a habitual disposition of a subject toward a form; in the case of the human body, it refers to an appropriate disposition of the parts of the body with respect to the requirements of its substantial form, the soul.

> Et hoc modo sanitas et pulchritudo, et huiusmodi, habituales dispositiones dicuntur.
>
> In this way, health and beauty and the like are called habitual dispositions. [46]

In this sense, beauty is a habit or state of being, a harmony deep within it. It is in this sense that it is described and justified in the question where Aquinas discusses whether the human body is appropriately made. [47] The human body, however, possesses another and more visible kind of beauty—namely, its external aspect and shape. This is the fourth species of quality, where form is taken in the sense of shape, *figura*. *Figura* signifies the boundary of any continuous quantity; it means the definition or limit which a thing possesses or has imposed upon it. In the case of the human body, its substantial *form* disposes its matter in accordance with an inner necessity and confers upon the matter a boundary or limit, which manifests itself externally in the accidental quality of *figura*. This quality can be perceived as something which has proportion and gives pleasure and may thus be defined as beautiful; although in reality, the true beauty of the human body is something deeper, so that its surface beauty should be called *formositas* rather than *pulchritudo*. This is why a human being, whose body is well formed but lacks the physical size which it would need if it is to have "integrity," can be called *formosus,* but not *pulcher.*

Turning now to artificial form, we find that the first type of quality (habit or disposition) and the fourth type (*figura,* shape) no longer have the same origin. We do still find, in the case of an artificial subject, that its matter has a disposition toward the requirements of its *form*—in other words, that it is an ontologically completed organism. But when it is worked with and fitted into a specific *figura,* this form is a product of artifice. In the case of the human body, the subject produces its accidents—its substantial *form* produces its shape—whereas in the case of artificial subjects, the subject is merely receptive of its shape: "when an accident is predicated of it on purely extrinsic grounds, the subject is merely the recipient" ("nam respectu accidentis extranei subjectum est susceptivum tantum").[48]

Artificial forms are produced by human beings, and artificial shape can alter the natural shape of a subject. When a block of stone becomes a statue, its original outline disappears and gives way to a different outline. But it must be kept in mind that, when this change takes place, the elements constitutive of the subject do not change; they are merely arranged in a particular *figura*. We saw in an earlier chapter, when discussing proportion, that a mixed body undergoes a metamorphosis of substance: the elements which become part of the mixed body lose their original substantial *form* and are reestablished in a single new substantial *form*.[49] In an artistic form, by contrast, the materials gathered together retain their substantial integrity. They are combined and arranged "commensurately," fashioned into a shape ("ad aliquam figuram redactis").[50]

All of this goes to show the limitations which Aquinas placed on the artist's work. But at the same time it shows again how, in this conception of the artist, the elements which he brings together and coordinates retain their individual qualities. Within the artistic order, they retain their emotive and significative potential. Thus, what counts in a stained-glass window is not just the abstract relations among the form and colors of the glass and the leads; what count also are the individual effects of the pieces of glass, the luminosity, color, thickness and density, and all the connotations of its material frame.[51]

Artificial form belongs to the relationships which sustain a thing as a fully formed organism. It is therefore the form of a coordinated whole, but not of the individual parts of that whole. Substantial *form* is the form of both the whole and its parts, but artificial form is not.

> Sicut forma domus, quae est forma totius et non singularium partium, est forma accidentalis.
>
> Thus the form of a house, which is the form of the whole and not of each part, is an accidental form.[52]

And elsewhere Aquinas writes that "art works upon material which nature provides" ("ars enim operatur ex materia quam natura ministrat").[53] Natural bodies are substantial with regard to both their matter and their form, but artificial bodies are substantial only with regard to their matter or material; their form, though based in the material, comes to it from outside.

It is a consequence of this that Aquinas does not refer to artistic production as "creation." His position is that man must have the humility to acknowledge that he does not bring forms into existence *ex nihilo,* since the forms which he produces are dependent upon a prexisting, concrete, and organic reality. In fact Aquinas suggests that they arise out of the preexisting reality, that they were already present there in potency.

> Materia artificialium est a natura, naturalium vero per creationem a Deo. Artificialia autem conservantur in esse virtute naturalium: sicut domus per soliditatem lapidum. Omnia igitur naturalia non conservantur in esse nisi virtute Dei.

> The material for art products comes from nature, while that of natural products comes through creation, by God. Moreover, art objects are preserved in being by the power of natural things; a home, for instance, by the solidity of its stones. Therefore, all natural things are preserved in being by nothing other than the power of God.[54]

These ideas were taken up in popular Scholasticism and in the encyclopedias. In the *Roman de la rose* Jean de Meun (who wrote his part of the poem shortly after Aquinas's *Summa*) wrote a long digression on art. Art, he says, does not produce true forms as nature does. Rather, it must go on its knees before nature (like a beggar, poor in learning but desirous to imitate her) and ask her to teach it how to capture reality in its images. But even when imitating the works of nature, art cannot create living things. It can create "knights on magnificent chargers, all clothed in armor of blue, of yellow or green, or striped with other colors; birds in the verdure; the fishes of all the oceans; savage beasts browsing in the forests; all the plants and flowers that children and young people go to gather in the woods in spring"[55]—art can create all of this, yet it cannot make them move or feel or speak.

The difference between Aquinas and Jean de Meun was this: the poet used his argument to show that alchemy was superior to art, on the ground that the alchemist was able to transmute substances. This is an indication that, beneath the modalities of Scholasticism, the lay culture of the time was already busy with the scientific and philosophical preoccupations of fifteenth-century Humanism.

Artistic Form and the Aesthetic

In Aquinas's philosophical system, man-made form possesses an aesthetic value. It is endowed with proportion and integrity in that it conforms with the form in the mind of its maker, and also, as an accidental form, with the requirements of the substantial *form* of the subject. In fact, the external shape given to a material must not exceed the possibilities inherent in the material, on pain of irregularity and failure. Also, artificial form thoroughly exploits these possibilities in the subject, in such a way that it brings about an integrated organism in which the duality of the natural and the artificial is almost unnoticeable.

Furthermore, the aesthetic character of artistic form is made possible by the objective existence of beauty in nature. We recall yet again that art, for Aquinas, imitates nature *in sua operatione:* the process which produces artistic form imitates the creative processes in nature, and the ontological structure of artistic form copies that of natural forms.

The labors of the artist confer actuality upon a preexisting formal design in his mind. He conceives of a form which then acquires concrete existence through an external process of manufacture governed by operative rules. The principal goal of artistic labor is that of actualizing something; its end is an actual existent, rather than an aesthetic reality. The aesthetic quality in an artistic form follows upon its ontological reality and is not the artist's primary aim. If he endeavors to make something beautiful, it is only because he first endeavors to make something perfect, which thus happens to be beautiful as well. Ontological perfection means a structural, formal perfection, which is for this very reason aesthetic in character. It is in this manner that beauty is coextensive with being.

The medieval preoccupation with function, with ensuring that a work of art was suitable for its intended purpose, gave rise to the most important of all the types of proportion, the proportion of a form to its end. Its various parts should come together in a whole which is adequate to the end which determined in the first place what kind of whole it was to be. The inclination of a form to its end is the basis of its harmonious qualities, that is, of its beauty. When Aquinas is discussing the nature of human beauty he writes:

> Quilibet autem artifex intendit suo operi dispositionem optimam inducere, non simpliciter, sed per comparationem ad finem.

> Every craftsman intends to give his work the best possible constitution, not indeed absolutely speaking, but in relation to its purpose.[56]

If a craftsman, he goes on, should construct a saw out of glass, because of some ill-conceived desire for beauty, it would be quite useless; it would therefore be imperfect, and thus ugly. Aesthetic quality follows from a perfection in the artist's work; it is a sign of its completeness but is not its specific end.

It is one thing to say that artistic form can have an aesthetic value. It is another thing to say that it has a specific type of aesthetic value, that is, a value which the artist intends and which he achieves in ways which are distinctive of art alone. In fact, many interpreters of Aquinas have been very prolix on the beauty of art, believing that his views contain an implicit notion of an aesthetic quality specific to art. They were trying to prove that Thomistic thinking was relevant in a cultural climate in which the aesthetic and the artistic were identified. Once again, a theoretical prejudice imposed itself upon historical interpretation.

On the Possible Autonomy of the Fine Arts

Despite the fact that they connected the artistic with the aesthetic, the medievals had little understanding of the *specifically* artistic. They lacked a theory of the fine arts. For all the variety in medieval "systems" of the arts, their aim was always to distinguish, not between the fine and useful arts, but between dignified arts and manual arts.

Aristotle had distinguished between the servile and the liberal arts,[57] but the idea of a system of the arts came to the Middle Ages from Galen's *Peri Technēs*. Several medieval authors devised such systems, among them Hugh of St. Victor, Rudolf of Longchamp, and Domenico Gundisalvi. Gundisalvi expounded his system, which was Aristotelian in type, in 1150.[58] He said that poetics, grammar, and rhetoric were superior arts, under the common name of eloquence. The mechanical arts were lower in character. Some writers even claimed that the word *mechanicae* derived from *moechari*, "to commit adultery"; this etymology is to be found in Anthony of Florence, and even in Hugh of St. Victor.[59] The servile arts were thought to be compromised by their material character and by the manual labor involved. Aquinas himself agreed with this view. The manual arts, he said, "are, after a fashion, servile" ("sunt quodammodo serviles"), whereas the liberal arts are superior and confer a rational order upon their material without being subject to the body, which is less noble than the mind. It is true, he goes on, that the liberal arts do not have the productive character of art as it is defined in the abstract; but they can be called arts all the same "because of a certain analogy" ("per quandam similitudinem").[60] In fact this leads to a paradox. As Gilson remarks, art arises for Aquinas when the reason takes an interest in *making* something; the more it is involved in making, so much the more is it an art. And yet, the more it realizes its true essence in the act of making, the less noble it is, and the more the art is a minor one.[61]

It is clear that this type of theory expressed an aristocratic viewpoint. The distinction between servile and liberal arts typified an intellectualistic mentality, for which the highest good was knowledge and contemplation. It reflected the ideology of a feudal and aristocratic society, just as in Greece it had reflected an oligarchical society, in which manual work, usually for wages, inevitably seemed inferior. Social factors made this theory so tenacious that, even when its external presuppositions ceased to hold, it still remained, a stubborn prejudice, difficult to eliminate, as we can see in the furious arguments during the Renaissance about the status of the sculptor.

Perhaps the medievals remembered Quintilian: "the learned understand the nature of art, the unlearned its voluptuousness" ("docti rationem artis intelligunt, indocti voluptatem").[62] Artistic theory provided definitions of art in terms of what could be experienced by the learned, whereas artistic practice and pedagogy had to do with *voluptas*. Any distinction between fine art and craft was prevented by the distinction between liberal and servile arts; and yet, the servile arts were considered as fine arts whenever they were

didactic, purveying truths of faith or of science through the pleasures of the beautiful. In this way, they came to be aligned with
those of the fine arts which were considered to be liberal. The result
was that Aquinas provided no definition of fine art. And, as we
have seen, the idea of an art designed simply to give pleasure was
mentioned only casually. He approved of women's hairstyles, of
games and diversions, and of verbal play and dramatic representations. Yet even here there were practical reasons. It is good, he said,
that a woman should adorn herself to cultivate the love of her hus-
band;[63] and games give delight "in that they lighten the harshness of our labors" ("inquantum auferunt tristitiam quae est ex labore").[64]

Stained glass, music, and sculpture were not beautiful simply
because they gave pleasure. They might give pleasure, or they
might give instruction; but in either case, the medievals took the
view that their true beauty lay in their conformity with their purpose. If a sound was meant to give pleasure, it had to possess proportion not just within itself, but also in respect of the listener, his
psychological needs and his desire for relaxation. A didactic form
possessed beauty not just through its inner proportion, but also
through its proportion to its educational goal. It was only when
these kinds of harmony were found that aesthetic pleasure could
arise.

The meaning and implications of this are clearest when we envis-
age the world in the manner of Thomas Aquinas. In his view, society displays a hierarchy of interrelated values, which are connected
with various ends, some immediate and some remote. Every human action, whether individual or social or supernaturally inclined,
progressively tends to the ultimate end. The drive toward perfection in things is an aspiration, whether conscious or confused, toward God.

> Unumquodque tendens in suam perfectionem, tendit in divi-
> nam similitudinem.

> Everything tending to its own perfection tends toward the di-
> vine likeness.[65]

Productive human actions are not isolated actions, but acquire
value from being part of the life of the City; and the terrestrial City

is an image and anticipation of the City of God. Values are not autonomous, or not in the sense that they are self-sufficient and can be pursued for their own sake. They are defined with reference to their consequences. Thus, although it is true that the *perfectio prima* makes possible the *perfectio secunda* (that is, adequacy to an end), the *perfectio secunda* presupposes, regulates, and actuates the *perfectio prima*.

> Similiter efficiens est prius fine, generatione et tempore, cum ab efficiente fiat motus ad finem; sed finis est prius efficiente in quantum est efficiens in substantia et completo esse, cum actio efficientis non compleatur nisi per finem.

> The efficient cause of a thing is prior to its end, both causally and temporally, for it is the efficient cause that produces movement toward the end. But the end is prior to the efficient cause because it has an effect upon the substance and the completion of its being; for the action of an efficient cause can be completed only through the end.[66]

Human art cannot eschew this hierarchy either. It is the City that gives it birth, and only within the City does it have goodness, truth, and beauty.

The Ambiguity of Art's Autonomy

Some of the things that Aquinas has said have led some people to talk enthusiastically about the autonomy of art. But this is to misunderstand him. Indeed, autonomy would be an absurd notion in a philosophical system based upon order and finality.

Aquinas does write that prudence has the good of mankind as its goal, whereas art aims only at the good of the object which is to be made.

> Bonum autem artificialium non est bonum appetitus humani, sed bonum ipsorum operum artificialium; et ideo ars non praesupponit appetitum rectum.

> The worth of things produced by art, however, does not consist in their being good for human appetite, but in the good of the products of art themselves.[67]

This statement should not be exaggerated. Aquinas defines art as *recta ratio factibilium,* and so, what counts in artistic labor is that the thing should be made well. All he means here is that no extraneous concerns should interfere with the process of manufacture, since its purpose is to give reality to the conceived form.

At this point, however, everything I have been saying about the concept of form should help us to see the issue in its true dimensions. It is completely accurate to say that the purpose of artistic labor is the actualizing of a conceived form in the material, and that there should be no extraneous concerns. But in fact what some might call extraneous concerns are already part of the design of the thing being manufactured. Let us return to Aquinas's example of the saw. The craftsman's job is to construct the saw honestly; his intentions, his mood, and his moral disposition have no bearing upon his work.

> Non enim pertinet ad laudem artificis, inquantum artifex est, qua voluntate opus faciat, sed quale sit opus quod facit.
>
> An artist as such is not commendable for the will with which he makes a work, but for its quality.[68]

However, the concept of a saw includes the notion of its use. A saw is used for sawing, and for sawing well, in the best manner possible, so that it can be of service to mankind. So it is made easy to handle, durable but not cumbersome, suited to the particular conditions of work, physical and social, in which it will be used. In other words, its purpose is also the rule of its manufacture. Its social function is its formal prescription. Its being referrable to something beyond itself becomes a constitutive element in its internal perfection.

The process of formation, then, is autonomous, but not the form itself. Or rather, the form is autonomous if it is understood as a form or perfection which includes a constitutive reference to something beyond itself. There is thus no analogy with such conceptions as "art for art's sake," or beauty as an "insular value" or an oasis, a kind of autonomous moment isolated from the total rhythm of life.[69] Beauty in Aquinas is found only in the interplay of ends; it is a moment within life and moves toward perfection, toward God as final and redemptive cause.

It is only within the general plan of the *Summa* that we can be clear about Aquinas's philosophy of art and beauty. Aquinas was a man of his own time, not our contemporary, and this must be a principle of our method. It is a historiographic principle, and indeed a moral principle for an interpreter, whose duty it is to respect both the texts and his readers. If this is forgotten, we will end by looking in Aquinas for quite absurd things. For example, it is often asked whether Aquinas thought of artistic creation as "imaginative" creation.[70] This is an obvious pseudo-problem, recognized the instant that we recall the very restricted sense of the term *imagination* in Thomistic psychology.[71] The question of art's "creativity" is also misconceived.[72] And so too are attempts to insist that, for Aquinas, the realm of the aesthetic is autonomous in respect of the moral realm, an insistence which is usually intended to make him a more "sympathetic" figure for the modern reader. Some have tried to show that Aquinas conceived of a perfect autonomy for art. For, in the first place, he thinks of beauty as a transcendental, so that anything beautiful is good. Also, when we look at the formal characteristics of beauty, it seems that the only thing required of a beautiful object is that it be formally perfect. As Stephen Daedalus puts it, "Aquinas is certainly on the side of the capable artist. I hear no mention of instruction or elevation."[73] And again, Aquinas asserts in one place that if a work of art lends itself to being enjoyed sinfully, it should be banned from the City;[74] and to this the response is made that Aquinas is not equating what is immoral with what is ugly. Rather, the work of art is beautiful but is banned because it is morally pernicious.

However, none of these arguments has anything more than a merely formal validity when seen in the light of what I said earlier: namely, that for Aquinas the formal concept of a work of art includes the notion of its end as a rule of its perfection. The work has beauty only if it is adequate to its end. The finality of a beautiful work of art involves both pleasure and instruction. If it exceeds or deviates from this type of proportion—if it inspires passion rather than delight or transmits falsehood rather than truth—it is for one and the same reason both ugly and immoral. It is not that the criterion of morality is surreptitiously converted into a criterion of aesthetic value (something that happens often enough in our own times); rather, the criterion of morality *is already* a formal rule of the aesthetic. It is not that moral circumstances alter aesthetic value, nor that aesthetic value alone is realized in the adequacy of a thing to its function. The situation is just the reverse of this. What concerned the medievals was not the specific nature of the aesthetic, but rather the perfection required by a thing's finality; therefore, a breach between art and morality could not occur. Whatever was beautiful was also good, but this did not mean that the good was an asymmetric condition of the beautiful. For the beautiful was also a condition of the good: if a thing is good but cannot be perceived as beautiful, it is imperfect and incomplete, thus not good and not fully suited to its function. And if it is good in itself and suited to its function, it is also beautiful. Neither value is subordinate. A concern for one is also a concern for the other.

Theoretically, therefore, it can also be claimed that a pernicious object—say, a pagan idol made for a blasphemous purpose—is adequate to its function and is therefore beautiful. Aquinas, however, would not have conceived of such a possibility. For the idol is adequate only to its immediate end. When considered in the world of ends as a whole, the idol does not fit harmoniously, but provokes imbalance and disquiet. It is adequate to the transmission of falsehood, but inadequate to mankind and to what is good for him. Its various purposes confer upon it a hideous disharmony, and so an aesthetic disvalue. The idol may be beautiful in color and proportion, but it does not fit in with the harmony of the universe. It stands out like a wrong note. It might be *formosus,* but never *pulcher.*[75]

Aquinas's aesthetic criteria can be used to defend the autonomy of beauty, if they are employed in a different spirit from his own. Joyce, for instance, does this. But the medieval desire for fullness, for perfect harmony, supersedes any such purely formal consideration of beauty. Formal values instead reflect their relations with higher levels in the universal hierarchy of ends.

Conclusions

Aquinas's views on these matters reflect the influence of Aristotle on both the philosophical and the theological levels. They should not be identified at all points with the medieval view in general. Or rather, Aquinas was rigorously aware of the implications of whatever he said, and so blocked off a number of ideas which were entertained in medieval times without having a place in any general system. In fact we must look outside the official philosophical thinking of the period for anomalies and enthusiasms which in time were destined to provoke a new conception of art and the artist.

The historian of medieval art theory should not dwell too much upon the pages of Aquinas. It is more useful to go back to the *Libri Carolini*,[76] where we find the earliest discussion of images, and thus the elements of a theory of iconography, an analysis *ante litteram* of the semiotic relation between iconic signs and their verbal basis, together with a defense in embryo of the autonomy of the artistic image and of the reasons for "pure visibility." It is also necessary to look at the technical manuals written for printers and master glassmakers, such as *De Coloribus et Artibus Romanorum* and *Mappa Clavicula*,[77] or the *Schedula Diversarum Artium* of Theophilus,[78] down to the mature work of Cennino Cennini.[79] There are also the literary manuals, in which we find a gradual emergence of the idea that poetics is an autonomous discipline, distinct from grammar and metrics.[80] There was a critical awakening in the twelfth century, reflected for instance in the works of John of Salisbury; there was also a controversy between *poetria nova* and ancient poetry, involving such movements as verbalism, antitraditionalism, and the school of Orléans.[81] In the twelfth and thirteenth centuries a number of treatises appeared—written by authors such as Matthew of Vendôme, Geoffrey of Vinsauf, Eberhard of Bethune, and John of Garland—in which the theory of art was enriched by observations which, though hardly philosophical (only nowadays would they form part of a philosophical aesthetics), were the product of practical experience. For instance, Geoffrey of Vinsauf spoke about the hardness and resistance of the material, which only strenuous effort could render docile to form.[82] This highlighted the element of struggle and dialogue with the raw material, which Scholastic theory seemed to ignore.[83] New ideas came also from Aristotelian poetics, due to the works of Averroës,[84] who discussed the nature of spectacle and of the imitative arts.[85] The *gaya ciencia* (art of poetry)[86] provided the outlines of a theory of poetic inspiration, which was to make great headway in the period immediately following. Little by little the Scholastic theory of art, with its system, its definitions of a life of practice which was rational and subject to rules discovered by the intellect, gave way to fresh ideas: invention, feeling, and adherence to the prescriptions of nature. Even though the treatises on art still maintained that reason should control the hand of the impetuous,[87] the artists themselves believed in the rules no longer. Chrétien de Troyes tells us that when Percival leaps upon his horse in full armor, it is explained to him that every art needs long and constant application. But the young Welsh knight is not impressed by the view which the whole of the Middle Ages accepted without discussion, and proceeds to acquit himself with the skill of a veteran. The poet explains that nature is responsible: "and when nature teaches us, and the heart is fully intent, nothing can be difficult where nature and the heart strive."[88]

It can be seen that we are here on the threshold of the modern period. But Aquinas's theories made no contribution to this evolution in sensibility and belief. Whatever he was able to give to aesthetics passed along other channels. We must abandon the attempt to reconstruct a Thomistic problematic of art, an attempt which has been made in some quarters without success. We must return instead to the problematic of form; this is where we discover Aquinas in his full philosophical vigor, full of rich suggestions, contradictory perhaps but always stimulating.

This digression on the problems of art has served merely to confirm that even in this area Aquinas's system remains consistent. But it is a system which hinges upon the relation between the three criteria of beauty and the concept of an aesthetic *visio,* a subject to which I return in the next chapter.

VII

Judgment and the Aesthetic *Visio*

The Function of the Aesthetic *Visio*

I said earlier that it was impossible to determine accurately the nature and the function of the aesthetic *visio* in Aquinas, without first of all defining its object. My subsequent analysis of the objective criteria of beauty involved an analysis of the formal character of the beautiful object, and so the general theory of form in its aesthetic aspect. This has been of central importance in clarifying the issue, to the point where an answer to the earlier question may now be sought.

If we take the first of the two problems, the function of *visio*, we can see at once how the analysis of form has amply clarified the question to be asked. The question is: what is the role of *visio* in the perception or the apprehension of beauty? Does it simply *confirm* that its object is in itself aesthetic, or does it *constitute* the object as an aesthetic object?

The act of aesthetic *visio* is an act in which I apprehend a formal reality. The apprehension causes pleasure, and the formal reality possesses clarity, integrity, and proportion. The formal reality is not specifically aesthetic, because proportion and integrity are criteria of ontological perfection or completeness; they pertain to essence and existence, not to the aesthetic. But if we take clarity to mean the capacity in a form to signify its own structure, then we see that form signifies itself as something with integrity and proportion, *but only to a perception of it as, precisely, a structure*. The ontological perfection or completeness of a thing, whenever the thing is looked at as a harmonious form, appears to us as beauty. It is in this sense that we can speak of beauty as the splendor of all the transcendentals together, so long we do not interpret the phrase in a rigidly objectivist manner. The splendor in question is not a "clarity in itself"—for clarity in itself is simply ontological perfection—but "clarity for us."

Beauty appears whenever the *visio* adopts an aesthetic demeanor toward its object; and yet the *visio* does not create beauty, for the objective conditions of beauty really subsist in things. It is therefore fair to say, in a very free paraphrase of Aquinas, that beauty in itself is "a state of equilibration between a perfect object and the intellect."[1] It follows that, even if everything is beautiful, man is not overwhelmed by beauty; he is not burdened by aesthetic harmony so total and continuous that, like the music of the spheres, it becomes irrelevant. Everything has within it the conditions of beauty, but it appears beautiful to us only if we concentrate our attention upon its formal structure.

Everything is beautiful, but this does not mean that we look at everything *sub specie pulchri*. When we do, we experience an ecstatic and fruitful moment, although this can happen only if we know how to quieten the urgencies of our other interests. And at the same time, this ecstatic moment does not make us ignore the basic urgencies of life: purpose, desire, meaning. Rather, it makes us grasp them in their perfection, not in their utility but in the harmonious modalities of their existence. The fact that the object relates to the subject does not mean, as some have claimed, an abolition of beauty's transcendental character. It allows the transcendental to show itself. Though on the other hand, *visio* is not just an affirmation of an aesthetic reality which is subsistent in itself. It is the aesthetic actuation of an ontological perfection which was aesthetic only in potential.

At the same time, and even if the universe possesses its beauty as a potential, human intervention is not indispensable for the transcendental quality in being to become real. For the universe, Aquinas tells us, is always beautiful in the eyes of God. The perfection of being, its beauty and its truth, translates into a beauty which is perennially actuated in God's vision of things and of himself. It is true that Aquinas does not state this explicitly, but it is supported by some of the things which he says about truth. It may be recalled that he distinguishes ontological truth from formal truth. Ontological truth means the very existence of a thing in its own determinate structure (and what else is this, in the end, but its beauty?).[2] Formal truth means the correspondence of a thing to the human intellect.

> Etiamsi intellectus humanus non esset, adhuc res verae dicerentur in ordine ad intellectum divinum. Sed si uterque intellectus, rebus remanentibus per impossibile, intelligeretur auferri, nullo modo ratio veritatis remaneret.

> Even if there were no human intellect, things could be said to be true because of their relation to the divine intellect. But if, by an impossible supposition, intellect did not exist and things continued to exist, then the essentials of truth would in no way remain.[3]

We can infer that, as God looks at things and at himself, with a specifically aesthetic knowledge, he apprehends every thing in its proper perfection, that is, as beautiful. And if *per impossibile* the divine gaze were extinguished, the beauty of the world would fall into darkness. In this way, the transcendental character of beauty combines smoothly with the irreplaceable and indispensable role of the aesthetic *visio*. In this way, Aquinas uses the dialectic of act and potency to evade both objectivism and subjectivism.

The Nature of the Aesthetic *Visio*

But if we now adopt an epistemological standpoint, we may ask: what exactly is the aesthetic *visio*? I have already rejected the view taken by some, that it is an intuition. But this was a view nevertheless which, though mistaken, attempted to cope with a particular need, a need which we can feel weighing upon us.

The need is as follows. When we confront the problem of beauty, we can see that it does not consist merely in sensation, nor in a pure abstraction. Knowledge of beauty is not a knowledge of archetypes, nor of substantial *forms* abstracted from matter. Whether we understand beauty to be the resplendence of form in matter, or think instead of a complete object signifying its organic quality, we always have to define the apprehension of it as an apprehension in which we grasp some principle of organization *of the sensible*. Beauty involves both *form* and a material together.

One answer to our question is this. Aesthetic seeing involves grasping the *form* in the sensible. It therefore occurs prior to the act of abstraction, because in abstraction the *form* is divorced from the sensible. However, we have already seen that knowledge of this type is not envisaged by Aquinas. Also, the act of abstraction, the *simplex apprehensio* through which the intellect formulates concepts, the act of knowledge prior to which the aesthetic intuition is supposed to occur, is in fact the epistemological *primum*. It is a natural, immediately spontaneous act in which, when the eye lights upon an object, the mind instantly takes possession of the seed of intelligibility within the object. This first epistemological step is not an intuition of the concrete, but a knowledge of the universal acquired through the agent intellect. *Simplex apprehensio* is an epistemologically complex act. First of all, an object stimulates our *sensus proprius;* then, it acts upon the *sensus communis;* as a result, it imprints an image of itself upon the senses, and this is a "phantasm." Aquinas says, however, that "phantasms, since they are likenesses of individuals and exist in corporeal organs, do not have the same mode of existence as the human intellect" ("phantasmata, cum sint similitudines individuorum, et existant in organis corporeis, non habent eundem modum existendi quem habet intellectus humanus").[4] So, when a phantasm occurs in the senses, the agent intellect acts upon it and abstracts from it its intelligible species; it then offers this to the possible intellect as a concept.[5] However, this cognitive movement has no chronological structure. It happens instantly and spontaneously. It cannot be divided into steps, not even in the imagination (only the intellect can analyse its parts). When the eye lights on something, the act of abstraction takes place.[6] It is absolutely impossible to posit an intuition of *form* in the concrete, *before* the abstraction.

Could it be the case, then, that aesthetic knowledge occurs *after* abstractive knowledge? And if so, how would it be defined? The situation here is extremely complicated. We are trying to define the modalities of knowledge of aesthetic value, and aesthetic value is rooted in the concreteness of things. But this has to be done within the limits of the Thomistic epistemology, which, as even Aquinas's disciples will admit, does not succeed in solving the problem of our knowledge of concrete individuals.

This is why some commentators introduced the notion of an "aesthetic intuition," as we saw earlier. They felt that Aquinas's system was of permanent relevance, and aesthetic intuition was intended to make some parts of the system more up-to-date and easier to deal with. If, however, we wish to remain within the strict confines of Thomistic philosophy, as we find it in the pages of Aquinas's works, we must reject any such notion as an intuition of *form* in the sensible. In fact the scope for movement within his philosophy is extremely limited.

We must, therefore, ask whether *simplex apprehensio* itself might possibly have an aesthetic character. Abstraction means the knowledge of an intelligible species. It is a type of knowledge which prescinds from individual circumstances, and from whatever accidents may attach themselves to the substance. To be sure, it does not prescind totally from the matter with which the form is linked.

> Unde et intellectus potest intelligere aliquam formam absque individuantibus principiis, non tamen absque materia, a qua dependet ratio illius formae: sicut non potest intelligere simum sine naso.

> The intellect is able to apprehend a form without its individuating principles. But it cannot apprehend it in abstraction from the matter, upon which the nature of the form depends. Thus, it cannot grasp the idea of a snub nose in abstraction from the nose.[7]

In this sense, knowledge of an abstract universal entails some reference to the matter in which the universal is made concrete.

> Ex cognitione formarum quae determinant sibi materiam cognoscitur etiam ipsa materia aliquo modo, scilicet secundum habitudinem quam habet ad formam.

> The knowledge of forms which are determinants of matter gives us some degree of knowledge of the matter, insofar as it is disposed to receive form.[8]

So if the apprehension of the beautiful consisted simply in this awareness of matter's engagement with form, the act of *simplex apprehensio* would provide the conditions for an aesthetic judgment. But the awareness of matter would be very slight, for Aquinas refers to it above as knowledge *aliquo modo*—that is, a rudimentary and approximate knowledge. Certainly, the concrete object does not come to be known in the act of abstraction. We are obliged to note, however, that the intellect attains to a certain knowledge of particulars as a result of abstraction, to be exact in the "reflection upon the phantasm" to which Aquinas often refers.

> Mens singulare cognoscit per quandam reflexionem, prout scilicet, mens cognoscendo obiectum suum, quod est aliqua natura universalis, redit in cognitionem sui actus, et ulterius in specimen quae est sui actus principium, et ulterius in phantasma a quo species est abstracta: et sic aliquam cognitionem de singulari accipit.

> The mind knows singulars through a certain kind of reflection, as when the mind, in knowing its object, which is some universal nature, returns to knowledge of its own act, then to the species which is the principle of its act, and, finally, to the phantasm from which it has abstracted the species. In this way, it attains to some knowledge about singulars.[9]

> Unde intellectus noster non directe ex specie quam suscipit, fertur ad cognoscendum phantasma, sed ad cognoscendum rem cuius est phantasma. Sed tamen per quandam reflexionem redit etiam in cognitionem ipsius phantasmatis, dum considerat naturam actus sui, et speciei per quam intuetur, et eius a quo speciem abstrahit, scilicet phantasmatis . . . Inquantum ergo intellectus noster per similitudinem quam accepit a phantasmate, reflectitur in ipsum phantasma a quo speciem abstraxit, quod est similitudo particularis, habet quamdam cognitionem de singulari secundum continuationem quamdam intellectus ad imaginationem.

> Consequently, from the species which it receives, our intellect is not applied directly to knowing the phantasm but rather the thing whose phantasm is presented. Nevertheless, by a certain reflection our intellect also returns to a knowledge of the phantasm itself when it considers the nature of its act, the nature of the species by which it knows, and, finally, the nature of that from which it has abstracted from the species, namely, the phantasm . . . Therefore, inasmuch as our intellect, through the likeness which it receives from the phantasm, turns back

upon the phantasm from which it abstracts the species, the phantasm being a particular likeness, our intellect gets some kind of knowledge of the singular because of its dynamic union with the imagination.[10]

But this kind of knowledge of the individual is markedly incomplete. Also, it fails to satisfy the requirements for an aesthetic experience. We have seen in earlier chapters what it is that we seek in an object if we are to contemplate it *sub specie pulchri*. We seek a complex formal reality, involving a structural tension among its elements—and not just among its empirical-physical elements, as if it were a wooden scaffolding, but also and especially in its metaphysical structure. Proportion is not just a concordance among the sensible parts: this is only one kind of proportion, and one of the most elementary. Proportion is something much more radical than that. By now we are familiar with its various kinds: the suitability of matter for the requirements of its *form,* a compatibility between accidental *forms* and the possibilities inherent in substantial *form,* and a compatibility between essence and existence, between a thing and its own nature, between action and the rational guide of action, between discourse and the principles of reason, and so on and so forth. Integrity, then, consists in the adequacy of a thing for what its nature determines that it ought to be. When we grasp its integrity we measure it against the concept of it and focus upon the perfect accord between what it is and what it ought to be. It is necessary, in short, to have a very profound knowledge of the object.

Looking at an object aesthetically means looking at its structure, physical and metaphysical, as exhaustively as possible, in all its meanings and implications, and in its proportionate relations to its own nature and to its accidental circumstances. It means, that is, a kind of *reasoning about* the object, scrutinizing it in detail and in depth. Only then can it be appreciated in its harmony and its formal structure.

We are thus compelled to come to the following conclusion. Aesthetic seeing does not occur before the act of abstraction, nor in the act, nor just after it. It occurs instead at the end of the second operation of the intellect—that is, *in the judgment.*

An examination of some passages in Aquinas will show us that judgment is the only act which can produce the exhaustive knowledge of a thing which is necessary if we are to contemplate it *sub specie pulchri*.

> Intellectus humanus non statim in prima apprehensione capit perfectam rei cognitionem; sed primo apprehendit aliquid de ipsa, puta quidditatem ipsius rei, quae est primum et proprium objectum intellectus; et deinde intelligit proprietates et accidentia et habitudines circumstantes rei essentiam. Et secundum hoc, necesse habet unum apprehensum alii componere vel dividere.

> The human intellect does not immediately, in first apprehending a thing, have complete knowledge; rather, it first apprehends only one aspect of the thing—namely, its whatness [*quidditas*], which is the primary and proper object of the intellect—and only then can it understand the properties, accidents, and relationships incidental to the thing's essence. Accordingly, it must necessarily either combine one apprehension with another or separate them.[11]

To see an object as beautiful we must discern its formal aspects, in their completeness. But seeing its completeness or perfection means seeing its ontological truth; it means judging it to be true, or predicating truth of it, by making our judgment adequate to that truth. Judgment says "This is so and so" in the sense that *this* is so and so, this *is* so and so, and *it is true* that this is so and so. In its logical aspect, judgment "is found primarily in an act of the intellect joining and separating, rather than in an act by which it forms the quiddities of things" ("prius invenitur in actu intellectus componentis et dividentis quam in actu intellectus quidditates rerum formantis").[12]

Judgment involves joining and separating, and the marking out of properties, accidents, and contexts. It is only by way of this kind of knowledge that I can measure accidental against substantial *form*, substantial *form* against its matter, the object against its function, and so on. During the course of abstractive knowing, my senses may be stimulated by sensible proportion, and I may experience an instinctive pleasure in it. But it is only in the act of judgment that I can determine whether a proportion measures up to my capacity to experience it and to my psychological needs, and whether it also conforms with (say) the laws of music and is adequate to what its nature demands. A quick and easy submission to the allure of harmony in shape and color can produce a pleasure that is aesthetic in embryo. But genuine, complete aesthetic pleasure occurs when we grasp the reasons for the harmony, the various ways in which it is realized, and all of its most intricate inner workings. This type of understanding comes about gradually; it relates to its object in such a way that a state of judgment, of one kind or another, precedes the flowering of aesthetic pleasure.

My consciousness has before it an interplay of structures, multiple interrelations of forms which combine into ever more inclusive forms. This profound and complex rule-governed order is something that I cannot grasp fully in an instant. I have to compare and separate, in a series of judgments which predicate of things their reality and their categorical richness.

This rule-governed order includes the proportion between essence and existence—a proportion rooted at such an ontological depth that its fundamental importance can be overlooked. But my seeing of a thing implies my determining that it has a structure of such a kind, and such a completeness, that the thing *is there*. Even in the case of an accidental, artificial form—say, a statue—it displays its most basic perfection to me when I grasp it as a subsisting thing, as a thing born to exist and maintained in existence, due to the formal stability which its maker has given it. Otherwise, it would collapse into nothingness, or reduce to the piece of marble that it originally was. But this essential preliminary determination of the thing's subsistence can be effected only in the judgment. Only the judgment leads me to the act of existence, the *ipsum esse* of a thing, permitting me to say: it is there.

> Prima operatio respicit quidditatem rei; secunda respicit esse ipsius.
>
> The first operation [of the intellect] considers the whatness [*quidd023itas*] of a thing; the second operation considers its being.[13]

Again, the mutual compatibility of substantial *form* and matter, and their coming to completion in a substance, is something that is fully manifest only to judgment. The forming of a judgment indicates that a particular *form* or act actually exists in a subject. The judgment "This is a tree" means that the property of being a tree belongs to some subject as its constitutive act. It means that I am considering the property of being a tree, not in an abstract way, but as something individuated, actual, and concrete in the object of the judgment; and I am able to enjoy the formal perfection of the tree only when I observe the manner and the degree in which the property is made concrete. The judgment that an object possesses integrity is also expressed by such judgments as "This is a tree." For the judgment signifies "This object presents itself to me as a tree because it is fully and harmoniously and truly adequate to our conception of a tree."

The intellect scrutinizes a thing in its objective truth in order to grasp it accurately and adequately. It strives to define the object, to explore it in its depths and in its meaning, in its substantial and its accidental structure. It knows the object in analytic detail, sees it as true, desires it as good. During the quest for the judgment of truth, there may well be concern for an aesthetic outcome; but a disinterested perception, concentrated upon formal values, occurs only after the judgment. Only then is there an aesthetic experience.

Aquinas uses the term *apprehensio* as well as *visio*. This is not a mistake, even though it suggests something immediate and nondiscursive. For the aesthetic *visio* is not the same thing as the *compositio*—the combining operation—which is a part of judgment. It is, rather, an "apprehension" of the structural harmony which *compositio* has brought to light. Thus, every intellectual endeavor which culminates in judgment has, in some degree, an aesthetic outcome. There is a striving, a laboring to become adequate to the truth of things, an intellectual toil. Then, when the labor stills itself in definition, the object delivers itself to aesthetic perception. We should recall again what Aquinas said about peace, the tranquillity of an order when it has been realized.

> Appetitum terminari ad bonum et pacem et pulchrum non est terminari in diversa.
>
> If appetite terminates in good and peace and the beautiful, this does not mean that it terminates in different goals.[14]

On the ontological level, peace is the perfection achieved when being is subjected to order. It means things becoming stable in form. It is a balance of energies. On the epistemological level, peace means the total delight of a contemplative perception which, freed from desire and effort, experiences love of the harmony which the intellectual judgment has shown to it.

> Pax autem importat remotionem perturbantium et impedientium adeptionem boni.

> Peace implies the removal of disturbances and obstacles to the obtaining of good.[15]

I cannot, therefore, agree with Maritain that aesthetic pleasure is a total, complete kind of pleasure because it is experienced prior to the labor of abstraction. On the contrary, aesthetic pleasure is total and complete because it is connected with a cessation of the efforts of abstraction and judgment. It signifies, not an *absence,* but a *cessation,* of effort. It is a sense of joy and triumph, of pleasure in a form which has been discerned, admired, and loved with a disinterested love, the love which is possible for a formal structure.[16] Here is Pareyson again.

> Interpretation has two aspects. On the one hand, it is an active process intended to grasp the true meaning of things, to fix the meaning in an image that is penetrating and exhaustive, to give it a shape that is vigorous and adequate . . . This process tends toward a state of quietude in which it stops and rests; and this is, precisely, the second aspect of interpretation. For on the other hand, interpretation means quietude and stasis—the quiet of discovery and success, the stasis of possession and satisfaction. . . . The eye, which before this was sharpening its gaze, now just looks and admires, intent, satisfied. It rests with pleasure upon the whole and upon the parts, happy to have discovered the law of coherence which gathers everything into a definite totality. It is contented at having understood the heart and nerve center and the nature of the breath which animates the form which it has put to the question.[17]

So, the final answer to the question of the aesthetic in Thomas Aquinas seems to have a paradoxical form; or so it seems in the light of modern aesthetics. The aesthetic *visio* comes to birth as a culmination and completion of intellectual knowledge at its most complex level. Beauty, in Aquinas's aesthetics, is not the fruit of psychological empathy, nor of the imaginative transfiguration or creation of an object. Instead, it sinks its roots deep into a complex knowledge of being. And so, intellectual travail is a necessary pathway to the knowledge of beauty.

VIII

Conclusion

The Central *Aporia* in Aquinas's Aesthetics

When Aquinas's aesthetic theory is considered in the light of the concept of form, it acquires, as we have seen, an organic quality. If parts of it are missing because not explicitly stated, it can be completed nonetheless through the relations and connections which belong to the system as a whole.

But let us look at what this entails. If we locate things in a certain system, which the system itself has not developed but which we can develop ourselves by following its internal logic, we may well arrive at conclusions which put the system into question. A medieval *summa* can be regarded as a kind of computer. If we put questions to it in the right way, it may well deliver answers which were unforeseen—but some of these answers may contradict the rules with which the computer operates.

If this were to happen to a computer, it would very likely have a breakdown. Medieval thinkers no doubt had a greater capacity for recuperation. They would in fact have had recourse to an *auctoritas*—some authoritative figure who could provide the justification for an eventual restructuring of the system, or who could furnish an appropriate quotation for covering up the contradiction.

Nowadays we are not inclined to attribute fantastical properties to the medieval computer-*summa*. What we do find in it is yet another demonstration of Gödel's theorem: every formal system has within it a little logical termite which nibbles away at it and spoils its perfect self-sufficiency. Aquinas's aesthetic system does not escape this fate—all the more, perhaps, because it achieved the highest possible degree of consistency.

Let us look at how this happens. The system shows (1) that every kind of form, terrestrial or supernatural, natural or artistic, can be an object of aesthetic experience; and (2) that natural substances are ontologically prior to artificial forms, divine creation prior to human productions. Thus, human productions are beautiful only in a superficial sense; their aesthetic value is deficient, as it were, in ontological density.

If all being is beautiful, and if beauty is grounded in the formal structure of the object of aesthetic *visio,* it follows that all being can become beautiful if looked at in this manner. But *can* it be looked at in this manner? An object is objectively beautiful if it is adequate to what it is supposed to be, and if it expresses what it is. We experience its beauty when we understand the manner in which it is adequate to itself, that is, when we see how it is proportionate to its function and to whatever is necessary for it to exist. It was not without reason that I claimed that the intellectual judgment is a necessary preliminary to aesthetic perception. To prepare ourselves for aesthetic perception we need a deep and exhaustive knowledge of the object; we must grasp its integrity and measure its reality against our concept of it.

However, the formal structure of a natural object is so complex that we know it fully only with the greatest difficulty. Philosophical investigation is a continuous, progressive endeavor to attain to a knowledge of things—yet it will never be "substantial knowledge," the knowledge which their Creator has of them. But it is certainly the case that the kind of knowledge that is needed for aesthetic experience is just this substantial knowledge, this creator's knowledge. With this kind of knowledge, we could grasp the object in all the complexity of its proportions, following the process in which they were acquired, and we could grasp its integrity because we would have a clear idea of what the object is supposed to be. But of course it is God who "informs" matter and guides the intimate coalescence of form and matter into a substantial reality; and it is God who measures the created object against his own eternal idea of it. Therefore, only God has the kind of knowledge of the formal structure of being which permits the perception of it *sub specie pulchri.*

When human beings look at the beauties of nature, they submit to the attractions of accidental form, the partial beauty of shape, of *figurae,* of surfaces. Most of the time they do not grasp the deep, substantial type of beauty, the beauty which consists in ontological perfection. It is extremely rare for man to be able to give this kind of total aesthetic judgment. Normally, it seems to be possible only for God or for angelic intellects.

The situation is different in the case of artificial form. Accidental form is so constituted that it is far more easily grasped. Aquinas writes, "Substantial forms are unknown to us in themselves; they are known through accidents" ("formae substantiales, quae secundum se sunt nobis ignotae, innotescunt per accidentia").[1] Accidents are immediately manifest, whereas substantial form has to be sought out, as a deep-seated matrix underlying surface phenomena. Also, mankind is disposed to find artificial forms the most congenial of the accidental forms.

> Formae artificiales accidentia sunt, quae sunt magis nota, quoad nos, quam formae substantiales, utpote sensui propinquiora.
>
> Artificial forms are accidents. They are known better by us than are substantial forms, because they are nearer to our senses.[2]

When the human intellect has an artificial form as its object, it has to employ a principle of order which is purely accidental. It is not the type of order which confers being upon the subject, but rather the order or design which gives it shape or figure. And the origin of this design is what Aquinas referred to as the form in the mind of its maker, *forma in mente artificis*. This is a human idea or conception which we find it easy to trace out, which we find to be knowable because it is connatural and congenial to us.

The maker knows his own work in its formation. But the process of divine creation is unknowable; all we can do is admire its effects. It is only the productive processes of human makers that we can retrace and comprehend. The practical intellect has a causal relation to objects and is therefore commensurate with those objects. Our understanding of forms that are accidental and artificial is such that we can easily infer the rules of production from the product of the rules. Artificial form thus emerges, from Aquinas's system, as something which is aesthetically more congenial to mankind than natural form. The beauty of artistic creations is more immediately perceivable; they belong more fully to the human world of the aesthetic.

By contrast, natural forms are beautiful in the eyes of God, but deductive necessity dictates that they *must* be closed off to human eyes. Aquinas's system *requires* him to make this claim, although it is not a claim which he himself has in mind. Nature must display the fullness of its proper perfection by its *claritas:* the existence of clarity is required by the system, but the system also requires that clarity *must* be in fact beyond our grasp. If we believed that we had grasped it, this would be a sign that our knowledge was not complete, not exhaustive. Aesthetic pleasure caused by natural forms is possible in theory, but, in virtue of the same theory, it is impossible in practice. Aesthetic pleasure caused by artificial forms is impossible in theory, but, in virtue of the same theory, it is the only such pleasure that the theory regards as a practical possibility.

This is the logical outcome of a process of deduction carried out according to the logic of the system. And it contradicts the system.

In compensation, we find here some explanation of why the Humanist culture of late medieval times destroyed the system from within. In fact it was only when post-Thomistic aesthetics called into question his concept of natural organic form, and of absolute substantial unity, that the circle of contradiction was broken. Out of the break there arose a new conception of art and beauty.

In the following pages I shall briefly indicate how this break occurred, and what came of it. I shall concern myself exclusively with what followed Aquinas chronologically, and not with what might be construed to solve his contradictions, or to subsume or improve upon his views. I am not engaging in speculative aesthetics, merely following the historical development of a problem.

The Dissolution of the Concept of Form in Post-Thomistic Scholasticism

John Duns Scotus defined beauty as follows.

> Pulchritudo non est aliqua qualitas absoluta in corpore pulchro sed est aggregatio omnium convenientium tali corpori, puta magnitudinis, figurae et coloris aggregatio omnium respectuum qui sunt istorum ad corpus et per se invicem.

> Beauty is not some kind of absolute quality in the beautiful object. It is rather an aggregate [*aggregatio*] of all the properties of such objects—for example, magnitude, shape, and color, and the sum of all the connections among themselves and between themselves and the object.[3]

Here, the term *aggregatio* might seem to refer us to the theory of proportion, except that Duns Scotus denies that beauty is an "absolute quality," and denies therefore that it is a substantial *form* inhering in the object as a whole. The reason for this becomes clear if we remember the Scotist doctrine that there is a plurality of forms. The unity of a composite object does not require a unity of *form*, but only the subordination of the forms of the parts, none of which is annulled, to an ultimate *form*.[4] This is just the opposite of Aquinas: one thinks of Aquinas's discussion of mixed bodies, where, in order to salvage something of the powers of the *forms* included in the composite, he had to engage in some tricky maneuvering. This was because his system could not allow the forms of the parts to retain any autonomy, within the shadow as it were of the composite's substantial *form*.

It is clear that, if one insists upon the existence of a relational structure of autonomous *forms,* the conception of beauty will become a more analytical one. And this analytical quality is further affected by another theory of Duns Scotus's, the theory of *haecceitas,* or "thisness." *Haecceitas* is an individuating property. Its function is not that of perfecting *form*—which cannot be other than universal—but rather of giving to the whole composite a concrete particularity, uniquely individual with respect to every other composite. It is quite different from Aquinas's *quidditas,* or "whatness," which makes substance exemplify a category, the typical rather than the individual. *Haecceitas* is a principle which completes a thing to the point where it is irreducibly concrete. "The ultimate specific difference," says Duns Scotus, "is simply to be different from everything else" ("ultima differentia specifica est primo diversa ab alia").[5] Particulars, therefore, are superior to essences. In Aquinas, the particular was more perfect than universal *form* because it had existence. In Duns Scotus, it is more perfect because it is a unique thing which is defined by its uniqueness. For Duns Scotus, something is included in the nature of the individual (*ratio individui*) which is lacking in shared nature (*natura communis*).

Illud autem inclusum est entitas positiva. Et facit unum cum natura. Ergo est per se praedeterminans illam naturam ad singularitatem.

It includes positively being something [*entitas positiva*]. This makes it one with nature. Therefore, nature is predetermined to particularity.[6]

We might wish at this point to examine whether this assertion of the absolute particularity of substance was homologous with the types of art which were contemporary with it. Aquinas's philosophy would seem more akin to the art of classical Gothic, which tended to represent the typical. Duns Scotus's would seem to be the philosophy of Flamboyant Gothic, with its liking for the particular, for individuality in the person, for a detailed and analytical mode of vision, for a sense of particularity opposed to the grand and unifying works of the preceding period. However, making connections of this kind is always dangerous. It is difficult to establish a point-by-point correspondence between theoretical propositions and works of art, just because they happen to be contemporary.[7] I shall therefore confine myself to noting that the theory of *haecceitas* would imply that we do not grasp a *form* by means of a purely intellectual act, but in an intuition; whereas the intellect, which can know particulars only in a confused manner, has to fall back upon universal concepts.[8] This shows that Scotist theory brings us to a new aesthetic world, even if Scotus himself did not care to follow his own principles to their ultimate conclusions.

We come next to William of Ockham. For Ockham, created things are absolutely contingent, and there is no regulation of things by ideas in the mind of God. Thus, it is no longer possible to conceive of a stable order in the universe. And if this is lacking, there is no conformity between the laws of the universe and the laws governing our perceptions, and the maker of things has no exemplary ideas to inspire him.

In Ockham's world, there is no "chain binding bodies together" ("quasi quoddam ligamen ligans corpora"). Bodies are absolutes, numerically distinct: "they do not become one because of their number" ("non faciunt unam rem numero"). The order that holds among them expresses their mutual relations, but not an essence which unifies them.[9] For Aquinas, form was a rational principle which organized the parts of a thing, fusing together with them in a particular—although, as an object of knowledge, it was separate from that particular. In Aquinas's theory, we are able to grasp the way in which the universal *form* combines with matter determined by quantity (*signata quantitate*) to produce the particular; but our grasp of the thing as an individual occurs only because we grasp its essence. Once the essence is known, the judgment can predicate of it that it subsists in *this particular* substance, and investigate it in all its relations. For Ockham, by contrast, the parts of an object are arranged in a certain manner, but "there is no object other than those complete parts" ("praeter illas partes absolutas nulla res est").[10] To be sure, there is a proportion of the parts to the whole,[11] but the notion involved here is much more rudimentary than the Thomistic concept of proportion which I have sought to expound in all its ontological richness.

It might still be possible, in the case of Ockham, to talk about "integrity" in things. But it is difficult to see how, if integrity implies universals, and universals are done away with by Ockham's nominalism. And again, it is hard to see how we can speak about beauty as a transcendental, if distinctions in terms of form and capacity can no longer be made. Ockham affirms that we can have intuitions of particulars;[12] but the maker's idea of the object which he wants to make is an idea of a single example of the thing, and not of its universal form.

We come finally to Nicholas of Autrecour and his critique of the concepts of causality, of substance, and of finality. This critique deprives the principles of Aquinas's aesthetics of their meaning. It affirms that we cannot know a cause from its effects; that one thing cannot be an end for another; that there are no hierarchical degrees of being, and things are simply different from other things; and that the judgments in which we arrange being in a hierarchy are just expressions of personal preference. If all of this were true, there would be no foundation for predications of organic unity, nor of dependence, appropriateness, adequacy for a purpose, *perfectio prima* and *perfectio secunda,* and so on.[13] Neither Ockham nor Nicholas of Autrecour discussed aesthetics; but we can see that they opened new pathways for philosophy. It was natural enough that after them, after the crisis of Scholasticism, anyone interested in the problems of art and beauty would find it easy to adopt positions such as those of Mannerism. Concepts such as wit and felicity underlined the particularity and uniqueness of beautiful things and of aesthetic experience. They indicated the same properties in the experience of artistic creation; now one could genuinely speak of art as "creative," rather than as imitative or merely productive.

This brief survey is the merest introduction to quite a different topic, namely the birth of modern conceptions of art. But it might be risky to stop at just this point, just when I have indicated the lines of fracture which caused a crisis in Scholasticism and opened up new perspectives. It is risky at least in this sense, that every chapter in the history of philosophy is constantly in danger of infection by Idealism (which is at the same time an aestheticizing tendency). Thus, historians are tempted to present philosophy as an epic poem or a bourgeois novel of the nineteenth century. We are shown the rise and fall of philosophies, the triumph of a rationality which is immanent in the forms of thought; and its various stages follow one another, not by chance, but in a dialectic in which each stage supersedes the stage preceding it. Thus, for example, Eckhart's theory of the image could be said to represent the "truth" of the matter, to translate the problems of art and beauty to a "more mature" level, and to put an end to the primitive, disingenous beginnings represented by the Scholastic systems.

In contrast to this vice of Idealist historiography, there is an opposite vice, one against which I have been struggling in this book. It is the neo-Scholastic vice of attempting to rescue, whole and entire, a body of thought which is valid and consistent only when applied to the problems of its own period.

It is difficult, but not impossible, to find a middle way between these two. But in order to do so, it is necessary to keep two things in mind, one historical, the other methodological. First of all, whenever a system of thought disintegrates, this never occurs just because an internal dialectical explosion, purely on the level of thought alone, produces contradictions within it, and causes it to be nullified in whatever supersedes it. Any system comes about as a response to specific social, political, and cultural questions, and to solicitations which are implicit in the relations of production and are mediated through the superstructure. Therefore, when a system breaks down, it does not do so just from within. It breaks down because of something *outside* it.

This indicates the conditions under which a system enters a state of crisis. But at the same time, it means refusing to countenance the complete disappearance of the mode of thought in question. If similar conditions should arise again, some of the forms of argument and systematic correlations might well recover their effectiveness. Historical reconstruction helps to restore the model of a particular way of thinking and, therefore, an image of one possible form that the world can have. In certain social and cultural circumstances, this can provide the conceptual instruments by means of which we can validly construct additional images of the world, in situations which are at least partly homologous.

This historical procedure immediately becomes the instrument of a method of theoretical analysis. Every so often we can usefully revisit our models of the thinking of the past and try out in new circumstances the conceptual instruments which at one time proved effective. Or we may discover that in fact we are already using them without knowing it. Thus, the reconstructed model can help us to avoid pathways which have already been found to lead nowhere, or it can indicate how to take new paths in a critical manner.

This is the twofold manner in which I now want to give an estimate of Aquinas's aesthetics: an estimate of what it was in its time, and of the ways in which it entered upon a crisis; and an estimate of his model for aesthetics, of what it can still say to us today.

Aesthetic Categories and Medieval Society

It seems to me that Aquinas's aesthetics was the most mature aesthetics which was possible for the medieval period. It represents the culmination of a long process of development. And yet, it came just at a point when new circumstances were changing the cultural conditions of philosophy.

To see how Aquinas brought medieval aesthetics to its peak, it is not enough just to look at the maturity of his ideas and methods. We must look also at the context in which the themes and methods were formed, and at how, even as Aquinas brought them to maturity, the context was changing. The new context functioned as a "code" for a philosophical message, and the traditional ideas being used by Aquinas had changed their meaning because of the changing context. A medieval philosopher could not be aware of this, for he lacked a sense of historical development in ideas and in systems of meaning. He operated with cultural entities such as classes, definitions, and names, but believed them to be ontological entities. He used a language inherited from tradition and believed that by making it consistent, within a system, he was putting it in the place assigned to it *ab aeterno*. But history, of course, had already assigned it a different place. It had altered in its meaning; tradition had not bestowed an atemporal deposit. Medieval aesthetics had undergone a development, even if for centuries it had manipulated the same concepts. The situation was changing under the very feet of the philosophers using the concepts, and the concepts changed in meaning, in function, and in efficacy, along with the situation. It is meaningless to say that there was a kind of transhistorical homogeneity in medieval aesthetics, just because Augustine and Denis the Carthusian both spoke of "beauty." It might as well be said that the concept of the state was no different in monarchical Rome and the kingdom of Burgundy because in both cases people used the word *king*.

If we restore to this supposedly perennial language its true historical character, we find that medieval aesthetics acquires a different sense. The history of its development takes on an interesting similarity to the history of European society in the centuries extending from the early Middle Ages to the collapse of Scholasticism.

This history began with a Pythagorean aesthetics of number, which was a reaction to the disorder of the barbarian invasions, and passed on to the "humanistic" aesthetics of the Carolingian Renaissance, which was mindful of the value of art and the beauty of the classical heritage. Then, with the emergence of a stable political order, there emerged also a systematic theological ordering of the universe; and once the crisis of the year 1000 was past, aesthetics became a philosophy of cosmic order. This was due to the earlier influence of Eriugena, representative of a northwestern culture already rich and mature even during the pre-Carolingian darkness. Then, while Europe was covering itself "with a white mantle of churches," the Crusades disturbed the provincialism of medieval life. The communal war effort produced a new civic consciousness, and philosophy opened itself to the myth of nature. People began to take a more scientific interest in natural objects, and beauty changed from being a property of the ideal order to being a property of concrete particulars. During the period between Origen, who insisted upon the physical ugliness of Christ, and the thirteenth-century theologians who made of Christ a dazzlingly beautiful prototype for artistic images, there was a maturing of the Christian ethos and the birth of a theology of the things of the earth. The cathedrals expressed the world of the *summae,* where everything was in its proper place: God and his angelic cohorts, the Annunication and the Last Judgment, death, human crafts, nature, even the devil, all subsumed in an order which measured and drew them within the circle of the substantial positivity of creation expressed in form.

At the high point of its evolution, medieval civilization attempted to capture the eternal essences of things, beauty as well as everything else, in clear if complex definitions. But this followed centuries of effort, for they still believed in a humanism of the eternal. In fact things were changing, and while philosophers were capturing essences, it appeared to the eyes of experience and of science that the essences had already changed. Systematic theory necessarily lagged behind these ferments and the tensions of practical life, and perfected its aesthetic image of political and theological order just when this order was being threatened on all sides: by nationalism, by vernacular languages, by a new type of mysticism, by social agitation, by theoretical doubts. At a certain point, Scholasticism—the doctrine of a universal Catholic state of which the *summae* were the constitution, the cathedrals the encyclopedias, and the University of Paris the capital—had to confront vernacular poetry (with Petrarch despising the "barbarians" of Paris), together with ferments of heresy and the *devotio moderna.*

Scholastic aesthetics could no longer serve, either for the northern medievalism then on the move, or for the new world which had in the meantime come to birth in Italy. This was a world in which Platonism and magic provided new explanations of the invisible, and in which the practice of humane letters had already for some time offered new and different kinds of guarantees and certainties.

There was also a new merchant class, which sought for its own forms of order—empirical, sectional, situational—since it was unable to see itself in that image of universal order of which Aquinas's aesthetics was a perfect model. It was unable to see itself, because the Thomistic model expressed the ideology of a system of relations of production, and a system of political relations, which they, the new men, were beginning to annul.

Scholasticism, and Aquinas himself together with his aesthetics, entered into crisis. This did not happen only because it produced within itself, as I showed earlier, its own internal logical contradictions. It happened also because it no longer corresponded to the people who had to employ it as an instrument of knowledge in their everyday lives. To be sure, Riegl has shown, in his study of the art of late antiquity,[14] that the aesthetic theories of a given period are an indication of its *Kunstwollen:* the formal characteristics of an art are reflected in the theoretical consciousness of its contemporaries; the concrete methods of making works of art, even styles, can be seen as models homologous with the historical situation in their own period. However, this correspondence functions only on some levels; on others, disparities may appear. The order in Aquinas's theological system reflected the architectural order in cathedrals—Panofsky is correct on this point[15]—and both were reflections of the order in a theocratic imperial system. But this political system no longer reflected the economic and social relations of the time. Many of the works of art gathered inside and outside the cathedrals were already pointing in new directions. They no longer corresponded rigorously to the various structural schemas just referred to.

In this way, medieval aesthetic theories could suddenly lose their significance. Often what they said was so general, and so perfect in its logical context, that they could refer to everything and to nothing. Their philosophy of beauty appears cut off from artistic practice as if by a sheet of glass. On the one hand there was a geometrically rational schema of what beauty ought to be, and on the other the unmediated life of art with its dialectic of forms and intentions. Still, this verbalism or "Idealism" of medieval aesthetics expressed the dualistic mentality of the age, its continuous tension between the theory of what ought to be the case and the contradictions of life. This dualism was a paradoxical aspect of a civilization which could make a public spectacle of the most extreme ferocity and wickedness, and which yet lived according to a code of piety, firm in its belief in God and sincere in its pursuit of a moral ideal which it contravened with great facility and candor. Nowadays we look at this rather critically. We take note of the contradictory aspects in their behavior and are unable to reconcile, within a single orthodoxy, Héloise and the characters in Chaucer, Boccaccio, and Gilles de Rais. But medieval philosophers tended to stress the points of convergence and unity, overcoming the contradictions by faith and hope. Their aesthetics, like all medieval thought, expressed an optimum convergence and looked at the world with the eyes of God.

The crisis arose when, in the late medieval period, man realized that God's interests (the God of Scholasticism, that is) did not coincide with his own interests. His own thinking on aesthetics was opposed to the theoretical system then associated with the notion of art, for it included a conception of the artist as an inventor and creator, someone who no longer submitted to the eternal laws of *recta ratio factibilium*. This was a change which had come about because, in everyday life, the citizens of the new self-governing communities were asserting their freedom and creativity as administrators, merchants, bankers, or independent artisans. In economic and political matters, they were turning their backs upon the various kinds of *recta ratio agibilium* which had been propounded in medieval ethics as if they were unique and unchangeable. The internal logic of a system of thought reveals its contradictions only in conjunction with these kinds of external factors. Otherwise, they can remain hidden almost indefinitely. Philosophy is skillful at keeping them in place, if life does not bring them to light.

This, then, is why the theoretical developments which I briefly indicated in the last section came about. Curiously, they seem rather like forerunners of modern aesthetics. And in fact, modern aesthetics conforms with a cognitive model brought to completion by the bourgeois society which was emerging at the time that medieval aesthetics was in crisis. Nonetheless, only an Idealist historian would claim that the new developments were logically more mature than Scholasticism, or more "true" in some theoretical sense. Modern aesthetics has constructed, out of these beginnings, various systems of thought which are just as detached from their historical circumstances as were those of the Scholastics. A barrier separated Aquinas's philosophy of beauty, and his conception of the artist as someone obediently applying the rules laid down by God, from his concrete historical circumstances. A similar barrier divides the modern conception of the artist—free, a creator, originator of independent worlds, priest of the Higher Reality of the Imagination—from the actual facts. These facts are: the commercialism of art, the dependence of the imagination upon technology, the materialist critique, the discoveries of Freud, the implications of cultural anthropology. The relation of Croce's aesthetics to the social realities of the Italy of his time was about as close as the relation of Aquinas's system of thought to the Magna Carta.

Whenever philosophy claims, "This is how things really are," it performs an act of mystification. Aquinas's image of an immutable reality was mystificatory, when confronted with facts that demanded something quite different. The image of reality found in modern aesthetics is also mystificatory, when confronted with other facts. We cannot say that either is an improvement on the other: each is a different and independent response made by the type of philosophy which wants to set before us a world which it has fully "explained"—rather than to change the world in knowing it, and to know it in changing it.

This brings us to the second element in my estimate of Aquinas's aesthetics. If we cannot say that one system of thought is more or less true than another, if all systems represent the effort to rationalize the historical relations found at a particular moment in the development of Western society, then they are all of equal value. Medieval and modern aesthetics are of equal value, provided that they are taken as explanatory models to point us in new directions, as a machinery with which to face the problems that now confront us.

I can therefore suggest a number of reasons why the model provided by Scholastic aesthetics is worth revisiting today. It offers us ways of explaining art in terms of intellect, as opposed to the emotivism of Romantic aesthetics. It offers us a more flexible conception of the relation between inventiveness in production and the rules of production, also the relation between materials and formal imperatives, and between the autonomy of aesthetic value and functional requirements. Scholastic aesthetics reminds us that art is connected with craft, and that there is an aesthetic aspect in production of every kind. It reminds us that aesthetic emotion depends upon complex operations of the intellect and involves systems of values, of ideologies, and thus of known cultural codes. One could continue in this vein. I have some doubt, however, about whether the reader will find the medieval model stimulating for the reasons which I have just given. But I must hope that books possess a life of a more varied kind than their authors' myopia concedes to them. A book is a kind of machine which the reader can freely use as a generator of intellectual stimulation. It is enough that the book should be truly a machine for thinking, that it should generate a variety of possible conclusions without its author's ordaining and limiting them in advance.

Thomistic Methodology and Structuralist Methodology

Despite what I have just said, I cannot refrain from looking now at one of the reasons why it is useful to revisit Aquinas's aesthetics. His aesthetics focused upon the notion of form, understood as something which can be broken down into elementary parts, the parts being united with one another by means of their relations. That it is also a synchronic aesthetics is quite evident, although I shall touch upon the reasons for this again.

Today, the human sciences study the formal structures of the objects which they investigate. They are also synchronic sciences, although unlike the medievals they employ this methodology in a critical fashion. Thus, reading Aquinas can have the following value: it can suggest methods of analysis which can be adopted today; and it can indicate a range of questions which have already been explored, so that it is not necessary to explore them again.

Structuralist reading of a medieval text is not just something that might be done for the fun of it. Structuralism can find not a little of its ancestry in the Scholastic *forma mentis:* for instance, there is the Structuralist claim to be an interdisciplinary discourse, its claim to be a kind of universal logic, its claim to reduce all human sciences to a single master science (linguistics, according to Structuralism) which the other sciences follow. All of this is Scholastic. And Scholastic thought, for its part, has two characteristics which connect it with Structuralist thought: it proceeds by way of binary divisions (true and false, *sic et non,* the dual structure of the *quaestio,* the dual structure of the *distinctio*); and it thinks synchronically. However, synchrony in medieval thought is not a methodological choice. Rather, it is something that derives of necessity from its metaphysical premises. It is the synchrony of being in the most general sense: being as the first object of the sciences, being in which there is no development, no becoming, therefore no diachrony. Invariably, medieval thought engaged in the synchronic analysis of the most general structure in things and pursued it to its utmost point and in all its possibilities. This very general structure was believed to be an ultimate common denominator in all phenomena, reflected in our linguistic behavior and our thinking as well as in the structure of natural objects. The laws of logic were also the laws of substance. Formal logic did not exclude ontology; for it was merely a *logica minor,* an instrument at the service of *logica major,* that is, the logic of things themselves.

This series of connections between Scholasticism and Structuralism does not mean that they were ideological relations. The homology between their operative procedures does not mean that either one of them should be overvalued or devalued in the light of the other. No one would want to suggest that Structuralism is a kind of neo-Scholasticism, or that Scholasticism was a kind of early Structuralism. All I want to do is to indicate some similarities in the two mental processes, or, better, to show two homologous models in action. I want to show that when the Scholastics tackled a problem, they solved it by devising a theoretical model of the object, and that the intellectual procedures which they employed in devising the model were akin to those of today's Structuralist methodologies.

Starting from these premises, it would be interesting to interpret the whole of Scholastic thought in the light of the Structuralist outlook. It would be quite a useful exercise, for Scholastic thinking would easily lend itself to a process in which the various aspects of things which it claims to define were reduced to explanatory models. In fact the claim of Scholastic thought is that it does resolve the real into explanatory models—except that these models are believed to be features of reality, not just constructs of the intellect. Still, in medieval disputes about universals, the opposition between nominalism and conceptualism was expressed in terms similar to those used nowadays in Structuralism. It is not altogether clear whether Structuralism would persevere to the end in denying an ontological significance to their epistemological models. At all events, both the Scholastics and the Structuralists engage in inquiries based upon the notion of universals.

It is not by chance that one of the most important issues in contemporary Structuralism is the investigation of linguistic universals. It matters little that these are universals of human psychology and are therefore brain structures, not Platonic universals. More important is the final outcome of this debate, namely the reaffirmation of an atemporality in the structures of the mind, the existence of a kind of *recta ratio dicibilium*—an idea which is remarkably close to the idea of a universal competence regulating the grammaticality of all possible utterances in every language.

Looking at these relations between Scholasticism and Structuralism, we may well consider that a medieval interpretation of Structuralism would help to demystify it. It would highlight its more perilous temptations. Another positive factor is that contemporary thought, which has spent too long in discussion of the creativity of the human spirit, now feels the need to discuss the question of a fixed order in the psyche. This investigation need not always or necessarily involve metaphysics; it can simply be a healthy reminder of the material conditions of the human intellect.

However, the former procedure—a Structuralist interpretation of the medievals—can hold surprises for us, and surprises which are of some interest. Also, Aquinas can provide examples of mental discipline in the solution of philosophical problems, an operative model for operative models of quite a different character and of different application. (Of course, we must be quite precise about this, and not confuse the two kinds of model.) For instance, we might think in this connection of his discussion of "mixed bodies" and the mixing of elements, a discussion which I used earlier in defining his conception of the artistic object.[16] For Aquinas, defining the artistic object—defining it vis-à-vis natural objects, and defining it within his own universe of problems and of language— meant also defining the opposition of nature and culture.

His explanation of nature had some affinity with the organic character of modern chemistry. It was that the various elements in a compound, which originally possessed their own autonomous substantial forms, fused together in a single new substantial form. (Hydrogen together with oxygen produces, not the sum of the two elements, but water, which is qualitatively different from either.) And yet, Aquinas said, the original forms subsisted as "virtues": though fused together in the compound, they persisted as active forces; they survived as a trace—just as the chemical elements in a chemical compound survive in the formula which denotes its structure. Aquinas's "mixed bodies" are just like chemical compounds, "a union of various things which have the capacity to mix together" ("miscibilium alteratorum unio").[17]

But in Aquinas's definition of the products of culture there was no fusion. The form which constituted such an object was a surface boundary, a *terminatio superficialis*. The original elements of which it was composed survived as substantial forms, ready for rearrangement in new correlations, for disposal in an infinity of combinations. This was art as *bricolage*.

This analogy might seem to be clever but superficial. And I should say at once that it is superficial up to a point. For in Structuralism, a structure is a system made up of the relations among "empty" values—values that are defined only by their difference from other values, and which for this very reason are able to feature in abstract models applicable across disciplines to a wide variety of phenomena. By contrast, Aquinas's "cultural" structure is one made up of relations among "full" elements—namely, substantial forms. Aquinas, therefore, was not a precursor of Structuralism. And yet, the analogy is not *just* clever and superficial. For when Aquinas faced the problem of defining the products of culture, he invented (and he did invent it—he didn't just apply it) an explanatory model which, when emptied of its content, was the same as the Structuralist model. That is, it offered the same possibility of conceiving of a compound as a system of values. Of course, for him the values were "full," but this does not detract from his solution to the problem. Indeed, the fact that they were "full" compelled him to define artifacts as surface forms which brought into relationship the systems in which other, substantial forms consisted: these substantial forms were present within the artistic form both in substance and in function, with everything which they were and which they represented before entering into the system of the accidental form. And this gives rise to the idea of a complex system as a *system of systems*. It is an idea which Structuralist aesthetics has taken over in order to explain the nature of composite operations which impose a formal relationship upon cultural data preceding the operation—complexes of ideas, networks of emotional stimuli, phonetic and lexemic series, suprasegmental levels, large syntagmatic strings which culture has previously endowed with their own particularity, and so on and so forth. And here too the preexisting levels become part of the new compound, and are modified thereby, without losing their original autonomy.

It is impossible to say whether Aquinas felicitously anticipated the methods of Structuralism, or whether Structuralism revived the Scholastic *forma mentis* through some kind of mediation, unconscious or explicit. (In something of the same way, generative grammar has revived the Port-Royal logic.) But we know, of course, that revisiting the thought of the past never involves just mastering its formal procedures. It also involves testing its results critically, in order at the very least to discover whether the formal procedures might not conceal material fallacies.

This is another good reason for this type of rereading of the past. In fact, many of the problematic points in contemporary Structuralism could be, if not resolved, at least clarified or avoided, if it were recognized that they originate in the exemplary models of Scholastic thought.

One of these problem areas involves the dialectic of diachrony and synchrony, and the reconciliation of formal logic with dialectical logic. To be sure, it would be easy to say that Scholasticism could never have posed this problem, because a sense of history was radically, if justifiably, extraneous to it. But it might be worth the trouble of asking whether Scholasticism's formal machinery was the effect or the cause of its deficiencies in dialectic.

Some time ago, a late disciple of Italian Idealism inquired whether it might not be possible to give a dialectical and historicist interpretation of Scholastic thought. In the case of this gentleman, it was probably a purely "ideological" enterprise, aimed at reconciling the devil with the deep blue sea for reasons of academic coexistence. In any event, he asked whether one might not interpret the Scholastic notion of *essentia* as a principle of continuous activity, as a mainspring of process. Now in fact, the idea which he had in mind does exist in Aquinas, but it is called *natura*, for "nature" means, precisely, substance conceived of as a principle of activity. However, in Scholasticism the term refers to a principle of an activity *which is always the same:* the activity is determined once and for all by the substantial structure of the particular in question.

Substance, in Aquinas, cannot change through time. It cannot break down in contradictions which would change it into something else. It cannot break down either by its own energy or through casual encounters with other substances. At the most, as we have seen, it can dissolve with other substances into the structure of a mixed body. But here, the active energies of the substances enter into a state of equilibrium with one another; they are not transformed into their opposites. In terms of modern chemistry, a mixed body is *something different*. In terms of hylomorphic theory, a mixed body is *something more:* it is a sum of its "virtues"—not, then, a transformation of its substances, for the substances live on as virtues. It is true that essence and matter are "active and passive in relation to one another" ("activa et passiva ad invicem").[18] but this does not mean that there is a dialectical relation between them. It means that there is a structural, synchronic, equilibrium of the two. If there has been an opposition, it occurred once only, in the act of their meeting, which gave birth to the concrete particular.

A methodology based on synchrony could never allow for dialectical becoming, except on one understanding (and it is an understanding with which the Scholastics would never have agreed). This is that the structures of synchronic equilibrium should be the products merely of definition; that we understand that the dialectical process of events is being frozen at a given moment, for purely cognitive reasons, so that we may discern the state of it, the field of relationships of which the process consists. We should understand that the synchronic reduction of the process, though necessary for debate about the events concerned, is in fact an impoverishment of the events and a "falsification" of them for our own purposes. It would follow that synchronic explanation and description were valid only if they were given in order to be then annulled and superseded, to be attempted afresh on a higher level.

Synchrony can be connected with dialectical diachrony only if it is understood that the facts themselves have a dialectical character, and that synchronic analysis is a purely methodogical instrument of a provisional nature. Synchrony, the static formalization of things, cannot connect with dialectic unless it is defined as a methodological moment, an indispensable moment but one which is subordinate to the larger dialectical enterprise.

The Scholastics, as I have said, or Thomas Aquinas anyway, would never have agreed with this. Indeed they could not, and could not have known how to, agree. However, the reinterpretation of the Scholastics' methodological universe ought to pose a similar problem to those who today profess to be Structuralists. But even if they do not agree, my discussion of the Scholastic model has shown at least that this Structuralist is a Scholastic.

The discussion could go on. The fact that it has gone on thus far is enough to show, perhaps, that this visit to the medieval philosophical world has not been without value—if, that is, it is always necessary to justify historical studies in terms of some immediate utility.

But of course we reinterpret a philosopher of the past for many reasons, many of which remain forever closed to people who simply make use of the reinterpretation, and others of which, as I have said, are known but not to the interpreter. Out of all the possible reasons, there is one that I wish to mention, now at the end of my labors. It is that anyone who makes use of the thinking of the past is enriched by an experience which is organic and complete, and is enabled subsequently to reconsider the world from a higher level of wisdom. However malformed and misplaced the tower which he has clambered up, he will see a larger vista; and not necessarily behind him.

As Bernard of Chartres remarked, with a genial, imperious, and spurious humility, we are dwarfs standing on the shoulders of giants.

Notes

Bibliography

Glossary

Index

Notes

Abbreviations

EEM   Edgar de Bruyne, *Etudes d'esthétique médiévale,* 3 vols. (Bruges, 1946).

PL   J.-P. Migne, ed., *Patrologiae Cursus Completus, Series Latina,* 222 vols. (Paris, 1844–90).

ST   St. Thomas Aquinas, *Summa Theologiae,* Blackfriars edition and translation, 60 vols. (London and New York, 1964–76).

Preface

1. The thesis was discussed with Luigi Pareyson, whose *Estetica* (Turin, 1954; 2d ed., Bologna, 1960) has heavily influenced the interpretative style of this book; also with Augusto Guzzo, one of the examiners, at the University of Turin's Philosophy Faculty. Parts of it appeared in Guzzo's journal *Filosofia,* before its publication by Edizioni di Filosofia. My thanks are due to Professor Guzzo, both for permission to reissue the book, and in particular for publishing a beginner's work in the first place. [Augusto Guzzo died in 1986; trans.]

2. Since this book was first published, there have been several studies dealing at least in part with Thomist aesthetics. Among those I have used and to which I refer in notes added to this edition are Rosario Assunto, *La critica d'arte nel pensiero medievale* (Milan, 1961); O. von Simson, *The Gothic Cathedral* (New York, 1956); E. J. Spargo, *The Category of the Aesthetic in the Philosophy of St. Bonaventure* (New York, 1953); W. Tatarkiewicz, *History of Aesthetics,* 3 vols. (The Hague, 1970–74), vol. II; Erwin Panofsky, *Gothic Architecture and Scholasticism* (London, 1957); Tullio Gregory, *Anima Mundi* (Florence, 1955); Etienne Gilson, *Painting and Reality* (London, 1957); William T. Noon, *Joyce and Aquinas* (New Haven, 1957); also various works by Graziella Federici Vescovini, Ananda Coomaraswamy, and Eugenio Garin. In taking account of these and other works, my aim has

been, not to update my book as though it had been written after the appearance of more recent works, but merely to enrich it through their additional insights.

3. This first appeared in my *Opera aperta* (Milan, 1962), and then as a separate work, *Le poetiche di Joyce* (Milan, 1966). The English translation is titled *The Aesthetics of Chaosmos* (Tulsa, 1982).

4. Umberto Eco, "Sviluppo dell'estetica medievale," in the anthology *Momenti e problemi di storia dell'estetica*, 4 vols. (Milan, 1959–61), vol. I; *Art and Beauty in the Middle Ages*, trans. Hugh Bredin (New Haven, 1986).

I. Aesthetics in Medieval Culture

1. Nelson Sella, *Estetica musicale in San Tommaso* (Turin, 1930).

2. "Almost all the developments of ancient Aesthetic were continued by tradition or reappeared by spontaneous generation in the course of the Middle Ages"; "It may be said that the literary and artistic doctrines and opinions of the Middle Ages have, with few exceptions, a value rather for the history of culture than for the general history of science"; Benedetto Croce, *Aesthetic*, trans. Douglas Ainslie (London, 1909), pp. 175, 179.

3. "The preeminence in the Middle Ages of theology, to which philosophy was but the handmaiden, meant that the problems of art lost the importance which they had been given, particularly in the works of Aristotle and Plato"; F. Biondolillo, *Breve storia del gusto e del pensiero estetico* (Messina, 1924), chap. 2.

4. These expressions, from Alexander Baumgarten's *Aesthetica*, 2 vols. (Frankfurt am Main, 1750–58), are quoted in Croce, *Aesthetic*, pp. 212–213.

5. Contemporary aesthetics is interested in the extent to which our experiences of art determine our aesthetic experiences in general. For the medievals this problem did not arise. The suspicion that natural objects appear beautiful to us because of some analogy with art can be sustained only in a world without God. If God exists, aesthetic pleasure in an object does not require any reference to the products of human artistic endeavor; the object is rather a product of divine workmanship, and indubitably so. On this question see Umberto Eco, *La definizione dell'arte* (Milan, 1968), in particular the chapter "L'estetica della formatività e il concetto di interpretazione." The view that all our "natural" experiences are shaped by cultural codes is discussed in my *La struttura assente: introduzione alla ricerca semiologica* (Milan, 1968), and later in my *A Theory of Semiotics* (Bloomington, Ind., 1979).

6. E. R. Curtius, *European Literature and the Latin Middle Ages*, trans. Willard R. Trask (London, 1953), examines the second of these two ele-

ments in medieval culture. Curtius is essential reading on medieval aesthetic sensibilities.

7. H. H. Glunz, *Die Literarästhetik des europäischen Mittelalters* (Bochum, 1937).

8. Eugenio Garin, *Medioevo e Rinascimento*, 2d ed. (Bari, 1961), chap. 2.

9. Edgar de Bruyne, *Etudes d'esthétique médiévale*, 3 vols. (Bruges, 1946) (cited hereafter as *EEM*). A summary of this work appeared under the title *L'esthétique du Moyen Age* (Louvain, 1947), translated as *The Esthetics of the Middle Ages* by E. B. Hennessy (New York, 1969). This short book, however, has no references to medieval texts (it refers us to the longer work) and is arranged thematically rather than chronologically, so that it is of little use for consultation purposes. More valuable is de Bruyne's *Geschiedenis van de Aesthetica*, 5 vols. (Antwerp, 1951–55), although the fact that it is written in Dutch makes it less accessible. Fortunately there is a Spanish translation, *Historia de la estética*, 2 vols. (Madrid, 1963); the entire second volume is devoted to Patristic and Scholastic aesthetics. The better-known *EEM* has also been translated into Spanish, *Estudios de estética medieval*, 3 vols. (Madrid, 1958). Among the most recent histories of aesthetics which deal in varying degrees with Aquinas are W. Tatarkiewicz, *History of Aesthetics*, 3 vols. (The Hague, 1970–74), vol. II; K. Gilbert and H. Kuhn, *A History of Esthetics*, 2d ed. (London, 1956), chap. 5; Raymond Bayer, *Histoire de l'esthétique* (Paris, 1961). Among the works and anthologies containing textual material are Rocco Montano, "L'estetica nel pensiero cristiano," in *Grande antologia filosofica*, ed. A. M. Moschetti and U. A. Padovani, 5 vols. (Milan, 1954), vol. V; Armando Plebe, *Estetica* (Florence, 1965); Elizabeth G. Holt, *A Documentary History of Art*, 2 vols. (New York, 1957), vol. I; Rosario Assunto, *Die Theorie des Schönen im Mittelalter* (Cologne, 1963). Only Assunto gives original and translation together.

10. "Their analyses were often conceptual rather than psychological. It would be unfair, however, to deny them any observational value. From the philosophical point of view, metaphysics had to come first; everything was considered in the light of being and its first principles"; *EEM*, III, 8.

11. Bernard Bosanquet, *A History of Aesthetics* (London, 1904), chap. 6.

12. Maurice de Wulf, *Art et beauté* (Louvain, 1943), chap. 9.

13. Curtius, *European Literature*, p. 224, n. 20.

14. Alcuin conceded that it was easier to love beautiful creatures, sweet fragrances, and lovely sounds (*species pulchras, dulces sapores, sonos suaves*) than to love God; *Rhetores Latini Minores*, ed. C. Halm (Leipzig, 1863), p. 550. But he added that if we take pleasure in these things in a proper manner—that is, using them as an aid to the greater love of God—then it is proper also to enjoy the love of beauty (*amor ornamenti*), sumptuous churches, and beautiful music and song.

15. *Consuetudines Carthusienses,* chap. 40 (*PL* 153, col. 717).

16. Hugh of Fouilloi, *De Claustro Animae,* I, 1 (*PL* 176, col. 1019).

17. This and the next three quotations are from St. Bernard of Clairvaux, *Apologia ad Guillelmum,* chap. 12 (*PL* 182, cols. 914–916). The translation is from G. G. Coulton, *Life in the Middle Ages,* 4 vols., 2d ed. (Cambridge, 1930), IV, 169–174. Part of this translation is reprinted in Holt, *Documentary History of Art,* I, 18–22.

18. E. R. Curtius maintains that before Dante there was nothing comparable in artistic value to the *Stabat Mater* and *Dies Irae; European Literature,* p. 390.

19. St. Augustine, *Confessions,* X, 33.

20. *ST,* II–II, 91, 2 ad 4. Denis the Carthusian expresses a similar view in his *De Vita Canonicorum,* 20 (*Opera Omnia,* 44 vols. [Tournai, 1896–1913], vol. XXXVII).

21. St. Bernard of Clairvaux, *Sermones in Cantica,* XXV, 6 (*PL* 183, col. 901). See *EEM,* III, 38.

22. Boethius, *De Consolatione Philosophiae,* III, 8.

23. On the *danse macabre,* see J. Huizinga, *The Waning of the Middle Ages,* trans. F. Hopman (Harmondsworth, 1965), chap. 11.

24. Gilbert of Hoyt, *Sermones in Canticum Salomonis,* XXV, 1 (*PL* 184, col. 129).

25. St. Bernard, *Sermones in Cantica,* LXXV, 11 (*PL* 183, col. 1193).

26. Hugh of St. Victor, *De Modo Dicendi et Meditandi,* 8 (*PL* 176, col. 879).

27. Hugh of St. Victor, *Soliloquium de Arrha Animae* (*PL* 176, col. 951).

28. Baldwin of Canterbury, *Tractatus de Vulnere Charitatis* (*PL* 204, col. 481).

29. Gilbert of Hoyt, *Sermones in Canticum Salomonis,* XXXI, 4 (*PL* 184, col. 163).

30. See Victor Mortet, *Recueil de textes relatifs à l'histoire de l'architecture, XIe–XIIe siècles* (Paris, 1911); Victor Mortet and Paul Deschamps, *Recueil de textes relatifs à l'histoire de l'architecture, XIIe–XIIIe siècles* (Paris, 1929).

31. Huizinga, *Waning of the Middle Ages,* pp. 254–255. Huizinga refers also to the occasion when Denis the Carthusian, on entering a church while the organ was playing, "was instantly transported by the melody into a prolonged ecstasy" (p. 256).

32. See Erwin Panofsky, *Abbot Suger on the Abbey Church of St.-Denis and Its Art Treasures* (Princeton, 1946). Parts of Panofsky's translation are reprinted in Holt, *Documentary History of Art,* I, 22–48. Suger's *De Rebus Administratione Sua Gestis* is in *PL* 186, cols. 1211–39. On Suger and medieval art collecting see F. H. Taylor, *The Taste of Angels: A History of Art Collecting from Rameses to Napoleon* (London, 1948).

33. Panofsky, *Abbot Suger*, p. 53.

34. Ibid., p. 79.

35. See Jules Guiffrey, *Inventaire de Jean, duc de Berry*, 2 vols. (Paris, 1894–96).

36. Panofsky, *Abbot Suger*, pp. 63–65.

37. Honorius of Autun, *Gemma Animae*, chap. 132 (*PL* 172, col. 586). See also William Durandus, *Rationale Divinorum Officiorum* (Treviso, 1479), I, part of which is reprinted in Holt, *Documentary History of Art*, I, 121–129; and St. Thomas Aquinas, *Commentarium in Quatuor Sententiarum P. Lombardi Libros*, III, 9, 1, 2; in *Opera Omnia*, ed. Roberto Busa, 7 vols. (Stuttgart, 1980). Aquinas's commentary on Lombard's *Sententiae* is cited hereafter by the book to which it refers, e.g., *Comm. in III Sent.* All quotations of Aquinas's work are from Busa's edition of *Opera Omnia*, except for those listed separately in the Bibliography.

38. For a wide-ranging account of the medieval aesthetic sensibility see Rosario Assunto, *La critica d'arte nel pensiero medievale* (Milan, 1961). On Patristic aesthetics see Quintino Cataudella, "Estetica cristiana," in the anthology *Momenti e problemi di storia dell'estetica*, 4 vols. (Milan, 1959, 1961), I, 81–114. On Scholastic aesthetics see Umberto Eco, "Sviluppo dell'estetica medievale," in ibid., pp. 115–229; translated by Hugh Bredin as *Art and Beauty in the Middle Ages* (New Haven, 1986). On medieval sensibilities other than the Scholastic, see Antonio Viscardi, "Idee estetiche e letteratura militante nel Medioevo," in *Momenti e problemi*, I, 231–253; and Giorgio Barberi-Squarotti, *Le poetiche del Trecento in Italia*, in ibid., pp. 255–324. Still a fundamental work is Julius Schlosser Magnino, *Die Kunstliteratur* (Vienna, 1924). Some useful remarks are to be found in G. Saintsbury, *A History of Criticism and Literary Taste in Europe*, 3 vols. (Edinburgh, 1900–04), vol. I, bk. 3. Another work deserving of repeated consultation is Marcelino Menéndez y Pelayo, *Historia de las ideas estéticas in España* (Madrid, 1883), chaps. 3–5; despite its title, this work ranges over the whole of European culture.

39. Reprinted in Aquinas, *Opera Omnia*, VII.

40. John of Meurs, *De Tonis*, in *Scriptores Ecclesiastici de Musica Sacra Potissimum*, ed. Martin Gerbert, 3 vols. (1784; reprint, Hildesheim, 1963), III, 311.

41. For example: "In genere enim consonantiarum est unum, quod est diesis, quod est minimum in consonantiis. Diesis enim est semitonium minus. Dividitur enim tonus in duo semitonia inaequalia, quorum unus dicitur diesis" ("The smallest element in harmony is a quarter-tone—smaller even than a semitone. For a tone is divided into two unequal parts, one of which is called a quarter-tone"); *Commentarium in Aristotelis Metaphysicam*, V, 8, 8, (cited hereafter as *Comm. Met.*).

42. "Se nascens dedit socium, / Convescens in edulium, / Se moriens in pretium, / Se regnans dat in praemium"; in *Officium de Festo Corporis Christi;* in *Opera Omnia,* VI.

43. *ST,* I-II, 1, 6 ad 1. See also *ST,* II-II, 168, 2c.

44. *ST,* II-II, 141, 4 ad 3.

45. Ibid. See also *Commentarium in Libros Aristotelis Ethicorum,* III, 19–20 (cited hereafter as *Comm. Eth.*).

46. *ST,* I, 91, 3 ad 3.

II. Beauty as a Transcendental

1. *De Veritate,* I, 1c.

2. The transcendentals have been of greater interest to the writers of Scholastic manuals than to historians. In fact it is a problem with few philological difficulties, and it is also one that has been formulated very clearly. For a discussion that is not without its subtleties, however, see Cardinal D. Mercier, *Cours de philosophie,* 3 vols., 5th ed. (Louvain, 1909–12), vol. II, *Métaphysique générale ou ontologie,* pp. 128–245. Mercier discusses among other things the accuracy of the terms *property* and *attribute,* which are usually employed to refer to the transcendentals. He himself suggests the term *passion* (p. 128)—better suited, in his view, for a property that belongs to being but is not absolutely identical with it.

3. See, for example, Aristotle, *Metaphysics,* III, 3; IV, 2; V, 6, 7; X, 2.

4. An early and explicit treatment of the theory of transcendentals is found in the *Summa de Bono* of Philip the Chancellor (d. 1236), which was influenced by, among other works, William of Auxerre's treatise *De Bono* (1220). Philip the Chancellor's *Summa* is discussed, with extensive quotations, in Henri Pouillon, "Le premier traité des propriétés transcendentales," *Revue Néoscholastique de Philosophie,* 42 (1939), 40–77.

5. "For with this our world has received its full complement of living creatures, mortal and immortal, and come to be in all its grandeur, goodness, beauty and perfection—this visible living creature made in the likeness of the intelligible and embracing all the visible, this god displayed to sense, this our heaven, one and only-begotten"; Plato, *Timaeus,* trans. A. E. Taylor (London, 1929), p. 100. These, the concluding words of the dialogue, were probably not known to the medievals, who were familiar with it partly in a fragment of Cicero's Latin translation, and more fully in the translation by Chalcidius, which ended at 53c. (Chalcidius' commentary on the work had a very considerable influence on medieval thought.) Still, this concluding passage reflects the spirit of the work and the spirit in which it was read. The development of its ideas in Scholasticism culminated in the twelfth-century school of Chartres; this school was marked

by what de Bruyne has defined as a genuine aesthetic *Weltanschauung*, grounded in Plato and structured in accordance with a mathematical conception of the universe (*EEM*, II, chap. 6).

6. See *EEM*, III, 217–218.

7. Dionysius the Areopagite (Pseudo-Dionysius), *The Divine Names*, IV, 7. The Latin text which Thomas Aquinas read (*De Divinis Nominibus*) and the object of his *Commentary* was basically the twelfth-century translation of Johannes Saracenus, which is given here. The English translation from the Greek original, in *The Divine Names and Mystical Theology*, is by John D. Jones (Milwaukee, 1980). The Saracenus translation is from *Dionysiaca*, ed. Philippe Chevallier, 2 vols. (Paris, 1937), I. I use the chapter divisions and subdivisions found in Jones.

8. "The God of Eriugena is like unto a principle which, incomprehensible in its simplicity, reveals itself at a stroke in the multiplicity of its consequences"; Etienne Gilson, *History of Christian Philosophy in the Middle Ages* (London, 1955), p. 119.

9. "Visibiles formas, sive quas in natura rerum, sive quas in sanctissimis divine scripture sacramentis contemplatur, non propter seipsas factas, nec propter seipsas appetendas seu nobis promulgatas, sed invisibilis pulchritudinis imaginationes esse, per quas divina providentia in ipsam puram et invisibilem pulchritudinem ipsius veritatis quam amat et ad quam tendit omne quod amat, sive sciens sive nesciens, humanos animos revocat" ("We contemplate visible forms, whether they be in nature or in the most holy sacraments in accordance with divine scripture, not because they have been created, not because we desire them if they are made known to us; rather, because they are images of invisible beauty, by means of which divine providence calls the minds of men to the pure and invisible beauty of the truth which we love, and which all that loves moves toward, whether knowingly or unknowingly"); John Scottus Eriugena, *Expositiones in Ierarchiam Coelestem*, ed. J. Barbet (Turnhout, 1975), I, 3.

10. M. D. Chenu, *Toward Understanding Saint Thomas*, trans. A.-M. Landry and D. Hughes (Chicago, 1964), p. 228.

11. Pseudo-Dionysius, *The Divine Names*, I, 4.

12. St. Thomas Aquinas, *Commentarium in Dionysii De Divinis Nominibus*, I, 2 (cited hereafter as *Comm. Div. Nom.*).

13. This and the next eight quotations from Aquinas are from *Comm. Div. Nom.*, IV, 5.

14. *Comm. Div. Nom.*, IV, 8.

15. *Comm. Div. Nom.*, IV, 1.

16. Pseudo-Dionysius, *The Divine Names*, IV, 7.

17. *Comm. Div. Nom.*, IV, 5.

18. "Licet verum et bonum supposito convertantur cum ente, tamen

ratione differunt" ("Though in their subject 'good' and 'true' are convertible with being, still they are notionally different"); *ST,* I, 16, 4c.

19. *Comm. Div. Nom.,* IV, 1.

20. *Comm. in I Sent.,* 31, 2, 1 ad 4.

21. *De Veritate,* quaest. 21.

22. *De Veritate,* 22, 1 ad 12.

23. See *ST,* I, 5, 1 and 3.

24. *Comm. Div. Nom.,* IV, 5.

25. *ST,* I-II, 27, 1 ad 3.

26. There are in the first place those who deny that beauty is a transcendental, basing this conclusion on certain formal statements by Aquinas. They accept that *pulchrum* is identical with *bonum,* but they maintain that it is merely a species of the good, and that there is at the most a logical distinction between them. These authors include Joseph Gredt, *Elementa Philosophiae Aristotelico-Thomisticae,* 2 vols. (Freiburg im Breisgau, 1932), II, 28; and Vincentio Remer, *Ontologia,* 9th ed., ed. Paulo Geny (Rome, 1947), pp. 114–121. Others are even more decisive in their denial. Cardinal D. Mercier, listing the transcendentals mentioned in *De Veritate,* reduces them to the One, the True, and the Good and ignores the Beautiful: "Il y a trois propriétés transcendentales et trois seulement"; *Cours de philosophie,* II, 236). Further on, however, he discusses beauty at some length, and attempts to justify its exclusion from the transcendentals (pp. 513–565). Similar views are held by de Wulf, *Art et beauté,* p. 140. The opposite view, however, is taken by A.-D. Sertillanges, *St. Thomas d'Aquin,* 2 vols. (Paris, 1925); by Edgar de Bruyne, *St. Thomas d'Aquin* (Paris and Brussels, 1928), who in fact considers Aquinas's commentary on Pseudo-Dionysius too explicit if anything; and Etienne Gilson, *The Philosophy of Saint Thomas Aquinas,* trans. Edward Bullough (Cambridge, 1924). A curious example of a rather forced "modern" interpretation is the Crocean judgment delivered by Nelson Sella: "Ontological beauty . . . is an external manifestation of the pure lyrical intuition of God (natural beauty) and of man (artistic beauty); but in the last analysis the beauty of art originates in the living fountain of Eternal Beauty"; *Estetica musicale in San Tommaso,* p. 14.

27. Marc de Munnynck, "L'esthétique de St. Thomas d'Aquin," in the anthology *San Tommaso d'Aquino* (Milan, 1923); Jacques Maritain, *Art and Scholasticism,* trans. J. F. Scanlan (London, 1930), chap. 5, nn. 56, 63b, 65.

28. Maritain, *Art and Scholasticism,* p. 24.

29. Ibid., p. 132.

30. The definition is so well chosen that it has been widely used by subsequent writers. It crops up again and again, though often by way of a convenient and elegant verbal evasion. It appears, for example, in R. Gar-

rigou-Lagrange, O. Derisi, M. R. Lerate, and L. Wencelius. The great influence of Maritain on those of his successors who have tackled the same problem has often relieved them from taking a closer look at Aquinas's actual words. Among the many who have accepted the definition is André Marc, in his "La méthode d'opposition en ontologie thomiste," *Revue Néoscolastique*, 33 (1931), 149–169, and more fully in his "Métaphysique du Beau," *Revue Thomiste*, 51 (1951), 112–134, and 52 (1952), 64–94. Marc has used it to refer to beauty conceived of as something generated by a dialectical tension among the transcendentals: "Beauty is a synthetic idea which combines these various aspects, showing them to relate to both the intellect and the will, the inner and the outer dimensions of the spirit. It adds pleasure to knowledge, just as it adds knowledge to the good. It is the goodness of truth and the truth of goodness, the splendor of the transcendentals reunited." The definition may owe something to the influence of Albertus Magnus's *De Pulchro et Bono*, which I discuss in this chapter in "Beauty as a Transcendental in Thirteenth-Century Philosophy."

31. The summary that follows is based upon the works of two writers who have, more than anyone else, studied this problem in historical terms: Henri Pouillon, in "La Beauté, propriété transcendentale chez les scholastiques," *Archives d'Histoire Doctrinale et Littéraire du Moyen Age*, 21 (1946), 263–329; and Edgar de Bruyne. Pouillon's article is a study of how the concept of beauty as a transcendental developed in the thirteenth century, and it is an essay in scholarship rather than in aesthetic theory. By contrast, because de Bruyne's interests in *EEM* are more specifically aesthetic, he often deploys interpretative rules which allow him to bring together viewpoints which Pouillon would consider to be in conflict. Pouillon's strength lies in the fact that most of the texts which he has assembled were previously unpublished. His judicious selections from various manuscripts make it a most valuable work, virtually an anthology. It is worth noting that de Bruyne and Pouillon worked closely with each other; each made use of the other's research, and both of them published in 1946.

32. *PL* 146, cols. 29–58. See *EEM*, II, 109.

33. Douai Ms. 434.

34. Quoted in Pouillon, "Le premier traité."

35. This example is taken from *EEM*, I, 359. See also Chevallier, *Dionysiaca*, I, 178–179.

36. *PL* 199, col. 259.

37. *EEM*, I, 359.

38. It is quite useful to relate the changes in medieval aesthetic sensibilities to improvements in the material conditions of life. Thus we may even connect the reevaluation of beauty to the cultivation of beans in the tenth

century. See Jacques Le Goff, *La civilisation de l'occident médiéval* (Paris, 1964).

39. Otloh of St. Emmeran, *Dialogus de Tribus Quaestionibus*, chap. 43 (*PL* 146, col. 120).

40. The passages quoted here are taken from Pouillon, "La Beauté."

41. Aristotle, *Rhetoric*, 1366a33.

42. This and the following quotation from Grosseteste are from Pouillon, "La Beauté."

43. Alexander of Hales, *Summa Theologica*, 4 vols. (Florence, 1924–48). The quotations given here are from Pouillon, "La Beauté."

44. These quotations, which are also in Pouillon, "La Beauté," are from St. Augustine, *De Diversis Quaestionibus*, LXXXIII, 30.

45. See Pouillon, "La Beauté," p. 275, n. 3. A similar idea is found in Plotinus, *The Enneads*, I, 6, 2.

46. Pouillon, "La Beauté," p. 279.

47. See F.-M. Henquinet, "Un Brouillon autographe de S. Bonaventure sur le commentaire des sentences," *Etudes Franciscains*, 44 (1932), 633–655, and 45 (1933), 59–82. The quotations given here are from Pouillon, "La Beauté."

48. Albertus Magnus' *De Pulchro et Bono* is printed in Aquinas, *Omnia Opera*, VII, 43–47. This little treatise was discovered by Abbot Uccelli in 1869, in the Biblioteca Nazionale in Naples. The handwriting was authentic, so it was immediately numbered among the works of Aquinas. Subsequently, when doubt was cast upon its authenticity, it was still sometimes held to incorporate Thomistic thinking (see, for example, Menéndez y Pelayo, *Historia de las ideas estéticas*, p. 141). Maritain was doubtful about it, yet he made use of it all the same. Others continued to exploit it as a Thomistic work without reservation. Even now, some of its ideas continue to be widely touted as Aquinas's views. This is all the more odd and irritating in that, as well as being firmly established as Albertus's work (the Neapolitan manuscript is a copy made by Aquinas as a student), its ideas are in fact at odds with those of Aquinas, certainly the Aquinas of the *Summa Theologiae*. See de Bruyne's penetrating discussion of the treatise in *EEM*, III, 153–161. Albertus Magnus's commentary on Pseudo-Dionysius, *Super Dionysium de Divinis Nominibus*, ed. P. Simon, is in his *Opera Omnia*, 12 vols. to date (Aschendorff, 1951–), XXXVII, 1.

49. Albertus Magnus, *De Pulchro et Bono*, I, 2c.

50. This kind of hylomorphic theory also provided a place for the various triads of terms that originated in the Book of Wisdom. Terms such as *dimension*, *species*, and *order* or *number*, *weight*, and *measure* could now be predicated of form. Perfection, beauty, and good are grounded in form, and if a thing is to be good and perfect it must possess all the properties

that govern form and that follow from it. Form is determined by dimension or quantity (*modus*), and is therefore in accordance with measure (*mensura*) and proportion. Form assigns a thing to its *species*, according to the proportioning of its constitutive elements or its *number*. Form, insofar as it is act, directs a thing to its proper end, the end appropriate to its *order*, by way of a particular inclination or weight (*pondus*). See *EEM*, III, 153–161.

51. Albertus Magnus, *De Pulchro et Bono*, IV, 1 ad 3.

52. *Comm. Div. Nom.*, IV, 1.

53. Ibid.

54. It is true that Aquinas borrowed much from Pseudo-Dionysius and was influenced by him. But Aquinas's world, whatever may be said about it, was not that of the Areopagite. I cannot agree with Bernard Bosanquet that "the neo-Platonic tradition was the principal element in the intellectual aesthetic of the Middle Ages"; *A History of Aesthetics*, p. 148. Nor can I accept the admittedly summary conclusions of G. M. Merlo: "The fact that the principal aesthetic ideas of St. Thomas can be found in his commentary on chapter IV of *The Divine Names* of the Alexandrian Pseudo-Dionysius shows that the Saint had a certain tendency to neo-Platonic thinking"; "Il misticismo estetico di S. Tommaso," *Atti dell'Accademia delle Scienze di Torino*, 1939–40.

III. The Function and Nature of the Aesthetic *Visio*

1. *ST*, I, 91, 3 ad 3.

2. St. Augustine, *De Vera Religione*, 32.

3. See *ST*, II–II, 141, 4 ad 3.

4. Eugène Viollet-le-Duc remarked that the statues in the King's Gallery in the cathedral at Amiens were designed to be seen at thirty meters from the floor. The eyes were placed far from the nose, and the hair was sculpted in great masses. At Reims the statues on the spires have arms that are too short, necks that are too long, lowered shoulders, and short legs. The ornamentation on the façade is the same. Thus, the mathematical laws of proportion were subordinated to the requirements of the eye. Sculpture was designed to occupy a particular place and to be seen at a certain distance. See in this connection Henri Focillon, *The Art of the West in the Middle Ages*, trans. Donald King, 2 vols. (London, 1963), II, 81. The same thing applied to stained-glass windows. Viollet-le-Duc has shown that light tended to "devour" the outlines of the colors, so that painters were compelled to exaggerate the forms and to enclose them in an outer form or zone, which in turn might be accentuated by means of leads. See Gino Severini, *Ragionamenti sulle arti figurative* (Milan, 1942).

5. See St. Augustine, *De Musica,* VI.

6. See *EEM,* II, 224, where the Victorine theory is said to have some affinity with the *Einfühlung* (empathy) theory.

7. Richard of St. Victor, *Benjamin Major,* I, 4 (*PL* 196, col. 67).

8. St. Bonaventure, *Itinerarium Mentis in Deum,* II, 5; in *Opera Omnia,* 10 vols. (Florence, 1882–1902), V.

9. *Comm. in I Sent.,* 1, 3, 2.

10. *Comm. in I Sent.,* 10, 1, 2.

11. This and the following quotation of William of Auvergne, *Tractatus de Bono et Malo,* are taken from Pouillon, "La Beauté."

12. William of Auvergne is discussed in Pouillon, "La Beauté," pp. 266–273, and original texts are given on pp. 315–319. His theory of the soul is discussed in *EEM,* III, 80–82. See also Gilson, *History of Christian Philosophy,* p. 256, where he writes that for William the soul "remains one and undivided, no matter what operations it may accomplish." He adds that this theory "exerted a profound influence in both England and France on the theologians of the fourteenth century, who, because they refused to distinguish the faculties from the essence of the soul, spoke of a cognitive function of the will." These considerations lead de Bruyne to emphasize his originality. According to de Bruyne's summary of William's views, there is a rational *habitus,* which prompts us to pass judgment upon the moral goodness of human actions, and a sensible *habitus,* which allows us to pass judgment upon the physical beauty of forms. Both of these become conscious of themselves in a state of "aspiration," in which the objective properties of things are grasped, not by way of abstraction, but in a feeling which is penetrated by love (*affectio*). Thus, the entire soul loves, and the entire soul knows, and the perception of beauty is also an act of the entire soul, in which knowledge and delighted feeling coincide. Apart from these theoretical viewpoints, however, William's emphasis on the sensible pleasure of objects led him to express certain ideas about the beauty of color, ideas which reflected the sensibility of his period and which were also an important feature of a line of thought which was to interest Aquinas. In several places, in his discussion of the beautiful "in itself" (*per seipsum*), William touched upon the beauty of color. Green, for instance (his own favorite colour), is especially pleasing because it lies in between white, which dilates the eye, and black, which causes it to contract. This pleasure, we should note, was an immediate and necessary pleasure, and the color was beautiful because of the pleasure. These remarks seem to reflect the widespread medieval taste for simple, brilliant colors. They were fond of many-colored combinations and compositions and sought decorative coloring in every kind of area and activity, in male and female sculpture, in painted illuminations, weapons, and standards. We shall return to this

matter when discussing the concept of *claritas*. An example of this delicate and childlike love of color is Jean de Joinville's *La vie de St. Louis* (also known as *Histoire de St. Louis*), which is filled with expressions of delight in the glitter of jewels, which are described in minute detail, and in the blue of the sea, the brightness of flame, the vermilion livery, striped with yellow, of a page, the golden weapons of a Saracen troop glittering in the hot sun, the gold and azure of paintings. We might refer also to St. Francis, who spoke of "the colored flowers and grass," to Guido Guinizelli's "visio de neve colorato in grana" ("snowy visage suffused with crimson"), to Dante's "dolce colore d'oriental zaffiro" ("soft color of the oriental sapphire"), or even to the goliardic *carmina*. In short, the medievals had a lively sense of the intrinsic beauty of colors (they were beautiful *per seipsum*), and this is particularly evident in William of Auvergne. William, in fact, envisaged a beauty which was undivided, immediately perceived without any concomitant critical awareness, and self-justifying. For Aquinas, by contrast, simple colors were connected with form and were beautiful for certain measurable and verifiable reasons. The medievals in general were convinced that color was one of the major categories of beauty. This belief, and their other sentiments about color, made an indelible mark upon Aquinas's aesthetics.

13. See Graziella F. Vescovini, *Studi sulla prospettiva medievale* (Turin, 1965). The text of *Liber de Intelligentiis* and parts of Witelo's *De Perspectiva* are in Clemens Baeumker, *Witelo* (Münster, 1908).

14. For the arguments summarized here and the passages quoted, see Baeumker, *Witelo*, pp. 143 and 172–175.

15. *ST*, I, 67, 1c. The reference at the end to a *visio Dei* might induce us to think that *visio* in the sense of intellectual knowledge refers to our intuition of God. But in fact there is a passage in *ST*, I-II, 77, 5 ad 3, which makes it clear that the term refers to all forms of apprehension ("omnes interiores apprehensiones").

16. *ST*, I-II, 27, 1 ad 3. This passage brings us to the much-debated question of human senses which are *maxime cognoscitivi*—that is, involved to the fullest extent with true knowledge. The distinction between these and the other senses may seem somewhat trite, and indeed is no more than a useful classification; and it is one which has been given a great variety of interpretations. When we consider Aquinas's use of it, the historical context suggests that he alluded to it because it first made its appearance in the thirteenth century. In the preceding century it was generally held that all the senses were vehicles of aesthetic pleasure; it was the Aristotelian revival which led to the distinction between the senses. For Aquinas, in fact, this distinction is less important than the distinction between interested and disinterested pleasure, and he devotes much more space to the latter. If we

look at his use of it in the passage quoted here, we can see that his only purpose is to emphasize the intellectual character of aesthetic knowledge; for, after making the distinction, he continues with the words "et sic patet"—"and so it is clear"—to introduce his assertion that beauty has a reference to the cognitive powers. Apart from his discussions of beauty, Aquinas makes virtually no reference to the superiority of one sense over another. Indeed, he describes the Beatific Vision as a state in which all the senses of the elect achieve a condition of perfect refinement; and, as it happens, the Beatific Vision is also an aesthetic vision of the First Beauty. In the *Supplement* to the *Summa Theologiae*, Part III, 83, 4 ad 3, we read: "The sense of smell in saints . . . is capable of knowing the most exquisite of odors . . . and also of distinguishing the finest differences in odor" ("sensus odoratus in sanctis . . . cognoscet non solum excellentias odorum . . . sed etiam minimas odorum differentias"). Incidentally, the lack of elegance in this passage should not be laid at Aquinas's door, since the *Supplement* was put together and partly written by Reginald of Piperno; vol. V of *Summa Theologica*, 6 vols. (Taurini: Marietti, 1937).

17. De Munnynck writes: "The term *placet*, [which refers to] the pleasure caused by the contemplation of an object, is absolutely essential to beauty, just as the intellect is essential to truth and just as the good entails a relation to the will. If one desires to reduce the definition of beauty to [a statement of] the analytic conditions of objective beauty, one must either introduce pleasure surreptitiously, or one must reduce beauty to something else—to truth, or even to being. *Quod visum placet* is the essential definition of beauty according to St. Thomas"; "L'esthétique de St. Thomas," p. 232. This author's enthusiasm for the phrase *visa placent* goes beyond anything that can be justified by the evidence. Two pages later he writes: "It is impossible to exaggerate the value and the astonishing fruitfulness of Aquinas's definition of beauty. It has an immediate relevance to the fundamental problems of contemporary aesthetics" (p. 234). De Munnynck comes to believe in an element of relativity in beauty because it is good and pleasurable (*bonum delectabile*), and is therefore affected by psychological and instinctual differences among people. But in his attempt to guarantee a minimal objectivity in the aesthetic judgment, he has devised a theory which is clever and interesting but which cannot be inferred from anything written by Aquinas. It is doubtful whether it is even consistent with Aquinas, although it might appear to bear the mark of Scholastic ideas. De Munnynck's theory is that beauty is relative to the subject, and that different subjects make aesthetic judgments relative to their differences. There is, however, an idea of a perfect human being, a limiting ideal for humanity, in which it is envisaged that every human faculty and quality is in harmony according to this perfection. It is this which guarantees a

possible aesthetic judgment which is perfect. Our everyday individual aesthetic judgments tend to this goal of total objectivity, which can be approached though never finally reached. The notion of this ideal can serve to regulate our own imperfect judgment—although how this happens, de Munnynck does not say. In short, he is trying to conciliate a certain kind of aesthetic theory—sociological, subjectivist, relativist—by arguing for the modernity and adaptability of Thomism. But in the end there is too much extraneous matter, to the neglect of the fundamental objectivism required by orthodox neo-Thomism.

18. A more moderate position is taken by Maurice de Wulf. C. Mazzantini takes an opposite view to that of de Munnynck but argues at the same time that the aesthetic judgment involves an agreement between subject and object; this agreement produces a universal and disinterested pleasure (he is being explicitly Kantian here) but is objectively based in the fact that the object is in its essence adapted for contemplation, because it possesses Aquinas's three formal conditions of beauty. See his *Linee fondamentali di una estetica tomista* (Rome, 1930).

19. Aquinas has often been taken as a precursor of Croce, on the basis of certain purely formal analogies between the two. In this interpretation, the term *intuition* is taken quite uncritically to mean the same as *visio*, and is thus deprived of all the richness (and confusion) of meaning which it possesses. Nelson Sella (*Estetica musicale*) puts us on our guard against this kind of thing by reminding us that for Croce intuition is a "form of the spirit" [a category of mental activity; *trans*.]. However, it is only since Descartes that philosophers have begun to look upon the mind as a *res cogitans, volens, sentiens et appetens*. In such a perspective, the Thomist distinction between a rational soul and a sensitive soul would be impossible. In fact, certain aspects of intuition in Croce's use of the word would be classified by Aquinas as aspects of sensation.

20. Beauty is "a lightning of the mind on a matter intelligently arranged"; Maritain, *Art and Scholasticism*, p. 20.

21. Ibid., p. 21.

22. "Firmly fixed in the intuition of sense, it [the intellect] is irradiated by an intelligible light granted to it of a sudden in the very sensible in which it glitters; and it apprehends this light not *sub ratione veri*, but rather *sub ratione delectabilis*, by the happy exercise it procures for it and the succeeding joy in appetite, which leaps out to every good of the soul as its own peculiar object. Only afterwards will it more or less successfully analyse in reflection the causes of such joy"; ibid. Elsewhere (pp. 124–127) Maritain exploits the expression *visum placet* in order to distinguish his own conception from the Kantian conception (in which beauty is defined as what gives pleasure without a concept). The term *visum*, he argues, does

not refer to a confused perception; nor is the intellect something alien to it. Rather, it is a process in which the mind grasps an idea, a form, a "ray of intelligibility." This intellectual element, however, is not expressible in a concept, but is graspable only in its matrix of the senses. If it were abstracted or considered in its own right we would lose the joy and delight, pass over to a state of knowledge, and break the spell of the aesthetic intuition. In order to define this intuitive state of mind, Maritain coins the expression *intellectualized sense:* aesthetic contemplation is essentially intellectual; but it is an apprehension of the intelligible which takes place without intellectual abstraction or reasoning. Feelings of love, of affective empathy, of delight, follow as the proper effect of this intuitive experience. Aesthetic emotion is thus "the satisfaction of our faculty of Desire reposing in the proper good of the cognitive faculty perfectly and harmoniously exercised by the intuition of the beautiful." It is a feeling which is determined completely by cognition, a sense of intellectual fullness brought about by the sensible intuition. He describes the aesthetic intuition as a "tonic" for the intellect, having remote analogies with the mystic graces. Maritain's theory of aesthetic intuition deserves its popularity, because of its plausibility, its *souplesse,* its explanatory skill. It does not, however, answer the purely historical question of whether Aquinas himself conceived of such a thing as intellectual intuition, an "intellectualized sense." Maritain's interpretation of the expression *visa placent* is extremely popular with neo-Thomists, many of whom take his definition of beauty as *id quod visum placet*—namely, the definition "Beauty is that which pleases when it is seen"—to be a correct quotation from Aquinas. In fact what Aquinas actually wrote was "Pulchra enim dicuntur quae visa placent"—that is, "things are called beautiful which please when they are seen." Aquinas's words refer to what we might call a sociological fact, whereas Maritain's version amounts to a metaphysical definition. We should not think of this as an out-and-out falsehood, for of course Maritain was concerned to construct a synthesis out of more than one Thomistic formula (one of which, as we have seen, describes beauty as *id cujus ipsa apprehensio placet*). Still, Maritain and his followers have been somewhat arbitrary in this matter, not least because *id quod visum placet* is presented on p. 19 of *Art and Scholasticism* as an actual quotation.

23. *De Veritate,* 2, 6 ad 3. De Bruyne's interpretation of this is as follows. "St. Thomas's [concept of] *apprehensio* has a universal import. When it refers to the perception of corporeal beauty, it is neither purely sensible nor purely abstractive; it is essentially intuitive, in the sense that it is, in its psychological aspect, a synthetic unity . . . Intuition is an act of the whole person, irrespective of how one conceives of the connection between the sensibility and the spirit"; *EEM,* III, 286. De Bruyne rejects Maritain's

view (already quoted in note 22) that aesthetic pleasure is "the satisfaction of our faculty of Desire reposing in the proper good of the cognitive faculty." He defines it rather as a pleasure of the cognitive faculty when it is active and expanding. He agrees that it is a pleasure produced by knowing, but for de Bruyne the activity of intuition is always a harmonious play of *all* the faculties whose end is determined by the intellect. It is synthetic and unitary. In other, earlier works of de Bruyne, where he is writing as a neo-Thomist philosopher rather than as a historical scholar, he describes aesthetic intuition as an instinctual synthesis, in which the intellect is both constitutive and immanent. It is not isolated from other psychic functions, nor separate from the abstractive synthesis. It exploits to the full both the sensible intuition and the feelings, and at the same time it submits to the influence of associative relations in things and their power to affect the emotions of sense. Aesthetic intuition grasps the truth, but not in a logical mode; it grasps the meaning of things and their relations without needing to perform an abstraction. It is thus a psychic synthesis whose unity is complex and dynamic, involving the coexistence of all the elements—representations and affections, simple and complex, higher and lower—which constitute the organic unity of the human consciousness. De Bruyne's theory suggests that his main theoretical interest is in rethinking both the psychological and the biological aspects of aesthetic experience. Even in his historical work he never loses an opportunity to locate in Aquinas's pages the possibility of a disinterested physical pleasure, of a free biological play. See in particular his "Du rôle de l'intelligence dans l'activité esthétique," in the anthology *Philosophia Perennis* (Regensburg, 1930), and his longer *Esquisse d'une philosophie de l'art* (Brussels, 1930).

24. M. D. Roland-Gosselin, "Peut-on parler d'intuition intellectuelle dans la philosophie Thomiste?" in *Philosophia Perennis*. It was no accident that Maritain made use of the concept of intuition. Not only was he influenced by Bergson, but he closely followed John of St. Thomas.

25. See *ST,* I, 84, 1, to 85, 3.

26. *ST,* I, 86, 1.

27. For Aquinas, only one form of intellectual intuition is possible for human beings, and that is an intuition of oneself. Even here, however, it is necessary to grasp the self at the moment when it is determined by the proper object of the mind, namely the species or nature of things. It can be known only in this act of self-reflection, because its primary act is the one in which the self and the species come into contact. Only subsequently can the intellect become conscious of itself as something in contact with a species. This point is very clearly expounded in Francesco Olgiati, *L'anima di San Tommaso* (Milan, 1923), pp. 105–106.

28. Roland-Gosselin points out that our everyday habits of mind, and

the speed of perception to which we have become accustomed, might give the impression of an intuitively immediate process. But, he maintains, "If we still want to speak of intuition—and there are the strongest reasons for doing so in aesthetics—we can use the term only in a derivative sense, by way of analogy with the [true] sense defined earlier"; "Peut-on parler d'intuition?" p. 723. For further critical comment on Maritain, see the essay "Storiografia medievale ed estetica teorica," in Eco, *La definizione dell'arte*.

IV. The Formal Criteria of Beauty

1. Only here do we find the term *integritas,* although a similar idea can be found in other works: see, for instance, *Comm. in I Sent.,* 31, 2, 1c. References to clarity and proportion, however, are frequent in the first and second parts of the *Summa.* For example, proportion is mentioned in I, 91, 3c., clarity in II-II, 142, 4c, and both together in II-II, 145, 2c and 180, 2 ad 3.

2. *Comm. Div. Nom.,* IV, 5.

3. Pseudo-Dionysius, *The Divine Names,* IV, 7.

4. "Unumquodque dicitur bonum inquantum est perfectum . . . Perfectum autem dicitur, cui nihil deest secundum modum suae perfectionis. Cum autem unumquodque sit id quod est per suam formam; forma autem praesupponit quaedam, et quaedam ad ipsam ex necessitate consequuntur; ad hoc aliquid sit perfectum et bonum, necesse est quod formam habeat, et ea quae praeexiguntur ad eam, et ea quae consequuntur ad ipsam" ("To be called 'good' things must be perfect . . . Being perfect means lacking nothing requisite to one's own mode of perfection. Now what a thing is its form determines, and form presupposes certain things and has certain necessary consequences. So, to be good and perfect, a thing must possess form and the prerequisites and consequences of form"); *ST,* I, 5, 5c.

5. Adelchi Baratono, *Arte e poesia* (Milan, 1945), pp. 154–155.

6. Luigi Pareyson, "Sui fondamenti dell'estetica," in *Teoria dell'arte* (Milan, 1965), pp. 65–76.

7. "Formal structure is characterized by the confining of the infinite in what is spatially and temporally finite, so that a multiplicity is gathered into an organic unity"; Enzo Paci, *Tempo e relazione* (Turin, 1954), p. 209.

8. "Life is form, and form is the modality of life"; Henri Focillon, *The Life of Form in Art* (New Haven, 1942), p. 2.

9. Pantheism and mysticism as in Goethe, relationism and organicism as in Whitehead.

10. Form "expresses a desire for fixity, for a standstill; but not in the manner of a standstill in the past. In reality the work is born of one change

and prepares another"; Focillon, *Life of Form in Art,* p. 16. Yet another relationist concept of form is that it has an emergent character which serves to impede relativization: "The resolution of things into centers of relationships gives way to forms. One must never forget that, although forms are determined by the process which has brought them about, they are nonetheless open and always in the course of formation"; Paci, *Tempo e relazione,* p. 27.

11. On this aspect of Aquinas's thought, see the accurate interpretation by Etienne Gilson, *Le Thomisme,* 5th ed. (Paris, 1948), particularly in chap. 1, where he discusses form and substance. See also Paul Grenet, *Le Thomisme* (Paris, 1953), chaps. 2 and 3.

12. *Summa contra Gentiles,* II, 54, 3.

13. Ibid., II, 54, 6. In the case of intellectual substances, which have form without matter, Aquinas says that the form is that which is (*quod est*). But here also the final perfection of something is produced by *ipsum esse,* by the act of existing.

14. Cicero, *Tusculan Disputations,* trans. J. E. King, 2d ed. (London and Cambridge, Mass., 1950), IV, 13.

15. St. Augustine, letter 3 (to Nebridius), in *Letters,* trans. Sr. Wilfred Parsons, 5 vols. (Washington, D.C., 1951), I, 9.

16. Hermann Diels, ed., *Die Fragmente der Vorsokratiker,* 5th ed., ed. W. Krantz (Berlin, 1934–54), 31, B122 (cited hereafter as Diels–Krantz); translated in part by Kathleen Freeman as *Ancilla to the Pre-Socratic Philosophers* (Oxford: Blackwell, 1948).

17. Philolaus of Tarentum, in Diels–Krantz, 44, B4; translation in Freeman, *Ancilla.*

18. Philolaus of Tarentum, in Diels–Krantz, 44, B6; translation in Freeman, *Ancilla.*

19. Views attributed to the Pythagoreans in Diogenes Laertius, *Lives of Eminent Philosophers,* trans. R. D. Hicks, 2 vols. (London and New York, 1925), VIII, 33.

20. Plutarch, *De Defectu Oraculorum,* 422B; translation by Isabel Bredin.

21. Theon of Smyrna on Archytas, in Diels–Krantz, 47, A19a; translation by Isabel Bredin.

22. Theon of Smyrna on Hippasus, in Diels–Krantz, 18, A13; translation by Isabel Bredin.

23. See Aristotle, *Topics,* 116b21; *Metaphysics,* 1078b1; Plato, *Philebus,* 26a6.

24. Pliny the Elder, *Historia Naturalis,* XXXIV, 55, trans. H. Rackham (London and Cambridge, Mass., 1952).

25. See Erwin Panofsky, "The History of the Theory of Human Proportions as a Reflection of the History of Styles," in *Meaning in the Visual*

Arts (Harmondsworth, 1970). See also Julius Schlosser Magnino, *La letteratura artistica,* trans. F. Rossi, 3d ed. (Florence, 1964), pp. 65–66.

26. Galen, *Placita Hippocratis et Platonis,* V, 3; quoted and translated in Panofsky, *Meaning in the Visual Arts,* p. 92.

27. Plato, *The Sophist,* 235e–236c, trans. H. N. Fowler (London and Cambridge, Mass., 1921).

28. These two passages, from Vitruvius, *De Architectura,* I, 2, are quoted and translated in Panofsky, *Meaning in the Visual Arts,* pp. 96–97.

29. See K. Svoboda, *L'esthétique de St. Augustin et ses sources* (Brno, 1927).

30. Because of Boethius, Pythagoras was considered in the Middle Ages to be the inventor of music: "primum omnium Pythagoras inventor musicae"; Engelbert Admontensis, *De Musica,* II, chap. 10, in *Scriptores Ecclesiastici,* II, 305.

31. Boethius, *De Institutione Musica,* ed. Godofredus Friedlein (Leipzig, 1867), I, 3; also in *PL* 63, cols. 1167–1300).

32. Boethius, *De Institutione Musica,* I, 3. For Boethius, consonance in music was an intelligible relation which at the same time could manifest itself only in the material form of acoustic vibration. Thus, an abstract relation has a physical source. "Consonantia, quae omnem musicae modulationem regit, praeter sonum fieri non potest, sonus vero praeter quendam pulsum percussionemque non redditur, pulsus vero atque percussio nullo modo esse potest, nisi praecesserit motus" ("Consonance regulates all musical modulations and cannot exist without sound. But there can be no sound unless something is struck or beaten, and no striking unless there is first some movement"); ibid. But, although the senses are the indispensable vehicle of notes and chords, only the intellect is able to discriminate and appreciate them. These are very reasonable observations, but Boethius goes on to draw rather extreme conclusions. Thus, he argues that the true musician is not the player of an instrument, who may be gifted and instinctive but is musically inexpert. He says the same about the composer of melody, at least if this is what he means by the term *poeta.* Some understand by this term a maker of the verses that are put to music; but de Bruyne takes it to mean a composer, and this is in fact its etymological sense. It could, of course, refer to someone who does both, a composer of songs or a troubadour. In any case, the true musician, for Boethius, is someone who knows the rules of music, a theorist whose skill in music is also a skill in mathematics, whose judgments are based on reason rather than on instinct. "Quod scilicet quoniam totum in ratione ac speculatione positum est, hoc proprie musicae deputabitur, isque est musicus" ("Thus, since this is established wholly by means of reason and thought, it is rightly classed as music; and such a person is a musician"); ibid., I, 34.

Here, the immediate aesthetic sensibility is valued less highly than an intellectualization of art. This attitude, in various—and usually more moderate—forms, was a constant in the medieval aesthetic consciousness. It reappears in Aquinas, in an intellectualist version tailored to his style of thinking.

33. Ibid., I, 8.

34. Ibid., I, 2. These arguments expose the limitations of Boethius' bias toward theory, which led him to say that a true musician was not someone who played music but someone familiar with the mathematical laws of sound. It has been observed that if each planet produced a different note of the scale, together they would produce a horrible dissonance. Medieval theorists, however, were concerned, not with this kind of problem, but rather with the perfection of numerical correspondences. The medievals approached their day-to-day experiences with a store of Platonic certainties. We may reflect that the ways of science are infinite if we recall that Renaissance scientists began to suspect that the earth moved because in so doing it would produce the eighth note of the scale. On the other hand, the theory of the music of the spheres produced also a more concrete conception of beauty—the beauty of cosmic cycles, of the regular play of time and the seasons, of the composition of the elements and the motions of nature, of biological rhythms and the humors; a beauty, in short, of the harmony of all things, macrocosm along with microcosm. See Boethius, *De Institutione Musica*, I, 2.

35. John Scottus Eriugena, *De Divisione Naturae*, III passim.

36. Honorius of Autun, *Liber Duodecim Quaestionum*, chap. 2 (*PL* 172, col. 1179).

37. Tullio Gregory, *Anima Mundi* (Florence, 1955), p. 214.

38. Plato, *Timaeus*, 30d and 31c.

39. See Gregory, *Anima Mundi*, p. 182.

40. William of Conches, *Dragmaticon*, I; quoted in Gregory, *Anima Mundi*, p. 178.

41. Alan of Lille, *The Plaint of Nature*, trans. James J. Sheridan (Toronto, 1980), p. 128.

42. Macrobius, *In Somnium Scipionis*, II, 2.

43. Vitruvius, *De Architectura*, III, 1.

44. See *EEM*, II, 343–368.

45. See H. O. Taylor, *The Medieval Mind*, 2 vols. (London, 1911), II, 347–348.

46. Hucbald of Saint-Amand, *Musica Enchiriadis*, chap. 9, in Gerbert, *Scriptores Ecclesiastici*, I, 159.

47. Franco of Cologne, *Ars Cantus Mensurabilis*, chap. 11, in *Scriptorum de Musica Medii Aevi*, ed. E. de Coussemaker, 3 vols. (Paris, 1864–67;

reprint, Hildesheim, 1963), I, 132. A *conductus* was a medieval composition for two or three parts, distinguished from the motet in being homophonic, not polyphonic. See also J. W. Vollaerts, *Rhythmic Proportions in Early Medieval Ecclesiastical Chant*, 2d ed. (Leiden, 1960).

48. See Saintsbury, *History of Criticism*, I, 404.

49. Two ninth-century examples are Aurelianus Reomensis and Remigius of Auxerre. See Gerbert, *Scriptores Ecclesiastici*, I, 23 and 68.

50. Geoffrey of Vinsauf, *The New Poetics*, trans. Jane Baltzell Kopp, in *Three Medieval Rhetorical Arts*, ed. James J. Murphy (Berkeley and London, 1971). See in particular p. 61.

51. See also Conrad of Hirschau, *Dialogus super Auctores*, ed. G. Schepss (Wurzburg, 1889); and Hugh of St. Victor, *Didascalicon*, chap. 10.

52. Edmond Faral, *Les arts poétiques de XIIe et du XIIIe siècle* (Paris, 1924), p. 60. See also Paolo Bagni, *La costituzione della poesia nelle arti del XII–XIII secolo* (Bologna, 1968); and Richard McKeon, "Rhetoric in the Middle Ages," in *Critics and Criticism*, ed. R. S. Crane (Chicago, 1952).

53. See Curtius, *European Literature*, p. 489.

54. See Louis Réau, "L'influence de la forme sur l'iconographie de l'art médiévale," in the anthology *Formes de l'art, formes de l'esprit* (Paris, 1951).

55. This was a special kind of theory connected partly with the idea of *homo quadratus* and partly with an esoteric mysticism of proportion. It appeared, for instance, in the cryptic form of the lapidary signs used by masonic guilds. For proportion in architecture see Matila Ghyka, *Le nombre d'or*, 2 vols. (Paris, 1952), II, chap. 2; Marius Schneider, *Singende Sterne* (Basel, 1955); O. von Simson, *The Gothic Cathedral* (New York, 1956); Paul Frankl, *The Gothic* (Princeton, 1960).

56. *Summa contra Gentiles*, III, 54, 14.

57. Ibid., II, 16, 8.

58. Ibid., II, 80–81, 8.

59. *Commentarium in Aristotelis Librum De Anima*, ed P. F. Angeli M. Pirotta (Taurini and Rome, 1948), I, 9, 144 (hereafter cited as *Comm. De Anima*).

60. *Summa contra Gentiles*, II, 53, 2.

61. *ST*, II-II, 141, 4 ad 3.

62. *ST*, II-II, 145, 2c.

63. *ST*, II-II, 142, 2c.

64. *ST*, II-II, 180, 2 ad 3.

65. See R. Garrigou-Lagrange, *Christian Perfection and Contemplation according to St. Thomas Aquinas* (St. Louis and London, 1937), where Aquinas is said to have taken this theory from Albertus Magnus, who wrote: "Deus quamvis autem sit simplex in substantia, est tamen multiplex in attributis. Et ideo, ex proportione motus ad actum resultat summa pulchritudo,

quod sapientia non discordat a potentia et sic de aliis" ("Although God is simple in his substance, he is complex in his attributes. Thus, the highest beauty comes from the proportion of motion to act: wisdom accords with power, and so too with the rest").

66. *ST*, I, 73, 1c.

67. Every type of order, then, is open to a number of finalistic interpretations, in which the accent is put upon the idea of an ultimate perfection which determines the order. "Order is a disposition which objects have toward one another, in accordance with the requirements of a goal"; L. Lachance, *Le concept de droit selon Aristote et St. Thomas* (Paris and Montreal, 1933), p. 176. For an exhaustive treatment of the concept of order see A. Silva-Tarouca, *Thomas heute* (Vienna, 1947).

68. "Digitorum quoque numerus perfectus est, et ordo decentissimus" ("The number of the fingers is perfect, and their order is most seemly"); Isidore of Seville, *Differentiarum*, II, 63, (*PL* 83, col. 79). The word *decentissimus* involves an aesthetic judgment, but the main emphasis of the passage is scientific and religious. Usually, Isidore talks about beauty only in connection with external ornament, the hair, the beard, and so on. This sentence, however, expresses a principle which we shall also find in Aquinas's aesthetics.

69. See *Summa contra Gentiles*, II, 16, 10.

70. Luigi Pareyson, *Estetica*, 2d ed. (Bologna, 1960), gives an interesting analysis of this kind of relation in works of art: "The parts of a work of art sustain a twofold type of relation among themselves—a relation of each to the other parts, and of each to the whole" (p. 86).

71. Silva-Tarouca, *Thomas heute*, p. 76, n. 7. This work is an interpretation of Aquinas's system in terms of the concept of order. I do not necessarily accept everything that the author says, but it is very relevant to the issue under discussion.

72. *EEM*, III, 304. This theory had its roots in Plato and Pythagoras. "For since God desired to make it resemble most closely that intelligible Creature which is fairest of all and in all ways most perfect, He constructed it as a Living Creature, one and visible, containing within itself all the living creatures which are by nature akin to itself"; *Timaeus*, 30d.

73. In *Comm. Div. Nom.*, IV, 6. The summary which follows is based upon this, and the quotations are taken from it.

74. *De Veritate*, XXII, 1 ad 12.

75. *ST*, I, 5, 4 ad 1.

76. Aristotle, *De anima*, 426a. The Latin translation given here, which was the version upon which Aquinas wrote his *Commentary*, is that of William of Moerbeke.

77. *Comm. De Anima*, III, 2, 597.

78. Aquinas was perhaps sharper than he knew. For in fact both the terms *proportio* and *ratio*, in the passage in question, were William of Moerbeke's renderings of one and the same Greek word, namely *logos*.

79. *ST*, I, 12. 1.

80. A great many commentators have stressed this psychological type of proportion. L. Taparelli d'Azeglio said that the contemplation of beauty is contemplation of a truth proportioned in respect of our cognitive abilities; "Delle ragioni del bello secondo la dottrina di San Tommaso d'Aquino," 19 articles in *Civiltà Cattolica*, 4 (1859–60), art. 6, p. 45. C. Mazzantini says that the chameleon ability of the intellect to become all things disposes it toward the object of knowledge. Things are independent of the act of knowledge, "but they are not by nature alien to our minds; if they were, they would remain impervious, obscure, opaque, unknowable"; *Linee fondamentali*, p. 331. Bernard Bosanquet connects proportion with Plotinian influences and concludes, "The ultimate ground of attraction in beauty is the affinity, revealed in symmetry, between the percipient and the perceived"; *A History of Aesthetics*, p. 147. It is easy to understand why this aspect of proportion is attractive to Marc de Munnynck. De Munnynck allows for an objective type of proportion, between matter and form; but he emphasizes the proportion between the knower and the known, which seems to him to be the foundation for a concept of subjective taste.

81. John Dewey, *Art as Experience* (New York, 1934), p. 216.

82. See also *ST*, I, 76, 4.

83. St. Thomas Aquinas, *Commentarium in Psalmos*, XLIV, 2 (cited hereafter as *Comm. in Psalmos*).

84. *ST*, I, 42, 3c.

85. For beauty as bodily size, see *Comm. Eth.*, IV, 8, 4. See also *Comm. in I Sent.*, 31, 2, 1c, where he writes: "To these two [qualities, clarity and consonance] Aristotle adds a third, when he says that beauty is found only in a large body; so that small men can be called correctly proportioned and well shaped, but not beautiful" ("His duobus addit tertium philosophus ubi dicit quod pulchritudo non est nisi in magno corpore; unde parvi homines possunt dici commensurati et formosi, sed non pulchri"). This passage has embarrassed and misled a number of commentators. De Bruyne confines himself to looking upon it as a clarification of the view that beauty is a superabundance, a richness of being. If this were the case, beauty would belong to the category of *formosus* (shapely, or "filled with form"). Cardinal Mercier, who is normally very acute, puts this point rather crudely: "In practice, a beautiful object is one which is spacious and potent and able to stimulate the faculties vigorously."; *Cours de philosophie*, II, p. 534. Elsewhere, integrity has been discussed in somewhat plainer

terms, by James Joyce for instance. It is well known that Joyce's aesthetics employs Thomistic concepts, and in particular the three formal criteria of beauty; although, of course, it is a purely formal Thomism adopted into the *forma mentis* of the great Irish writer. Harry Levin has described Joyce as a realist in the medieval sense of the term and says that his thought is Scholastic in all ways save for its premises. Joyce interprets the three criteria, not as objective properties of things, but rather as stages in our aesthetic encounter with them. Integrity is the first stage, a moment of synthesis in which the object is isolated and considered as something separate from everything else; it is grasped as integral and as a *thing*. As he says in *Stephen Hero*, the object's integrity is the first quality of beauty, and "it is declared in a simple sudden synthesis of the faculty which apprehends." He gives a more detailed account of it in *A Portrait of the Artist as a Young Man*: "Look at that basket, he said . . . In order to see that basket, said Stephen, your mind first of all separates the basket from the rest of the visible universe which is not the basket. The first phase of apprehension is a bounding line drawn about the object to be apprehended . . . But, temporal or spatial, the aesthetic image is first luminously apprehended as selfbounded and selfcontained upon the immeasurable background of space and time which is not it. You apprehend it as *one* thing. You see it as one whole. You apprehend its wholeness. That is *integritas*." It is clear that to understand Aquinas's term in this fashion is to strip it of its original ontological character. When the three criteria, especially the first two, are taken in an epistemological sense, their importance dwindles. It should be noted also that what Joyce is describing here does constitute part of the Thomist epistemology, except that it cannot be separated from the *simplex apprehensio* nor from the act of judgment which grasps the concrete individual existence of objects. Aquinas's notion of the aesthetic *visio* certainly implies a process in which an object becomes a specific object of consciousness. But this process traces, as it were, an ideal boundary of the object, whereas the three criteria (proportion, integrity, clarity) refer above all to its internal structure. They have to do with volume rather than with outline. See Umberto Eco, *The Aesthetics of Chaosmos* (Tulsa, 1982), and William T. Noon, *Joyce and Aquinas* (New Haven, 1957).

86. *ST,* I, 73, 1c.
87. *ST,* I, 39, 8c.
88. *Comm. in IV Sent.*, 44, 3, 1a, c.
89. Pareyson, *Estetica*, p. 85.
90. *Comm. De Anima*, II, 8, 332.
91. Pareyson, *Estetica*, p. 86.
92. *ST,* I, 16, 1c.
93. Pareyson, *Estetica*, p. 87. The analogy between Pareyson's theory

and Aquinas's is not wholly fortuitous. Pareyson's theory of a *forma formante* presupposes a metaphysics of construction. Thus, the existence of a divine Artificer is ground for the fact that when a form is invented, it already possesses, as it springs into being, an intentionality. This intentionality is the kind that leaves it open to various outcomes. It is not the type of principle of order found in Scholastic realism, but rather a matrix of possible ways of ordering things, based upon the divine laws of the universe—and these are open laws, laws of process. On this feature of Pareyson's aesthetics, see Umberto Eco, "L'estetica della formatività," in *La definizione dell'arte*.

94. *ST*, II-II, 145, 2c.

95. Bosanquet, *A History of Aesthetics*, p. 147.

96. *Comm. in IV Sent.*, 48, 2, 3c.

97. See *Comm. De Anima*, II, 14. For a wide-ranging study of the whole matter see J. de Tonquédec, *Questions de cosmologie et de physique chez Aristote et St. Thomas* (Paris, 1950).

98. *ST*, II-II, 142, 4c.

99. *ST*, II-II, 180, 2 ad 3.

100. *ST*, II-II, 145, 2c.

101. Chrétien de Troyes, *Arthurian Romances*, trans. W. W. Comfort (London, 1914), p. 21.

102. See above, Chapter III, note 12.

103. Many examples from French and Provençal poetry are given in *EEM*, III, 9–10.

104. Huizinga, *Waning of the Middle Ages*, p. 259. See in general chap. 19.

105. Hugh of St. Victor, *De Tribus Diebus*, chap. 12 (*PL* 176, col. 821; the treatise appears in *PL* as Book VII of *Didascalicon* but is in fact a separate work). The reference to William of Auvergne is in *EEM*, III, 86.

106. *ST*, I, 39, 8c.

107. See Panofsky, *Abbot Suger*, Introduction.

108. See Giovanni Getto, "Poesia e teologia nel *Paradiso* di Dante," in *Aspetti della poesia di Dante* (Florence, 1966), pp. 193–235.

109. St. Hildegard, *Liber Divinorum Operum*, I, 4, 13 (*PL* 197, cols. 812–813). See also Charles Singer, ed. *Studies in the History and Method of Science* (Oxford, 1917), p. 33.

110. Pseudo-Dionysius, *The Celestial Hierarchy*, XV, 2 (in Chevallier, *Dionysiaca*); and *The Divine Names*, IV, 4–6.

111. See Menéndez y Pelayo, *Historia de las ideas estéticas*, chap. 3. Von Simson, *The Gothic Cathedral*, gives a useful account of the relations among Platonism, the aesthetics of light (which connected with the aesthetics of proportion), and the poetics of medieval architecture.

112. St. Augustine, *De Quantitate Animae*, chaps. 8–11. See Svoboda, *L'esthétique de St. Augustin*, p. 59.

113. Robert Grosseteste, *Commentarium in Hexaemeron;* quoted in Pouillon, "La Beauté."

114. Robert Grosseteste, *Commentarium in Divinis Nominibus;* quoted in Pouillon, "La Beauté."

115. Robert Grosseteste, *De Luce*, in *Die philosophischen Werke des Robert Grosseteste*, ed. L. Baur (Münster, 1912), p. 51. The translation, *On Light*, is by Clare C. Riedl (Milwaukee, 1942), p. 10. In addition to the analogy with Bergson, we might note certain parallels between Grosseteste's metaphysics of energy and "fields of light" and some of the concepts found in modern physics.

116. The best account of Grosseteste's aesthetics is *EEM*, III, chap. 4. The most complete bibliography on Grosseteste is S. Gieben, "Bibliographia universa Roberti Grosseteste ab an. 1473 ad an. 1969," *Collectanea Franciscana*, 39 (1969), 362–418.

117. St. Bonaventure, *Commentarium in II Sententiarum;* 12, 2, 1 arg. 4; in *Opera Omnia*, 10 vols. (Florence, 1882–1902).

118. Ibid., 13, 2, 2c.

119. *ST*, I, 67, 3c.

120. *Comm. De Anima*, II, 14, 421. On this topic see de Tonquédec, *Questions de cosmologie*. In late Scholasticism, the concept of light lost its hard metaphysical sense and became an imprecise metaphor. See Denis the Carthusian, *De Venustate Mundi et Pulchritudine Dei*, in *Opera Omnia*, 44 vols. (Tournai, 1896–1913), XXXIV. On Bonaventure's aesthetics see E. J. Spargo, *The Category of the Aesthetic in the Philosophy of St. Bonaventure* (New York, 1953).

121. This and the following quotations of Albertus Magnus's *De Pulchro et Bono* are from the text printed in Aquinas, *Opera Omnia*, VII, 43–47.

122. *EEM*, III, 166.

123. Pseudo-Dionysius, *The Divine Names*, IV, 7.

124. *Comm. Div. Nom.*, IV, 5.

125. Ibid. See also ibid., IV, 6: "Forma autem est quaedam irradiatio proveniens ex prima claritate; claritas autem est de ratione pulchritudinis" ("Form is a certain radiance that comes from the first clarity; and clarity belongs to the nature of beauty").

126. *ST*, I, 67, 3c.

127. *ST*, I, 57, 4 ad 1.

128. *ST*, III, 45, 2c.

129. Aquinas also attributes to *claritas* an expressive or communicative quality in itself. See, for example, *ST*, II-II, 132, 1c, where it signifies a "manifestation"—that is, expression—of a state of internal beauty.

130. Sometimes the requirements of a particular system have led to an impoverishment of the concept of clarity. Maurice de Wulf, for example, asserts that clarity is a quality which pertains especially to art, since a work of art causes the ideal to shine forth in the sensible and the material (*Art et beauté*, p. 79). However, although clarity may in fact mean this, it is not its only meaning. Taken in an ontological sense it means something more. The notion of making the ideal present, when interpreted on the ontological rather than the artistic level, can only mean that substantial *form* is manifested in matter. But in fact clarity seems to me to refer to the manifestation of the *whole* of a work, the work which has been perfected by its organizing *form*—the manifestation, that is, of an ordered organism. De Wulf himself was not unaware of this when he wrote: "Yes, the work of art ought to be resplendent: because of the multiplicity of its elements, because of the variety of relations which unites them, because of the principle of unity which binds them" (p. 80). For Maritain, *claritas* was an ontological splendor, not a conceptual clarity. It referred, not to a clarity and intelligibility "for us," but to a clarity and luminosity *in se*. *Form* is the principle of a thing's intelligibility, but it is an intelligibility which has no reference to something else; rather, it is a real internal structure, and therefore a "mystery"; see *Art and Scholasticism*, p. 41. This element of ontological mystery, which is something peculiar to Maritain's aesthetics, would require separate discussion. It gradually developed into the theory that art is a manifestation of being because of a connaturality between the depths of human subjectivity and the real; see Maritain, "De la connaissance poétique," *Revue Thomiste*, 44 (1938), 87–98. In other words, poetic knowledge is conceived of as creative intuition; see Maritain, *Creative Intuition in Art and Poetry* (Princeton, 1953). In his interpretation of Aquinas, Maritain adopts the objectivist tone of Albertus Magnus's *De Pulchro et Bono*. I am in agreement with him on the definition of intelligibility *in se*: defined as the splendor of form, it is an element from Albertus which is present also in Aquinas. However, it is an element which was absorbed into Aquinas and superseded in the view that *visio* brings ontological clarity to aesthetic consciousness (thus making it clarity "for us"), and that ontological clarity can be assimilated to form in the broad sense. I am in more substantial agreement with de Bruyne. He interprets *claritas* as expressiveness, except that he inclines to emphasize the notion of an organizing idea which is incarnated in the sensible: "Clarity . . . is expressive of the principle of organization which is called substantial form." Thus, the beauty of a person consists in the resplendence of his essential and permanent nature (his *form*) in his transient appearances. The essence of the aesthetic is just this appearance of universal value embodied in the individual (see *EEM*, III, 307). Here again, however, I must advance the usual reservation: *claritas*

does indeed mean this, but this does not exhaust its meaning. It is not just that an organism signifies the universal which gives it life. It also signifies *itself*, in its combination of universality with contingency, in the reality of its concrete form. A more felicitous account of clarity, albeit one lacking in scientific rigor, and more an intuition than a proper interpretation, is to be found in Joyce's *A Portrait of the Artist as a Young Man*: "The connotation of the word, Stephen said, is rather vague. Aquinas uses a term which seems to be inexact. It baffled me for a long time. It would lead you to believe that he had in mind symbolism or idealism, the supreme quality of beauty being a light from some other world, the idea of which the matter is but the shadow, the reality of which it is but the symbol. I thought he might mean that *claritas* is the artistic discovery and representation of the divine purpose in anything or a force of generalization which would make the esthetic image a universal one, make it outshine its proper conditions. But that is literary talk. I understand it so. When you have apprehended that basket as one thing and have then analysed it according to its form and apprehended it as a thing you make the only synthesis which is logically and esthetically permissible. You see that it is that thing which it is and no other thing. The radiance of which he speaks is the scholastic *quidditas*, the *whatness* of a thing. This supreme quality is felt by the artist when the esthetic image is first conceived in his imagination. The mind in that mysterious instant Shelley likened beautifully to a fading coal. The instant wherein that supreme quality of beauty, the clear radiance of the esthetic image, is apprehended luminously by the mind which has been arrested by its wholeness and fascinated by its harmony is the luminous silent stasis of aesthetic pleasure"; (Harmondsworth, 1960), pp. 212–213. If we think of *quidditas* as substance, in the sense which I have defined earlier, then this interesting passage in Joyce is acceptable at the very least as a persuasive suggestion. See Eco, *The Aesthetics of Chaosmos*.

V. Concrete Problems and Applications

1. St. Hilary, *De Trinitate*, II, 1 (*PL* 10, 51).

2. *ST*, I, 35, 2c. The whole of question 35 deals with the matter under discussion.

3. *ST*, I, 35, 1 ad 2. Aquinas's reference is to St. Hilary, *Liber de Synodis*, 13 (*PL* 10, col. 490), where St. Hilary uses *similitudo* as a synonym for *species*.

4. Aquinas is careful to say that "among the divine persons imitation indicates not subordination but simply likeness" ("imitatio in divinis personis non significat posterioritatem, sed solam assimilationem"); *ST*, I, 35, 1 ad 3.

5. "Ipsa autem forma significatur per speciem, quia per formam un-umquodque in specie constituitur" ("Form signifies species, for a thing belongs to a species because of its form"); *ST*, I, 5, 5c.

6. This is an ancient idea which goes back to Plutarch. But here in Aquinas, as has been noted, it is grounded in proportion. Also, Aquinas's presentation of the theory implies a conception of the image as something regenerative, for it introduces form in place of the deformed. The beauty which is absent from an ugly object comes to actuality in its image, in virtue of the fact that the image conforms with the object.

7. *Summa contra Gentiles*, II, 72, 3 and 4.

8. *ST*, I-II, 54, 1c.

9. *De Ente et Essentia*, 1.

10. *De Veritate*, 26, 10c.

11. A phrase which Aquinas takes from Aristotle's *De anima*.

12. These were traditional theories, which Aquinas revivified by putting them in a more critical context. In Isidore, by contrast, they had an ingenuous, almost pictorial character: "Caput namque ad coelum refertur, in quo sunt duo oculi, quasi duo luminaria solis et lunae . . . Jam vero in capitis arce mens collocata est, tamquam in coelo Deus, ut ab alto speculatur omnia, atque regat . . . Factus est autem homo ad contemplationem coeli rigidus, et erectus, non sicut pecora in humum prona, atque vergentia" ("For his head points to the sky, and has two eyes, just like the two luminaries the sun and the moon . . . The mind is situated in the body's summit, the head, just as God is in heaven, whence he observes and rules all things . . . Man has been made straight and erect so that he may contemplate heaven, not like cattle which are bent and inclined to earth"); *Differentiarum*, II, 48, 49, 50 (*PL* 83, cols. 77–78).

13. "This distinction between man and brute is outwardly expressed by the difference of the relation of the head to the body. In the case of the lower brutes both are deformed: in all brutes the head is directed towards the earth, where the objects of its will lie; even in the higher species the head and the body are still far more one than in the case of man, whose head seems freely set upon his body, as if only carried by and not serving it. This human excellence is exhibited in the highest degree by the Apollo of Belvedere; the head of the god of the Muses, with eyes fixed on the far distance, stands so freely on his shoulders that it seems wholly delivered from the body, and no more subject to its cares." This passage, which was written about six centuries after Aquinas, comes from A. Schopenhauer, *The World as Will and Idea*, 3 vols. (London, 1883), I, 230.

14. *Comm. De Anima*, I, 9, 135.

15. *ST*, I, 25, 6 ad 3.

16. *ST*, II-II, 91, 1c.

17. *ST,* II-II, 91, 1 ad 2.

18. *ST,* II-II, 91, 2c. These were views which Aquinas took directly from St. Augustine. In his *Confessions,* Augustine discoursed at some length on the mystical emotions which sacred music could inspire in him. "At times indeed it seems to me that I am paying them greater honour than is their due—when, for example, I feel that by those holy words my mind is kindled more religiously and fervently to a flame of piety because I hear them sung than if they were not sung: and I observe that all the varying emotions of my spirit have modes proper to them in voice and song, whereby, by some secret affinity, they are made more alive"; *The Confessions of St. Augustine,* trans. F. J. Sheed (London and New York, 1944), X, 33. The whole of this chapter is devoted to music and its psychological effects.

19. Plato, *The Republic,* III; Aristotle, *Politics,* VIII.

20. Boethius, *De Institutione Musica,* I, 1.

21. *ST,* II-II, 91, 2c.

22. *ST,* II-II, 141, 4 ad 3.

23. See *ST,* II-II, 91, 2 ad 2. I am not paraphrasing Aquinas here, but drawing out the implications of what he says.

24. *ST,* II-II, 91, 2 ob. 4.

25. *ST,* II-II, 91, 2 ad 4.

26. See *ST,* II-II, 141, 2c.

27. *ST,* II-II, 91, 2 ad 5. Augusto Guzzo, in his essay "Il gregoriano e Palestrina," emphasizes that medieval song is essentially religious, and its aesthetic character is secondary. "Christian music in the earliest centuries was not intended to be art; if it was art, this happened naturally, but its primary orientation was not artistic. It was practical rather than artistic purposes which determined and ratified it . . . Even in the centuries when Gregorian chant was at the summit of its artistic involvement, this was a matter of the external sound rather than the internal sentiment"; *Studi di arte religiosa* (Turin, 1932), pp. 181–183.

28. See G. Vecchi, ed., *Poesia latina medievale* (Parma, 1952), pp. 104, 118, 374. See also P. Wagner, "La sequenza ed il suo svolgimento profano," in *Antologia della storia della musica,* ed. Andrea della Corte, 4th ed. (Turin, 1945).

29. It is clear, from the fact that Aquinas considers the matter of the *histriones,* that he had in mind the light verse which I referred to above.

30. *ST,* I-II, 32, 2 ad 3; see also *ST,* I-II, 60, 5c.

31. See Huizinga, *Waning of the Middle Ages,* chap. 15. On medieval symbolism see also Eugenio Battisti's "Simbolo e classicismo," in his *Rinascimento e Barocco* (Turin, 1960).

32. Alan of Lille, *De Incarnatione Christi (Rhythmus Alter)* (*PL* 210, col. 579).

33. See Henri Focillon, *The Year 1000* (New York, 1971); Le Goff, *Civilisation de l'occident médiéval;* Lewis Mumford, *The Condition of Man* (London, 1944), pp. 138–139.

34. For a rich and well-documented survey of medieval symbolism see Louis Réau, *Iconographie de l'art chrétien,* 3 vols. (Paris, 1955–59), I, Introduction and pp. 67–245.

35. Macrobius, *In Somnium Scipionis,* I, 14.

36. Richard of St. Victor, *Benjamin Major,* II, 12 (*PL* 196, col. 90).

37. Eriugena, *De Divisione Naturae,* V, 3 (*PL* 122, cols. 865–866).

38. Huizinga, *Waning of the Middle Ages,* p. 194.

39. Ibid., pp. 195, 197, 198.

40. See Etienne Gilson, *La philosophie au moyen age,* 2d ed. (Paris, 1944), chap. 5; Arnold Hauser, *The Social History of Art,* 2 vols. (London, 1951), I; F. Ulivi, "Il sentimento francescano delle cose e S. Bonaventura," *Lettere Italiane,* 14 (1962), 1–32.

41. I am conscious of the controversial nature of this statement. In fact there is as yet no agreed-upon definition of the concept of analogy as it is used in Aquinas. My interpretation receives support from Gilson's view that analogy operates in the judgment rather than in conceptualization. See Gilson, *Le Thomisme,* p. 153. F.-A. Blanche, by contrast, adopts an extreme position by defining analogy as something which mediates between the concept and the symbol, and by seeking ontological and metaphysical reasons for analogical resemblance. See his "L'analogie," *Revue de Philosophie,* 1931, pp. 248–271. On the concept of analogy see also Ralph McInerny, *The Logic of Analogy* (The Hague, 1971); and Enzo Melandri, *La linea e il circolo. Studio logico-filosofico sull'analogia* (Bologna, 1968).

42. Huizinga, *Waning of the Middle Ages,* p. 196.

43. Pseudo-Dionysius, *De Caelesti Hierarchia,* chap. 2.

44. Several authors claimed that both types of allegory were to be found in the Bible. See the Venerable Bede, *De Schematibus et Tropis,* in Halm, *Rhetores Latini Minores,* pp. 616–617; and Hugh of St. Victor, *De Scripturis et Scriptoribus Sacris,* V (*PL* 175, cols. 13–15).

45. St. Jerome, *Epistolae,* 54, 20 (*PL* 22, col. 619).

46. Origen, *In Ezechielem Homiliae,* IV, 1.

47. Origen, *In Genesin Homiliae,* IX, 1.

48. Gilbert of Stanford, *Commentarium in Canticum,* 20, 225; quoted in J. Leclerq, "Le commentaire de Gilbert de Stanford sur le Cantique," *Studia Anselmiana,* 20 (1948), 225.

49. St. Augustine, *De Doctrina Christiana,* bk. III and passim.

50. For example, Honorius of Autun, *De Imagine Mundi* (*PL* 172, cols. 115–187).

51. *ST,* I, 1, 9.

52. *ST,* I-II, 101, 2 ad 2.

53. *ST,* I, 1, 9 ad 1.

54. *ST,* I, 1, 9c.

55. See ibid. For the next part of my argument, see *ST,* I, 1, 10, and *Quaestiones Quodlibetales,* VII, 6 (cited hereafter as *Quaest. Quod.*).

56. Aquinas includes three other traditional senses under the heading of the literal sense—namely, the historical, etiological, and analogical senses. See *ST,* I, 1, 10 ad 2.

57. *ST,* I, 1, 10c.

58. *Quaest. Quod.,* VII, 6, 3c.

59. *Quaest. Quod.,* VII, 6, 2c.

60. *Quaest. Quod.,* VII, 6, 1c.

61. *Quaest. Quod.,* VII, 6, 3c.

62. *Quaest. Quod.,* VII, 6, 3 ad 2.

63. *Ibid.*

64. *See ST,* I, 1, 10 ad 3.

65. *ST,* I, 1, 10 ad 3.

66. *ST,* I, 1, 10c.

67. *ST,* I-II, 101, 102, and 103.

68. *ST,* I-II, 103, 4c.

69. In fact Aquinas is inclined at times to ascribe a parabolic value to the Old Testament ceremonies as well.

70. *ST,* I-II, 102, 2c.

71. *ST,* I-II, 101, 2 ob. 2.

72. Ibid.

73. *ST,* I-II, 101, 2 ad 2.

74. *ST,* I-II, 101, 2 ad 1.

75. Synod of Arras, chap. 14, in *Sacrorum Conciliorum Nova et Amplissima Collectio,* ed. J. D. Mansi, 53 vols. (Paris and Leipzig, 1901–27), XIX, col. 454.

76. *ST,* I, 1, 10 ad 3.

77. See Emile Mâle, *Religious Art in France,* trans. Marthiel Mathews (Princeton, 1978). Mâle enables us to grasp in its entirety the sociocultural conditioning underlying the psychological mechanism of allegorical interpretation. He shows how the cathedral statues can be understood only by reference to the contents of medieval encyclopedias, such as Vincent of Beauvais's *Speculum Majus.* See also Emile Mâle, "Le Portail de Senlis," in *Art et artistes du moyen age* (Paris, 1947).

78. In deducing Aquinas's poetics, I have looked at his texts very super-

ficially. I could instead have employed the criteria of analogy and homology—the first by comparing philosophical theories with concrete works of art, the second by showing a structural homology between the form of Scholastic systems and the forms of medieval art. The first of these is the one preferred by Assunto, *La critica d'arte,* in the chapter "Idee e gusto di Tommaso d'Aquino." Here Assunto compares philosophical theories with works of art of the same period and takes the former as a justification or a critical analysis of the latter. He thus feels able to say that Aquinas displays "a preference for realism and for the classical"—a view with which I am inclined to agree. He goes on: "The precedence of the true over the beautiful, which is one of the cardinal points in his aesthetics, seems to provide a theoretical justification of the art of southern Italy, both during and after the period of Frederick II, with which Aquinas must have been acquainted from his youth." And the three criteria of beauty, Assunto adds, reflect the taste of Nicolas Pisano (p. 253). It is all too easy, in this kind of comparison, to attribute to a Scholastic concept such as *verum* a meaning which has been altered in the light of modern criticism, and to arrive at a notion such as "realism." This is always risky. After all, it might be discovered that Aquinas (who lived as much in France as in Italy) considered the idealized Gothic statue-columns of the Ile de France to be more "true" than Tuscan sculpture. However, this brings us to another issue, which belongs to the history of taste and the theoretical problem of the correspondence, or parallelism, between the philosophical and the artistic consciousness in a given period.

A different tack is taken by Panofsky, *Gothic Architecture and Scholasticism,* who examines structural analogies between the plan of a Gothic cathedral and the system of relations found in a Scholastic *Summa.*

On Aquinas's poetry see J. P. Foucher, *La littérature latine du Moyen Age* (Paris, 1963), especially the chapter "Les hymnes de St. Thomas d'Aquin."

79. *Literary Criticism of Dante Alighieri,* ed. and trans. Robert S. Haller (Lincoln, Neb., 1973), p. 99.

80. Ibid., p. 100.

VI. The Theory of Art

1. *ST,* I-II, 57, 4c.

2. Alexander of Hales, *Summa Theologica,* II, 12.

3. Cassiodorus, *De Artibus et Disciplinis Liberalium Litterarum,* Preface (*PL* 70, col. 1151).

4. John of Salisbury, *Metalogicon,* I, 12.

5. Isidore of Seville, *Etymologiae,* I, 1.

6. *ST,* I-II, 57, 3c.

7. Hugh of St. Victor, *Didascalicon*, I, 9.

8. William of Conches, *Commentarium in Timaeum;* quoted in *EEM,* II, 266.

9. *ST,* I, 117, 1c.

10. John of Salisbury, *Metalogicon,* I, 11 (ed. Clement C. J. Webb [Oxford, 1929]). This definition is ascribed by John to Isidore of Seville, but is more likely to have been taken from Hugh of St. Victor. The last phrase, *per se valens,* is rendered as "immarent" in the translation by Daniel D. McGarry (Berkeley, 1962).

11. See Erwin Panofsky, *Idea: A Concept in Art Theory* (Columbia, S.C., 1968); Schlosser Magnino, *Die Kunstliteratur,* p. 67; Arnold Hauser, *Modernism* (London, 1960).

12. The conception of art as intuition, imagination, feeling, and enlightenment was not unknown in the ancient world. See Augusto Rostagni, "Sulle tracce di un'estetica dell'intuizione presso gli antichi," in *Scritti Minori,* 3 vols. (Turin, 1955), I, 356–371. But there can be no doubt that what counted in Scholasticism was, instead, the Aristotelian tradition.

13. Mussato said that poetry was a form of knowledge that came from heaven, a gift from God: "It was a science sent down from heaven, just as law comes from that same God" ("haec fuit a summo demissa scientia caelo, cum simul excelso ius habet illa Deo"; epistle 4, quoted in Curtius, *European Literature,* p. 215. For a discussion of Albertino Mussato see Curtius, pp. 215–221). He held that the poets of the ancient world were prophets of God, and that in this sense poetry ought to be called a second theology: "quisquis erat vates, vas erat ille dei" ("whosoever was a poet, he was a prophet of God"; epistle 7, quoted in ibid., p. 216). Aquinas had referred to Aristotle's distinction between the early cosmological poets, whom Aristotle called "theologians," and philosophers (Aristotle, *Metaphysics,* 983b–984a); but Aquinas himself held that only philosophers (who for Aquinas were also theologians) were repositaries of divine knowledge. Poets, by contrast, "are liars, as the proverb has it" ("mentiuntur, sicut dicitur in proverbio vulgari"; *Comm. Met.,* 1, 3, 12. He was rather condescending about the mythical poets—Orpheus, Musaeus, and Linus—saying that they "give us to understand," by way of similitude and fable ("sub fabulari similitudine"), that water is the origin of things; *Comm. Met.,* 1, 4, 15. The proto-humanists, however, set out to add the somewhat dubious notion of the poet theologian to Scholastic terminology. The idea originated in arguments with people who supported Aristotelian intellectualism, such as the Thomist Giovannino of Mantua. Hidden beneath traditional views, they smuggled in an entirely new concept of poetry. Petrarch, Boccaccio, and Coluccio Salutati were on the same line of thought. Curtius (*European Literature,* chap. 12) refers to the piquancy of the way in

which Humanism dusted off a theological idea in its struggle with the Thomistic cultural heritage. See also Manlio Dazzi, *Il Mussato preumanista* (Vicenza, 1964), and G. Vinay, "Il Mussato e l'estetica medievale," *Giornale Storico della Letteratura Italiana*, 1949.

14. Garin, *Medioevo e Rinascimento*, p. 50. In Garin's view, the medieval period had a conception of poetry as noetic intuition, as distinct from its conception of philosophy as dianoetic explanation.

15. See Menéndez Y Pelayo, *Historia de las ideas estéticas*, pp. 303–304.

16. Avicenna, *Livre des directives et remarques*, trans. A.- M. Goichon (Paris, 1951), pp. 514–515.

17. See Curtius, *European Literature*, pp. 474–475.

18. See A. K. Coomaraswamy, "Meister Eckhart's View of Art," in *The Transformation of Nature in Art* (Cambridge, Mass., 1934). For Eckhart, an image that has been expressed is "an emanation of form" ("formalis emanatio") and "knows its own emerging forth" ("sapit proprie ebullitionem"). It is not distinct from the exemplar, but shares its life with it; it is in it and identical with it. "Ymago cum illo, cujus est, non ponit in numerum, nec sunt duae substantiae . . . Ymago proprie est emanatio simplex, formalis, transfusiva totius essentiae purae nudae; est emanatio ab intimis in silentio et exclusione omnis forinsici, vita quaedam, ac si ymagineris res ex se ipsa intumescere et bullire in se ipsa" ("An image, and the thing of which it is an image, are not separate; they are not two substances . . . An image is strictly an emanation, simple, formal, a pouring forth of the whole of an essence, pure and naked. It is an emanation from the depths, in silence, excluding everything exterior. It has a kind of life. A thing's image grows out of itself and grows upon itself"); A. Spamer, ed., *Texte aus der deutschen Mystik des XIV und XV Jahrhundert* (Jena, 1912), p. 7. See also G. Faggin, *Maestro Eckhart e la mistica preprotestante* (Milan, 1946), chap. 4.

19. *De Veritate*, III, 1, s.c. 7. The first sentence is a quotation from St. Augustine.

20. Ibid., III, 1c.

21. Ibid., III, 2c.

22. Ibid., III, 5c.

23. Ibid., III, 7c.

24. See *ST*, I, 15, 3 ad 4; also *De Veritate*, III, 7c. Similar ideas are to be found in Vincent of Beauvais, *Speculum Doctrinale*, 160–173 (*Speculum Maius*, 4 vols. [Venice, 1591]), and they had an influence upon Leon Battista Alberti. See E. R. de Zurko, "Alberti's Theory of Form and Function," *Art Bulletin*, September 1957.

25. *ST*, I, 15, 1c.

26. *ST*, I, 15, 2c.

27. *De Veritate*, III, 2c.

28. On the evolution of the terms *phantasia* and *imaginatio* in medieval psychology, see M. D. Chenu, "Imaginatio. Note de lexicographie philosophique," *Miscellanea Mercati*, 2 (1946), 593–602.

29. *ST*, I, 78, 4c.

30. See *Comm. De Anima*, III, 4, 632 and 633; 5, 641–647; 6, 664–665.

31. *ST*, I, 78, 4c.

32. *ST*, I, 12, 9 ad 2.

33. Ibid.

34. *Comm. De Anima*, III, 4, 635.

35. *ST*, I, 84, 6 ad 2.

36. *Comm. Div. Nom.*, IV, 5.

37. *Commentarium de Coelo et Mundo*, I, 6, 9; *ST*, III, 2, 1c.

38. Croce, *Aesthetic*, p. 99.

39. *Commentarium in Libros Posteriorum Analyticorum*, I, 1, 5.

40. *Comm. De Anima*, II, 1, 218. See in this connection *ST*, I, 77, 6c.

41. St. Bonaventure, *Commentarium in III Sententiarum*, 37, 1, dub. 1.

42. *ST*, III, 66, 4c.

43. St. Thomas Aquinas, *De Principiis Naturae*, 1, in *Opuscula Omnia necnon Opera Minora*, ed. R. P. Joannes Perrier (Paris, 1949). I substitute *quia* for *quamvis* in the second-last line. The text given in Roberto Busa differs in some respects from the text quoted here.

44. Silva-Tarouca, *Thomas heute*, p. 78.

45. *ST*, I-II, 49, 1c. Cf. Aristotle, *Metaphysics*, 1022b10–12.

46. *ST*, I-II, 50, 1c.

47. *ST*, I, 91, especially article 3.

48. *ST*, I, 77, 6c.

49. *De Mixtione Elementorum*; *ST*, I, 76, 4c.

50. *ST*, III, 2, 1c.

51. Aquinas appears to minimize this when he writes, in *ST*, II-II, 96, 2 ad 2: "The natural forces of things result from their substantial forms, which come to them under the action of the heavens; and so, through the same influence, they have certain active forces. On the other hand, the forms of artifacts result from the conception of the artist, and since they are nothing else but things of composition, order and shape . . . theirs is not one single natural active force" ("virtutes naturales corporum naturalium consequuntur eorum formas substantiales, quas sortiuntur ex impressione caelestium corporum: et ideo ex eorumdem impressione sortiuntur quasdam virtutes activas. Sed corporum artificialium formae procedunt ex conceptione artificis: et cum nihil aliud sint quam compositio, ordo et figura"). However, Aquinas says this only to rebut the presumptions of necromancy; his point is that the shapes produced by magic have no operative virtue. He adds in fact that "they have no power because they are

artificial, but only because of their natural matter" ("nullam virtutem sortiuntur inquantum sunt artificialia, sed solum secundum materiam naturalem"). This passage tends to confirm my interpretation, that the artistic shape exploits and coordinates the active powers of the coordinated natural elements.

52. *Summa contra Gentiles*, II, 72, 3.

53. *Comm. De Anima*, II, 1, 218. See also *ST*, I, 77, 6c.

54. *Summa contra Gentiles*, III, 65, 6; translated as *On the Truth of the Catholic Faith* by Anton C. Pegis, James F. Anderson, Vernon J. Bourke, and Charles O'Neil, 4 vols. (New York, 1955–57).

55. Jean de la Meun, *Roman de la rose*, lines 16807–18.

56. *ST*, I, 91, 3c.

57. Aristotle, *Politics*, VIII, 2.

58. Domenico Gundisalvi, *De Divisione Philosophiae*, ed. Ludwig Baur (Münster, 1903).

59. Hugh of St. Victor, *Didascalicon*, I, 9.

60. *ST*, I-II, 57, 3 ad 3.

61. Etienne Gilson, *Painting and Reality* (London, 1957), p. 31.

62. Quintilian, *Institutio Oratoria*, IX, 4.

63. *ST*, II-II, 169, 2c.

64. *ST*, I-II, 32, 1 ad 3.

65. *Summa contra Gentiles*, III, 21, 6.

66. *De Principiis Naturae*, 11.

67. *ST*, I-II, 57, 4c.

68. *ST*, I-II, 57, 3c.

69. M. Menéndez Y Pelayo is inclined to this kind of interpretation: "He never suggests that art has any aim other than art itself, nor any methods other than its own; thus, it seems fair to say that he would not have been put out of countenance, as his followers were, by the concept of form without an end— a concept which, since the time of Kant, we are accustomed to apply to art" (*Historia de las ideas estéticas*, p. 139).

70. V. del Gaizo writes: "We do not want to make St. Thomas think in a way that was impossible in the thirteenth century, but rather to see what he would have thought if he were alive in our own times"; Spunti tomistici per un'estetica moderna," *Humanitas*, 2 (1947), 373. This involves speculation about the reactions of a particular human being to particular historical circumstances and is psychologically and philosophically foolhardy. And there is nothing in the practice of history to give it any support.

71. Croce foresaw and discussed the possibility of identifying the modern concept of imagination with that of ancient and medieval times. His history of aesthetics provides a number of well-founded objections to it. See Croce, *Aesthetic*, p. 171.

72. Creativity, however, can also mean the ability to use material means in producing creations of the spirit—that is, bringing into being new entities and new worlds through an act of miraculous creation, or of "con-creation," since it involves divine inspiration. We find such a conception in G. M. Merlo, although Merlo tends to give an Augustinian tinge to Aquinas and to make his thought more mystical than it is. He writes: "The artist infuses the form of beauty into something, thus producing a work of art and imitating the creative processes of nature. This form—the form which is essence and beauty and the splendor of the Divine Beauty—is found by the artist within himself, but it has been directly given to him by God"; "Misticismo estetico di S. Tommaso." It is clear that this view is based upon a strongly Augustinian conception of the intellect. Against Merlo's interpretation we can cite the keen medieval awareness that artistic skill is acquired by study and application, and also the fact that the medievals had no concept of an autonomy or specificity of fine art. If this latter point were taken into account, Merlo's theory would have to be generalized to the point of conceding a mystical illumination in the case of barbers and shipbuilders.

73. Joyce, *Stephen Hero* (p. 84). Of course, the pious intent of the young Stephen Daedalus was to make the doctrine of art for art's sake seem acceptable to his Thomist tutors.

74. *ST,* II-II, 169, 2 ad 4.

75. There is one passage in Aquinas which is sometimes cited in order to show that he conceived of the possibility of beauty's being divorced from morality: "Everyone loves beauty. Carnal people love carnal beauty, and spiritual people love spiritual beauty" ("Omnis homo amat pulchrum: carnales amant pulchrum carnale; spirituales amant pulchrum spirituale"; *Comm. in Psalmos,* 25, 5. But when he writes *carnale* it is clear that he does not mean something morally negative. The purely physical beauty of an animal or a natural object is "carnal." As for spiritual beauty, we know that for Aquinas this referred to what was beautiful deep within itself (*radicaliter*), and was therefore more honorable and sought after by "spiritual people." There is a very clear acount of this point in Virgilio Melchiorre, "Il bello come relazionalità dell'essere in S. Tommaso," in *Arte ed esistenza* (Florence, 1956), pp. 215–230. When Aquinas writes, "An image is called beautiful if it represents a thing, even an ugly thing, faithfully" ("Aliqua imago dicitur esse pulchra si perfecte repraesentat rem quamvis turpem"; *ST,* I, 39, 8c), we should not put the stress upon the ugliness that is represented, but rather upon the perfection of the representation. The representation must gather and define the ugliness in its place in the hierarchy of ends.

76. *Libri Carolini, PL* 98, cols. 941–1350. The authorship of this work is

examined in Ann Freeman, "Theodulf of Orleans and the *Libri Carolini*," *Speculum*, 32 (1957), 663–705. An examination of the views expressed therein can be found in Assunto, *La critica d'arte*.

77. See Schlosser Magnino, *Die Kunstliteratur*, pp. 26–27.

78. Theophilus, *De Diversis Artibus* [*Schedula Diversarum Artium*], ed. and trans. C. R. Dodwell (London, 1961). For a discussion of this work, see *EEM*, II, 413–417.

79. Cennino Cennini's *Il libro dell'arte*—translated by Daniel V. Thompson as *The Craftman's Book* (New York, 1933)—is discussed in Schlosser Magnino, *Die Kunstliteratur*, p. 91, and Panofsky, *Meaning in the Visual Arts*, pp. 102–103.

80. See Curtius, *European Literature*, pp. 148–154.

81. See G. Paré, A. Brunet, and P. Tremblay, *La Renaissance du XIIe siècle* (Ottawa, 1933). See also Mario Dal Pra, *Giovanni di Salisbury* (Milan, 1951).

82. "The mass of the subject matter, like a lump of wax, is at first resistant to handling; but if diligent application kindles the intellect, suddenly the material softens under this fire of the intellect and follows your hand wherever it leads"; *The New Poetics*, trans. Kopp, p. 41.

83. There is one place in Aquinas where he suggests that in every completed form there is a rebellious appetite for new forms; see *In Libros Physicorum*, I, 9. Elsewhere he refers to the fact that not every imitation is a perfect copy of its model, and this suggests that the artistic idea must be formed in such a way that it is already adapted to this limitation; see *De Veritate*, III, 2c.

84. It was only through the commentary of Averroes that Aristotle's *Poetics* was known to the Middle Ages, since William of Moerbeke did not include it in his translation of 1272. See E. Franceschini, "La Poetica di Aristotele nel secolo XIII," *Atti dell'Istituto Veneto*, 1934–35 and also his "Ricerche e studi su Aristotele nel medioevo latino," in the anthology *Aristotele nella critica e negli studi contemporanei* (Milan, 1956).

85. See Menéndez Y Pelayo, *Historia de las ideas estéticas*, p. 310–344.

86. See ibid., p. 416.

87. Geoffrey of Vinsauf, *The New Poetics*, p. 34.

88. Chrétien de Troyes, *Le conte du Graal (Perceval)*, ed. Félix Lecoy (Paris, 1972), lines 1477–80.

VII. Judgment and the Aesthetic *Visio*

1. This phrase, which in the original reads "adaequabilitas rei perfectae et intellectus," is from M. Febrer, "Metafisica de la belleza," *Revista de filosofia*, 7 (1948), 91–134. Other definitions which he gives are: "perfec-

tion in being comformable with the intellect; the aptitude in a perfect object for being apprehended by the intellect; perfection in a thing as the ground of its relation with the reason." We can see that these involve the concept of a proportion between subject and object.

2. This means that the objective conditions of beauty might be confounded with truth. However, it does not follow, as L. Taparelli d'Azeglio has said, that beauty is simply the pleasure we feel in contemplating truth. Aesthetic pleasure arises only when we contemplate a true thing in its formal aspects, when the true is seen as the beautiful, when we concentrate upon structural features. In this kind of scenario, aesthetic pleasure cannot be reduced to the hedonistic pleasure we feel when our need for theoretical knowledge is satisfied.

3. *De Veritate*, I, 2c.

4. *ST,* I, 85, 1 ad 3.

5. "Virtute intellectus agentis resultat quaedam similitudo in intellectu possibili ex conversione intellectus agentis supra phantasmata, quae quidem est repraesentativa eorum quorum sunt phantasmata, solum quantum ad naturam speciei" ("In virtue of the agent intellect and by its turning to senses images [which in turn represent the realities of which they are images], a likeness is effected in the possible intellect, but only with respect to the specific nature"); *ST,* I, 85, 1 ad 3. "Dico autem intentionem intellectam id quod intellectus in seipso concipit de re intellecta. Quae quidem in nobis neque est ipsa res quae intelligitur; neque est ipsa substantia intellectus; sed est quaedam similitudo concepta in intellectu de re intellecta, quam voces exteriores significant; unde et ipsa intentio verbum interius nominatur, quod est exteriori verbo significatum" ("Now, I mean by the intention understood what the intellect conceives in itself of the thing understood. To be sure, in us this is neither the thing which is understood nor is it the very substance of the intellect. But it is a certain likeness of the thing understood conceived in the intellect, and which the exterior words signify. So, the intention itself is named the interior word, which is signified by the exterior word"); *Summa contra Gentiles,* IV, 11, 6.

6. "This simple and direct apprehension of reality by the intellect does not presuppose any activity which is conscious and reflective. It is an operation of a being which acts in accordance with its nature, and in the manner of an external reality, rather than the free activity of a spirit which dominates and enriches that activity"; Gilson, *Le Thomisme,* pp. 325–326.

7. *Comm. De Anima,* III, 8, 717.

8. *De Veritate,* X, 4c.

9. *De Veritate,* X, 5c.

10. *De Veritate,* II, 6c.

11. *ST,* I, 85, 5c.

12. *De Veritate*, I, 3c.

13. *Comm. in I Sent.*, 19, 5, 1 ad 7.

14. *De Veritate*, XXII, 1 ad 12.

15. Ibid.

16. Aesthetic delight or *delectatio* can therefore be said to have a dual nature, and in this way we can reconcile Maritain's view with that of de Bruyne. On the one hand there is pleasure when desire stills itself in the act of our cognitive powers; on the other, there is pleasure when the cognitive powers can operate without hindrance. In fact Aquinas writes, "For pleasure, two things are necessary: attaining some appropriate good thing, and knowing that one has attained it" ("ad delectationem duo requiruntur: scilicet consecutio boni convenientis et cognitio hujusmodi adeptionis"); *ST*, I-II, 32, 1c.

17. Pareyson, *Estetica*, pp. 161–162. Here again I am reproducing a theoretical account which has no interpretative relevance to Aquinas's texts. In fact Pareyson's account of knowledge takes the form of a hermeneutic theory, while that of Aquinas can be defined as an epistemology of a univocal and necessary conformity of the intellect with its object. However, I wish to underline here the relation between intellectual discovery and aesthetic experience, a relation which Pareyson describes in a way that helps us to understand better the meaning I am attempting to elicit from Aquinas.

VIII. Conclusion

1. *ST*, I, 77, 1 ad 7.

2. *Comm. de Anima*, II, 2, 235.

3. John Duns Scotus, *Opus Oxoniense (Quaestiones in Libros [P. Lombardi] Sententiarum)*, I, 17, 3, 13; in *Opera Omnia*, Wadding edition, 13 vols. (1639; reprint, Paris, 1891–95).

4. See ibid., IV, 11, 3, 46.

5. Ibid., II, 3, 6, 13.

6. Ibid., II, 3, 6, 2.

7. See above, Chapter V, note 78.

8. See Duns Scotus, *Opus Oxoniense*, IV, 45, 3, 17 and 21.

9. William of Ockham, *Quodlibeta*, VIII, 8; in *Opera Plurima*, 4 vols. (London, 1962); facsimile of Lyons edition, 1494–96.

10. William of Ockham, *Ordinatio*, XXX, 1.

11. William of Ockham, *In I Sententiarum*, XXXV, 5.

12. William of Ockham, *Ordinatio*, Prologue, 1.

13. See Mario Dal Pra, *Nicola di Autrecourt* (Milan, 1951).

14. A. Riegl, *Spätrömische Kunstindustrie* (Vienna, 1901).

15. See Panofsky, *Gothic Architecture and Scholasticism*.

16. See, in Chapter IV, "The Concept of Proportion in Aquinas," 8; and, in Chapter VI, "The Ontology of Artistic Form."

17. *Comm. Met.*, I, 12, 15.

18. *Summa contra Gentiles*, II, 56, 3.

Bibliography

Works by St. Thomas Aquinas

Commentarium in Aristotelis Librum De Anima. Edited by P. F. Angeli M. Pirotta. Taurini and Rome, 1948.

De Principiis Naturae. In *Opuscula Omnia necnon Opera Minora,* edited by R. P. Joannes Perrier. Paris, 1949.

The Disputed Questions on Truth [De Veritate]. Translated by Robert W. Mulligan. 3 vols. Chicago, 1952.

On the Truth of the Catholic Faith [Summa contra Gentiles]. Translated by Anton C. Pegis, James F. Anderson, Vernon J. Bourke, and Charles O'Neil. 4 vols. New York, 1955–57.

Opera Omnia. Edited by Roberto Busa. 7 vols. Stuttgart, 1980.

Summa Theologiae. Blackfriars edition and translation. 60 vols. London and New York, 1964–76.

Supplement to the *Summa Theologiae,* Part III. Vol. V of *Summa Theologica.* 6 vols. Taurini, 1937.

Works by Other Ancient and Medieval Authors

Adam Belladonna. *Liber de Intelligentiis.* In Clemens Baeumker, *Witelo.* Münster, 1908. Pages 1–71.

Alan of Lille (Alan de Insulis). *De Incarnatione Christi.* PL 210, cols. 578–579.

——— *The Plaint of Nature [De Planctu Naturae].* Translated by James J. Sheridan. Toronto, 1980.

Albertus Magnus. *De Pulchro et Bono.* In St. Thomas Aquinas, *Opera Omnia,* edited by Roberto Busa. 7 vols. Stuttgart, 1980. VII, 43–47.

——— *Opera Omnia.* 12 vols. to date. Aschendorff, 1951–.

Alexander of Hales. *Summa Theologica.* 4 vols. Florence, 1924–48.

Augustine, St. *The Confessions of St. Augustine.* Translated by F. J. Sheed. London and New York, 1944.

———— *Letters*. Translated by Sister Wilfred Parsons. 5 vols. Washington, D.C., 1951.

Avicenna. *Livre des directives et remarques*. Translated by A.-M Goichon. Paris, 1951.

Baldwin of Canterbury. *Tractatus de Vulnere Charitatis*. PL 204, cols. 477–484.

Bede, the Venerable. *De Schematibus et Tropis*. In *Rhetores Latini Minores*, edited by C. Halm. Leipzig, 1863. Pages 607–618.

Bernard of Clairvaux, St. *Apologia ad Guillelmum*. PL 182, cols. 895–918.

———— *Sermones in Cantica*. PL 183, cols. 785–1198.

Boethius. *De Institutione Musica*. Edited by Godofredus Friedlein. Leipzig, 1867.

Bonaventure, St. *Opera Omnia*. 10 vols. Florence, 1882–1902.

Cassiodorus. *De Artibus et Disciplinis Liberalium Litterarum*. PL 70, cols. 1149–1220.

Cennini, Cennino. *The Craftsman's Book*. [*Il libro dell'arte*]. Translated by Daniel V. Thompson. New Haven, 1933.

Chrétien de Troyes. *Arthurian Romances*. Translated by W. W. Comfort. London, 1914.

Cicero. *Tusculan Disputations*. [*Tusculanae Disputationes*]. Translated by J. E. King. 2d ed. London, 1950.

Conrad of Hirschau. *Dialogus super Auctores*. Edited by G. Schepss. Wurzburg, 1889.

Consuetudines Carthusienses. PL 153, cols. 631–760.

Dante Alighieri. *Literary Criticism of Dante Alighieri*. Edited and translated by Robert S. Haller. Lincoln, Neb., 1973.

Denis the Carthusian. *Opera Omnia*. 44 vols. Tournai, 1896–1913.

Diogenes Laertius. *Lives of Eminent Philosophers*. Translated by R. D. Hicks. 2 vols. London and New York, 1925.

Dionysius the Areopagite (Pseudo-Dionysius). *De Divina Hierarchia* and *De Divinis Nominibus*. In *Dionysiaca*, edited by Philippe Chevallier. 2 vols. Paris, 1937. Translated by John D. Jones as *The Divine Names and Mystical Theology*. Milwaukee, 1980.

Domenico Gundisalvi. *De Divisione Philosophiae*. Edited by Ludwig Baur. Münster, 1903.

Engelbert Admontensis. *De Musica*. In *Scriptores Ecclesiastici de Musica Sacra Potissimum*, edited by Martin Gerbert. 3 vols. 1784. Reprint. Hildesheim, 1963. II, 287–369.

Die Fragmente der Vorsokratiker. Edited by Herman Diels. 5th ed. edited by W. Krantz. Berlin, 1934–54.

Franco of Cologne. *Ars Cantus Mensurabilis*. In *Scriptorum de Musica Medii*

Aevi, edited by E. de Coussemaker. 3 vols. 1864–67. Reprint. Hildesheim, 1963. I, 117–136.

Geoffrey of Vinsauf. *The New Poetics [Poetria Nova].* Translated by Jane Baltzell Kopp. In *Three Medieval Rhetorical Arts,* edited by James J. Murphy. Berkeley, 1971. Pages 32–108.

Gilbert of Hoyt. *Sermones in Canticum Salomonis. PL* 184, cols. 11–252.

Hilary, St. *De Trinitate. PL* 10, cols. 9–472.

Hildegard, St. *Liber Divinorum Operum. PL* 197, cols. 742–1038.

Honorius of Autun. *De Imagine Mundi. PL* 172, cols. 115–187.

—— *Gemma Animae. PL* 172, cols. 541–738.

—— *Liber Duodecim Quaestionum. PL* 172, cols. 1177–86.

Hucbald of Saint-Amand. *Musica Enchiriadis.* In *Scriptores Ecclesiastici de Musica Sacra Potissimum,* edited by Martin Gerbert. 3 vols. 1784. Reprint. Hildesheim, 1963. I, 152–212.

Hugh of Fouilloi. *De Claustro Animae. PL* 176, cols. 1017–1182.

Hugh of St. Victor. *Didascalicon.* Edited by C. H. Buttimer. Washington, D.C., 1939. Translated by Jerome Taylor. New York, 1961.

—— *De Modo Dicendi et Meditandi. PL* 176, cols. 878–880.

—— *De Scripturis et Scriptoribus Sacris. PL* 175, cols. 9–28.

—— *De Tribus Diebus. PL* 176, cols. 811–838. Printed as book VII of *Didascalicon.*

—— *Soliloquium de Arrha Animae. PL* 176, cols. 951–970.

Isidore of Seville. *Differentiarum. PL* 83, cols. 9–98.

Jerome, St. *Epistolae. PL* 22, cols. 325–1192.

Joinville, Jean de. *La vie de Saint Louis [Histoire de St. Louis].* Edited by Noel L. Corbett. Quebec City, 1977.

John Duns Scotus. *Opera Omnia,* Wadding edition, 13 vols. 1639. Reprint. Paris, 1891–1985.

John of Meurs. *De Tonis.* In *Scriptores Ecclesiastici de Musica Sacra Potissimum,* edited by Martin Gerbert. 3 vols. 1784. Reprint. Hildesheim, 1963. III, 308–312.

John of Salisbury. *Metalogicon.* Edited by Clement C. J. Webb. Oxford, 1929. Translated by Daniel D. McGarry. Berkeley, 1962.

John Scottus Eriugena. *De Divisione Naturae.* Edited by I. P. Sheldon-Williams. 2 vols. Dublin, 1968–72. Translated by Myra L. Uhlfelder as *On the Division of Nature.* Indianapolis, 1976.

—— *Expositiones in Ierarchiam Coelestem.* Edited by J. Barbet. Turnhout, 1975.

Libri Carolini. PL 98, cols. 941–1350.

Macrobius. *In Somnium Scipionis.* Edited by J. Willis. Leipzig, 1970. Translated by W. J. Stahl as *Commentary on "The Dream of Scipio."* New York, 1952.

Origen. *Opera Omnia*. Edited by C. and C. V. Delarue. 25 vols. Berolini, 1831–48.

Otloh of St. Emmeran. *Dialogus de Tribus Quaestionibus*. PL 146, cols. 61–134.

———— *Liber de Tentationibus Suis et Scriptis*. PL 146, col. 29–58.

Patrologiae Cursus Completus, Series Latina. Edited by J.-P. Migne. 222 vols. Paris, 1844–90.

Plato. *The Sophist*. Translated by H. N. Fowler. London and Cambridge, Mass., 1921.

———— *Timaeus*. Translated by A. E. Taylor. London, 1929.

Pliny the Elder. *Historia Naturalis*. Translated by H. Rackham. 10 vols. London and Cambridge, Mass., 1952.

Plutarch. *De Defectu Oraculorum* [in Greek]. In *Sur la Disparition des oracles*, edited by Robert Flaceliere. Paris, 1947.

Quintilian. *Institutio Oratoria*. Translated by H. E. Butler. 4 vols. London, 1920–22.

Rhetores Latini Minores. Edited by C. Halm. Leipzig, 1863.

Richard of St. Victor. *Benjamin Major*. PL 196, cols. 63–202.

Robert Grosseteste. *De Luce*. In *Die philosophischen Werke des Robert Grosseteste*, edited by L. Baur. Münster, 1912. Translated by Clare C. Riedl as *On Light*. Milwaukee, 1942.

Scriptores Ecclesiastici de Musica Sacra Potissimum. Edited by Martin Gerbert. 3 vols. 1784. Reprint. Hildesheim, 1963.

Suger, Abbot. *De Rebus Administratione Sua Gestis*. PL 186, cols. 1211–39. Translation in Erwin Panofsky, *Abbot Suger on the Abbey Church of St.-Denis and Its Art Treasures*. Princeton, 1946.

Synod of Arras. In *Sacrorum Conciliorum Nova et Amplissima Collectio*, edited by J. D. Mansi. 53 vols. Paris and Leipzig, 1901–27. XIX, cols. 423–460.

Texte aus der deutschen Mystik des XIV und XV Jahrhundert. Edited by A. Spamer, Jena, 1912.

Theophilus. *De Diversis Artibus* [*Schedula Diversarum Artium*]. Edited and translated by C. R. Dodwell. London, 1961.

Vitruvius. *De Architectura*. Edited by V. Rose. Leipzig, 1899. Translated by Frank Granger. 2 vols. London, 1931–34.

William of Auvergne. *Tractatus de Bono et Malo*. Reprinted in part in Henri Pouillon, "La Beauté, propriété transcendentale chez les scolastiques." *Archives d'Histoire Doctrinale et Littéraire du Moyen Age*, 21 (1946), 263–329.

William Durandus. *Rationale Divinorum Officiorum*. Treviso, 1479. Book I translated in J. M. Neale and B. Webb, *The Symbolism of Churches and Church Ornaments*. Leeds, 1843. Pages 53–69.

William of Ockham. *Opera Plurima*. 4 vols. London, 1962. Facsimile of Lyons edition, 1494–96.

Witelo. *De Perspectiva*. Reprinted in part in Clemens Baeumker, *Witelo*. Münster, 1908.

Modern Works

Adler, M. *Art and Prudence*. New York, 1937.

Assunto, Rosario. *La critica d'arte nel pensiero medievale*. Milan, 1961.

—— *Die Theorie des Schönen im Mittelalter*. Cologne, 1963.

Baeumker, Clemens. *Witelo*. Münster, 1908.

Bagni, Paolo. *La costituzione della poesia nelle arti del XII–XIII secolo*. (Bologna, 1968).

Balthasar, N. "Art, esthétique, beauté." *Revue Néoscolastique*, 34 (1933), 70–116.

Baratono, Adelchi. *Arte e poesia*. Milan, 1945.

Barberi-Squarotti, Giorgio. "Le poetiche del trecento in Italia." In *Momenti e problemi di storia dell'estetica*, by various authors. 4 vols. Milan, 1959–61. I, 255–324.

Battisti, Eugenio. *Rinascimento e Barocco*. Turin, 1960.

Bayer, Raymond. *Histoire de l'esthétique*. Paris, 1961.

Biondolillo, F. *Breve storia del gusto e del pensiero estetico*. Messina, 1924.

Bizzarri, R. "Abbozzo di una estetica secondo i principi della scolastica." *Rivista Rosminiana*, 29 (1935), 183–196.

—— "San Tommaso e l'arte." *Rivista di Filosofia Neoscolastica*, 26 (1934), 88–98.

Blanche, F.-A. "L'analogie." *Revue de Philosophie*, 1931, pp. 248–271.

Borgese, G. A. "Sommario di storia della critica letteraria dal Medioevo ai nostri giorni." In *Poetica dell'unità*. Milan, 1952.

Bosanquet, Bernard. *A History of Aesthetics*. London, 1904.

Bullough, Sebastian. "St. Thomas and Music." *Dominican Studies*, 4 (1951), 14–34.

Callahan, L. *A Theory of Aesthetics according to the Principles of St. Thomas of Aquino*. Washington, D.C., 1927.

Cataudella, Quintino. "Estetica cristiana." In *Momenti e problemi di storia dell'estetica*, by various authors. 4 vols. Milan, 1959–61. I, 81–114.

Ceriani, G. "La gnoseologia e l'intuizione artistica." *Rivista di Filosofia Neoscolastica*, 26 (1934), 285–300.

Chailley, J. *Histoire musicale du Moyen Age*. Paris, 1950.

Chenu, M. D. "Imaginatio. Note de lexicographie philosophique." *Miscellanea Mercati*, 2 (1946), 593–602.

————— *Toward Understanding Saint Thomas*. Translated by A.-M. Landry and D. Hughes. Chicago, 1964.

Chiocchetti, E. *San Tommaso*. Milan, 1925.

Coomaraswamy, A. K. "Meister Eckhart's View of Art." In *The Transformation of Nature in Art*. Cambridge, Mass., 1934.

————— "St. Thomas Aquinas on Dionysius and a Note on the Relation of Beauty to Truth." *Art Bulletin*, 20 (1938), 66–77.

Coulton, G. G. *Life in the Middle Ages*. 4 vols. 2d ed. Cambridge, 1930.

Croce, Benedetto. *Aesthetic*. Translated by Douglas Ainslee. London, 1909.

Curtius, E. R. *European Literature and the Latin Middle Ages*. Translated by Willard R. Trask. London, 1953.

Dal Pra, Mario. *Giovanni di Salisbury*. Milan, 1951.

————— *Nicola di Autrecourt*. Milan, 1951.

Dazzi, Manlio. *Il Mussato preumanista*. Vicenza, 1964.

de Bruyne, Edgar. "Du rôle de l'intelligence dans l'activité esthétique." In *Philosophia Perennis*, by various authors. Regensburg, 1930.

————— *Equisse d'une philosophie de l'art*. Brussels, 1930.

————— *L'esthétique du Moyen Age*. Louvain, 1947.

————— *Études d'esthétique médiévale*. 3 vols. Bruges, 1946.

————— *Geschiedenis van de Aesthetica*. 5 vols. Antwerp, 1951–55.

————— *St. Thomas d'Aquin*. Paris and Brussels, 1928.

de Coussemaker, E. *Scriptorum de Musica Medii Aevi*. 4 vols. 1864–67. Reprint. Hildesheim, 1963.

del Gaizo, V. "Spunti tomistici per un'estetica moderna." *Humanitas*, 2 (1947), 373–386.

de Munnynck, Marc. "L'esthétique de St. Thomas d'Aquin." In *San Tommaso d'Aquino*, by various authors. Milan, 1923.

Derisi, O. *Lo eterno y lo temporal en el arte*. Buenos Aires, 1942.

de Tonquédec, J. *Questions de cosmologie et de physique chez Aristote et St. Thomas*. Paris, 1950.

Dewey, John. *Art as Experience*. New York, 1934.

de Wulf, Maurice. *Art et beauté*. Louvain, 1943.

de Zurko, E. R. "Alberti's Theory of Form and Function." *Art Bulletin*, September 1957.

Eco, Umberto. *The Aesthetics of Chaosmos*. Tulsa, 1982.

————— *La definizione dell'arte*. Milan, 1968.

————— "Sviluppo dell'estetica medievale." In *Momenti e problemi di storia dell'estetica*, by various authors. 4 vols. Milan, 1959–61. I, 115–229. Translated by Hugh Bredin as *Art and Beauty in the Middle Ages*. New Haven, 1986.

————— *A Theory of Semiotics*. Bloomington, Ind., 1979.

Faggin, G. *Maestro Eckhart e la mistica preprotestante*. Milan, 1946.

Faral, Edmond. *Les arts poétiques du XIIe et du XIIIe siècle*. Paris, 1924.

Febrer, M. "Metafisica de la belleza." *Revista de Filosofia*, 7 (1948), 91–134.

Focillon, Henri. *The Art of the West in the Middle Ages*. Translated by Donald King. 2 vols. London, 1963.

—— *The Life of Form in Art*. New Haven, 1942.

—— *The Year 1000*. New York, 1971.

Foucher, J. P. *La littérature latine du Moyen Age*. Paris, 1963.

Franceschini, E. "La Poetica di Aristotele nel secolo XIII." *Atti dell'Istituto Veneto*. 1934–35.

—— "Ricerche e studi su Aristotele nel medioevo latino." In *Aristotele nella critica e negli studi contemporanei*, by various authors. Milan, 1956.

Frankl, Paul. *The Gothic*. Princeton, 1960.

Freeman, Ann. "Theodulf of Orleans and the *Libri Carolini*." *Speculum*, 32 (1957), 663–705.

Freeman, Kathleen. *Ancilla to the Pre-Socratic Philosophers*. Oxford, 1948.

Garin, Eugenio. *Medioevo e Rinascimento*. 2d ed. Bari, 1961.

Garrigou-Lagrange, R. *Christian Perfection and Contemplation according to St. Thomas Aquinas*. St. Louis and London, 1937.

Getto, Giovanni. "Poesia e teologia nel *Paradiso* di Dante." In *Aspetti della poesia di Dante*. Florence, 1966, pp. 193–235.

Ghyka, Matila. *Le nombre d'or*. 2 vols. Paris, 1952.

Gilbert, K., and H. Kuhn. *A History of Esthetics*. 2d ed. London, 1956.

Gilby, T. *Poetic Experience: An Introduction to Thomist Aesthetics*. New York, 1934.

Gilson, Etienne. *History of Christian Philosophy in the Middle Ages*. London, 1955.

—— *Painting and Reality*. London, 1957.

—— *La philosophie au moyen age*. 2d ed. Paris, 1944.

—— *The Philosophy of St. Thomas Aquinas*. Translated by Edward Bullough. Cambridge, 1924. Translation of 3d ed. of *Le Thomisme*.

—— *Le Thomisme*. 5th ed. Paris, 1948.

Glunz, H. H. *Die Literarästhetik des europäischen Mittelalters*. Bochum, 1937.

Gredt, Joseph. *Elementa Philosophiae Aristotelico-Thomisticae*. 2 vols. Freiberg im Breisgau, 1932.

Gregory, Tullio. *Anima Mundi*. Florence, 1955.

Grenet, Paul. *Le Thomisme*. Paris, 1953.

Guiffrey, Jules. *Inventaire de Jean, duc de Berry*. 2 vols. Paris, 1894–96.

Guzzo, Augusto. *Studi di arte religiosa*. Turin, 1932.

Hauser, Arnold. *Modernism*. London, 1960.

—— *The Social History of Art*. 2 vols. London, 1951.

Henquinet, F.-M. "Un Brouillon autographe de S. Bonaventure sur le commentaire des sentences." *Etudes Franciscains*, 44 (1932), 633–655; 45 (1933), 59–82.

Holt, Elizabeth G. *A Documentary History of Art*. 2 vols. New York, 1957.

Huizinga, J. *The Waning of the Middle Ages*. Translated by F. Hopman. Harmondsworth, 1965.

Improta, G. *Contributo dell'Angelico Dottore San Tommaso alla dottrina ed all'evoluzione del bello e dell'arte estetica*. Naples, 1933.

Joyce, James. *A Portrait of the Artist as a Young Man*. Harmondsworth, 1960.

—— *Stephen Hero*. London, 1944.

Koch, J. "Zur Aesthetik des Thomas von Aquin." *Zeitschrift für Aesthetik*, 25 (1931), 266–271.

Lachance, L. *Le concept de droit selon Aristote et St. Thomas*. Paris and Montreal, 1933.

Le Goff, Jacques. *La civilisation de l'occident médiéval*. Paris, 1964.

Lerate, M. R. "Los fundamentos ontológicos del orden estético." *Actes du XIe Congrès International de Philosophie*, 10 (1953), 212–214.

Lingueglia, P. "Le basi e le leggi dell'estetica secondo San Tommaso." In *Pagine d'arte e di letteratura*. Turin, 1915.

Mâle, Emile. *Art et artistes du moyen age*. Paris, 1947.

—— *Religious Art in France*. Translated by Marthiel Mathews. Princeton, 1978.

Marc, André. "Métaphysique du Beau," *Revue Thomiste*, 51 (1951), 112–134; 52 (1952), 64–94.

—— *La méthode d'opposition en ontologie thomiste*." *Revue Néoscolastique*, 33 (1931), 149–169.

Marchese, V. *Delle benemerenze di S. Tommaso verso le belle arti*. Genoa, 1874.

Maritain, Jacques. *Art and Scholasticism*. Translated by J. F. Scanlan. London, 1930.

—— *Creative Intuition in Art and Poetry*. Princeton, 1953.

—— "De la connaissance poétique." *Revue Thomiste*, 44 (1938), 87–98.

Mazzantini, C. *Linee fondamentali di una estetica tomista*. Rome, 1930.

McInerny, Ralph. *The Logic of Analogy*. The Hague, 1971.

McKeon, Richard. "Rhetoric in the Middle Ages." In *Critics and Criticism*, ed. R. S. Crane. Chicago, 1952.

Melandri, Enzo. *La linea e il circolo. Studio logico-filosofico sull'analogia*. Bologna, 1968.

Melchiorre, Virgilio. "Il bello come relazionalità dell'essere in S. Tommaso." In *Arte ed esistenza*. Florence, 1956, pp. 215–230.

Menéndez y Pelayo, Marcelino. *Historia de las ideas estéticas in España*. Madrid, 1883.

Mercier, Cardinal D. *Cours de philosophie*. 3 vols. 5th ed. Louvain, 1909–12.

Merlo, G. M. "Il misticismo estetico di S. Tommaso." *Atti dell'Accademia delle Scienze di Torino*, 1939–40.

Montano, Rocco. "L'estetica nel pensiero cristiano." In *Grande antologia filosofica*, edited by A. M. Moschetti and U. A. Padovani. 5 vols. Milan 1954. V, 151–205.

Mortet, Victor. *Recueil de textes relatifs à l'histoire de l'architecture, XIe–XIIe siècles*. Paris, 1911.

Mortet, Victor, and Paul Deschamps. *Recueil de textes relatifs à l'histoire de l'architecture, XIIe–XIIIe siècles*. Paris, 1929.

Müller, W. *Das Problem der Seelenschönheit im Mittelalter*. Berlin, 1926.

Mumford, Lewis. *The Condition of Man*. London, 1944.

Nemetz, A. A. "Art in St. Thomas." *New Scholasticism*, 25 (1951), 282–289.

Noon, William T. *Joyce and Aquinas*. New Haven, 1957.

Olgiati, Francesco. *L'anima di San Tommaso*. Milan, 1923.

———— "L'arte e la tecnica nella filosofia di San Tommaso." *Rivista di Filosofia Neoscolastica*, 26 (1934), 156–165.

———— "L'arte, l'universale e il giudizio." *Rivista di Filosofia Neoscolastica*, 27 (1935), 290–300.

———— "San Tommaso e l'arte." *Rivista di Filosofia Neoscolastica*, 26 (1934), 90–98.

———— "San Tommaso e l'autonomia dell'arte." *Rivista di Filosofia Neoscolastica*, 25 (1933), 450–456.

———— "La *simplex apprehensio* e l'intuizione artistica." *Rivista di Filosofia Neoscolastica*, 25 (1933), 516–529.

Paci, Enzo. *Tempo e relazione*. Turin, 1954.

Pancotti, V. *San Tommaso e l'arte*. Turin, 1924.

Panofsky, Erwin. *Abbot Suger on the Abbey Church of St.-Denis and Its Art Treasures*. Princeton, 1946.

———— *Gothic Architecture and Scholasticism*. London, 1957.

———— *Idea: A Concept in Art Theory*. Columbia, S.C., 1968.

———— *Meaning in the Visual Arts*. Harmondsworth, 1970.

Paré, G., A. Brunet, and P. Tremblay. *La Renaissance du XIIe siècle*. Ottawa, 1933.

Pareyson, Luigi. *Estetica*. 2d ed. Bologna, 1960.

———— *Teoria dell'arte*. Milan, 1965.

Philippe, M. D. "Situation de la philosophie de l'art dans la philosophie aristotélico-thomiste." *Studia Philosophica*, 13 (1953), 99–112.

Plé, R. "Ontologie de la forme." *Revue de Philosophie*, 36 (1936), 329–342.

Plebe, Armando. *Estetica*. Florence, 1965.

Pouillon, Henri. "La Beauté, propriété transcendentale chez les scolastiques." *Archives d'Histoire Doctrinale et Littéraire du Moyen Age*, 21 (1946), 263–329.

———— "Le premier traité des propriétés transcendentales." *Revue Néoscolastique de Philosophie*, 42 (1939), 40–77.

Réau, Louis. *Iconographie de l'art chrétien*. 3 vols. Paris, 1955–59.

———— "L'influence de la forme sur l'iconographie de l'art médiévale." In *Formes de l'art, formes de l'esprit*, by various authors. Paris, 1951.

Remer, Vincentio. *Ontologia*. 9th ed., ed. Paulo Geny. Rome, 1947.

Riegl, A. *Spätrömische Kunstindustrie*. Vienna, 1901.

Roland-Gosselin, M. D. "Peut-on parler d'intuition intellectuelle dans la philosophie Thomiste?" In *Philosophia Perennis*, by various authors. Regensburg, 1930.

Rostagni, Augusto. "Sulle tracce di un'estetica dell'intuizione presso gli antichi." In *Scritti Minori*. 3 vols. Turin, 1955. I, 356–371.

Saintsbury, G. *A History of Criticism and Literary Taste in Europe*. 3 vols. Edinburgh, 1900–04.

Schlosser Magnino, Julius. *Die Kunstliteratur*. Vienna, 1924. Translated by F. Rossi as *La letteratura artistica*. 3d ed. Florence, 1964.

Schneider, Marius. *Singende Sterne*. Basel, 1955.

Schopenhauer, A. *The World as Will and Idea*. 3 vols. London, 1883.

Sella, Nelson. *Estetica musicale in San Tommaso*. Turin, 1930.

Sertillanges, A.-D. *St. Thomas d'Aquin*. 2 vols. Paris, 1925.

Severini, Gino. *Ragionamenti sulle arti figurative*. Milan, 1942.

Silva-Tarouca, A. *Thomas heute*. Vienna, 1947.

Singer, Charles, ed. *Studies in the History and Method of Science*. Oxford, 1917.

Spargo, E. J. *The Category of the Aesthetic in the Philosophy of St. Bonaventure*. New York, 1953.

Svoboda, K. *L'esthétique de St. Augustin et ses sources*. Brno, 1927.

Taparelli d'Azeglio, L. "Delle ragioni del bello secondo la dottrina di San Tommaso d'Aquino." 19 articles in *Civiltà Cattolica*, 4 (1859–60).

Tatarkiewicz, W. *History of Aesthetics*, 3 vols. The Hague, 1970–74.

Taylor, F. H. *The Taste of Angels: A History of Art Collecting from Rameses to Napoleon*. London, 1948.

Taylor, H. O. *The Medieval Mind*. 2 vols. London, 1911.

Trias, M. "Nota sobre la Belleza como transcendental." In *Actas des I° Congreso Nacional de Filosofia*, III (Mendoza, 1949).

Ulivi, F. "Il sentimento francescano delle cose e S. Bonaventura." *Lettere Italiane*, 14 (1962), 1–32.

Valensise, P. *Dell'estetica secondo i principi dell'Angelico Dottore*. Rome, 1903.

Vallet, P. *L'idée du Beau dans la philosophie de St. Thomas d'Aquin*. Louvain, 1887.

Valverde, J. M. "Introducción a la polémica aristotélico-tomista sobre la transcendentalidad metafisica de la belleza." *Revista de Ideas Estéticas, 52* (1955), 305–317.

Van Groenewoud, A. "De schoonheidsleer van der H. Thomas van Aquino." *Bijdragen van Philosophische en Theologische Faculteites der Neederlandische Jezuiten* (1938), 273–311.

Vanni Rovighi, S. *Elementi di filosofia*. Milan, 1948.

Vecchi, G., ed. *Poesia latina medievale*. Parma, 1952.

Vescovini, Graziella F. *Studi sulla prospettiva medievale*. Turin, 1965.

Vinay, G. "Il Mussato e l'estetica medievale." *Giornale Storico della Letteratura Italiana*, 1949.

Viscardi, Antonio. "Idee estetiche e letteratura militante nel Medioevo." In *Momenti e problemi di storia dell' estetica*, by various authors. 4 vols. Milan, 1959–61. I, 231–253.

Vollaerts, J. W. *Rhythmic Proportions in Early Medieval Ecclesiastical Chant*. 2d ed. Leiden, 1960.

Von Simson, O. *The Gothic Cathedral*. New York, 1956.

Wagner, P. "La sequenza ed il suo svolgimento profano." In *Antologia della storia della musica*, edited by Andrea della Corte. 4th ed. Turin, 1945.

Wencelius, L. *La philosophie de l'art chez les néoscolastiques de langue française*. Paris, 1932.

Zimmerman, R. *Geschichte der Aesthetik als Philosophische Wissenschaft*. Vienna, 1858.

Glossary

Abstraction   The mental process of extracting a universal concept from the matter and the sensible conditions of the individual or individuals which instantiate it.

Act and *potency*   Translations of Aristotle's *energeia* and *dynamis*. Every finite thing consists of *act*, that is, its actuality, its existential completeness, and of *potency*, that is, its capacity to receive actuality. (*Active potency*, however, means the capacity to confer, rather than just receive, actuality.)

Agent intellect   The function of the intellect which consists in the abstraction of concepts.

Appetite   The inclination of a thing toward some good.

Apprehension   See Simplex apprehensio.

Cause   That which is responsible for existence, action, or change. The four kinds of cause are: *efficient cause:* the agent which produces an effect; *material cause:* that out of which something is made or effected; *formal cause:* the actuating principle which determines what a thing is, often synonymous with substantial form (an *accidental formal cause* determines the accidental properties of a thing); *final cause:* the end or purpose of a thing.

Divine names   The attributes of God, expressed or expressible in human language.

Essence and *existence*   The essence of a thing is its nature, that which is known when we have a concept of it. Essence is in itself a potency; existence makes it actual.

Exemplary idea   An idea of the essence of a thing, in accordance with which an agent intentionally brings it into being.

Form and *matter*   Translations of Aristotle's *morphē* and *hylē*. Every material thing is composed of form, the factor which determines what a thing is, and matter (*materia prima*), the material factor which receives a form and individuates it. Neither can exist independently of the other. Matter is in potency to receive forms, and forms confer actuality upon matter. Form in this sense is strictly speaking *substantial form;* *accidental form* means an accidental property.

Hylomorphism (or *hylemorphism*)   The Aristotelian and Scholastic doctrine that bodies consist of prime matter and substantial form.

Judgment   The mental act of affirming or denying that an object present to consciousness genuinely instantiates the concept of that object. In a more superficial sense, a judgment is the expression of this mental act, and consists in affirming or denying a predicate of a subject.

Kalokagathia   A noun derived from the composite *kalos kagathos,* which itself is an abbreviation of *kalos te kai agathos* ("beautiful and good"). It refers to the coexistence in anything or, more usually, anyone, of the highest aesthetic and moral value, and was an ideal in both classical and medieval culture.

Matter   See *Form* and *matter.*

Participation   The possession of existence or of a property that comes from elsewhere. Thus, the intellect participates in the light of divine truth, and all created things participate in being.

Perfection   Completeness, the state of fully actualizing a form. Strictly speaking, this is *perfectio prima;* a thing has *perfectio secunda* when it fulfills its purpose. However, each of these perfections necessarily entails the other.

Phantasm   A mental sensible representation, a sense-image. "Reflection on the phantasm" is sometimes thought to refer to an act in which the agent intellect takes a phantasm as its object of consciousness, in order to abstract a concept from it. Recent work, however, suggests that the phrase is used by Aquinas to refer to an act in which the possible intellect returns, after the abstraction, to the image of the object in order to understand, incompletely and defectively, its singularity.

Possible intellect   the function of the intellect which consists in receiving and in knowing the concepts which have been abstracted by the agent intellect.

Potency   See *Act* and *potency.*

Ratio   An almost untranslatable word, some of whose meanings are: reason; the ability to reason; the ability to know and understand; intelligibility; definition; form; essence; species; logical structure. The expression *sub ratione,* followed by the genitive, means something like "from the point of view of."

Simplex apprehensio   Direct awareness of an object, the first step in the act of knowledge.

Species   (1) Form, or essence, considered as an object of knowledge; (2) a particular sort or kind; (3) beauty of appearance, comeliness.

Subject   Any object considered as the recipient or possessor of attributes.

Substance   translation of Aristotle's *ousia*. A thing which exists on its own, and not in something else. See, in Chapter IV, "The Concept of Form."

Transcendental   In Scholasticism, a transcendental property is one which is predicable of anything, and is so called because it "transcends" the Aristotelian categories.

Index